IRAN
AND THE WEST

A Critical Bibliography

VOLUME 2
ARTICLES, JOURNALS & CATALOGS

By

Cyrus Ghani

MAGE PUBLISHERS
WASHINGTON DC

To Caroline

Library of Congress Cataloging-in-Publication Data

First digital paperback edition

ISBN Volume 1: 1-933823-08-9
ISBN Volume 2: 1-933823-09-7

Printed and manufactured in U.S.A.

Mage books are available at bookstores,
through the internet or directly from the publisher:
Mage Publishers, 1032-29th Street, NW, Washington, DC 20007
202-342-1642 • as@mage.Com • 800-962-0922
Visit mage online at
WWW.MAGE.COM

CONTENTS
VOLUME 1

VOLUME 2

VOLUME 2

Illustrated Art Sale Catalogues
Pamphlets, Articles, Journals,
Occasional Papers, Museum
Catalogues, Newspaper and News
Magazine Articles

<u>ILLUSTRATED ART SALE CATALOGUES</u>
<u>IN CHRONOLOGICAL ORDER.</u>

<u>AMERICAN ART ASSOCIATION ANDERSON GALLERIES Inc.</u>
The Emile Tabbagh Collection: Early Mediterranean and Near Eastern Art.
Sale: 3 and 4 January 1936, New York; 127 pp.

Sale conducted by Hiram H. Parke, Otto Bernet and H.E. Russell, Jr.

<u>PARKE-BERNET GALLERIES Inc.</u>
The Dikran Kelekian Collection: Part I. Near Eastern Art, including the celebrated collection of Antique Textiles, Egyptian and Classical Antiquities, Medieval and Renaissance Art.
Sale: 21, 22 and 23 October 1953, New York; 130 pp.

<u>HOTEL DRUOUOT</u>
Art Persan. Collection Sevadjian.
Sale: 23 November 1960, Paris; 16 pp.

<u>SOTHEBY and Co.</u>
Catalogue of Egyptian, Western Asiatic Greek, Etruscan and Roman Antiquities, also Islamic Pottery.
Sale: 18 June 1968, London; 94 pp.

<u>SOTHEBY and Co.</u>
Catalogue of Persian, Turkish and Arabic Manuscripts, Indian and Persian Miniatures.
Sale: 25 and 26 November 1968, London; 149 pp.

<u>SOTHEBY and Co.</u>
Catalogue of Western and Oriental Manuscripts and Miniatures.
Sale: 11 December 1968, London; 67 pp.

<u>SOTHEBY and Co.</u>
Catalogue of Important Oriental Manuscripts and Miniatures.
Sale: 18 July 1969, London; 163 pp.

<u>SOTHEBY and Co.</u>
Catalogue of Highly Important Oriental Manuscripts and Miniatures.
Sale: 7 December 1970, London; 82 pp.

<u>SOTHEBY and Co.</u>
Catalogue of Oriental Manuscripts and Miniatures.
Sale: 9 December 1970, London; 63 pp.

<u>CHRISTIE'S</u>
Western, Hebrew and Oriental Manuscripts and Miniatures.

Sale: 16 December 1970, London; 95 pp.

CHRISTIE'S
Objects of Art and Clocks, Animalier Bronzes, Fine Continental Furniture, Tapestries, Eastern Rugs and Carpets.
Sale: 6 May 1971, London; 50 pp.

SOTHEBY and Co.
Catalogue of Oriental Manuscripts and Miniatures.
Sale: 13 July, 1971, London; 102 pp.

SOTHEBY and Co.
Catalogue of Oriental Manuscripts and Miniatures and Printed Books.
Sale: 14 July 1971, London; 58 pp.

CHRISTIE'S
Oriental Books, Printed and Manuscript, Miniatures and one Hebrew Manuscript.
Sale: 21 July 1971, London; 94 pp.

SOTHEBY and Co.
Catalogue of Oriental Manuscripts and Miniatures.
Sale: 7 December 1971, London; 63 pp.

SOTHEBY and Co.
Catalogue of an interesting collection of Oriental Miniatures.
Sale: 11 April 1972, London; 36 pp.

SOTHEBY and Co.
Catalogue of Oriental Manuscripts and Miniatures.
Sale: 11 April 1972, London; 29 pp.

SOTHEBY and Co.
Catalogue of Important Mughol Miniatures.
Sale: 26 March 1973, London; 44 pp.

SOTHEBY and Co.
Catalogue of Indian and Persian Miniatures.
Sale: 27 March 1973, London; 45 pp.

SOTHEBY and Co.
Catalogue of Important Oriental Miniatures and A Mughol Manuscript.
Sale: 10 July 1973, London; 46 pp.

SOTHEBY and Co.
Catalogue of Fine Oriental Miniatures and Manuscripts.
Sale: 11 July 1973, London; 78 pp.

SOTHEBY and Co.
     Catalogue of Fine Oriental Miniatures and Manuscripts.
     Sale: 11 December 1973, London; 76 pp.

MAGGS BROS. Ltd.
     Oriental Miniatures and Illumination.
     Sales: 1974-1978, London.
     Bulletin # 22; Vol.VII, Part 1, March 1974; 88 pp.
     Bulletin # 23; Vol.VII, Part 2, March 1975; pp. 95-154.
     Bulletin # 24; Vol.VII, Part 3, December 1975; pp. 159-219.
     Bulletin # 26; published for the Tenth Californian Antiquar-
     ian Bookfair; September 1976; 8 pp.
     Bulletin # 27; June 1977; 58 pp.
     Bulletin # 28; February 1978; 8 pp.

SOTHEBY and Co.
     Catalogue of Fine Oriental Miniatures and Manuscripts.
     Sale: 9 July 1974, London; 48 pp.

SOTHEBY and Co.
     Catalogue of Oriental Manuscripts; Indian and Persian
Miniatures.
     Sale: 27 November 1974, London; 129 pp.

SOTHEBY and Co.
     Catalogue of Fine Oriental Miniatures and Manuscripts.
     Sale: 10 December 1974, London; 75 pp.

SOTHEBY PARKE BERNET Inc.
     The Lester Wolfe Collection of Persian Pottery and Metalwork.
     Sale: 14 March 1975, New York; 52 pp.

SOTHEBY and Co.
     Catalogue of Important Oriental Manuscripts and Miniatures.
     Sale: 7 April 1975, London; 104 pp.

SOTHEBY and Co.
     Catalogue of Oriental Miniatures and Manuscripts and An
Important Qajar Painting.
     Sale: 8 April 1975, London; 44 pp.

SOTHEBY and Co.
     Catalogue of Good Continental Furniture, Tapestries, Textiles,
Works of Art, Rugs and Carpets.
     Sale: 18 April 1975, London; 42 pp.

SOTHEBY PARKE BERNET Inc.
     Antiquities and Islamic Works of Art (Greek, Roman, Egyptian,
Western Asiatic, Islamic Antiquities and Works of Art).
     Sale: 2 May 1975, New York; 93 pp.

SOTHEBY and Co.
      Fine Oriental Miniatures, Manuscripts, and Qajar Paintings.
      Sale: 7 July 1975, London; 78 pp.

CHRISTIE'S
      Fine Oriental Miniatures and Manuscripts.
      Sale: 10 July 1975, London; 48 pp.

CHRISTIE'S
      Persian and Islamic Works of Art (An Important Mamluk glass
vase, Fine Persian Lacquer and Metalwork, Persian and Islamic
Pottery).
      Sale: 14 July 1975, London; 32 pp.

SOTHEBY PARKE BERNET Inc.
      Fine Oriental Rugs and Carpets.
      Sale: 27 September 1975, New York; 32 pp.

CHRISTIE'S
      Fine Oriental Miniatures, Manuscripts and Qajar Paintings,
Maps and Books on Persia and the Middle East.
      Sale: 4 December 1975, London; 52 pp.

CHRISTIE'S
      Persian and Islamic Works of Art (Fine Persian Lacquer and
Metalwork, Persian and Islamic Pottery and Textiles).
      Sale: 8 December 1975, London; 27 pp.

SOTHEBY'S
      Catalogue of Fine Oriental Miniatures, Manuscripts and Qajar
Paintings.
      Sale: 9 December 1975, London; 91 pp.

SOTHEBY'S
      Catalogue of Islamic Ceramics, Metalwork, Arms and Armour,
Glass and other Islamic Works of Art.
      Sale: 12 April 1976, London; 95 pp.

SOTHEBY'S
      Catalogue of Important Oriental Manuscripts and Miniatures.
      Sale: 12 April 1976, London; 95 pp.

SOTHEBY'S
      Catalogue of Fine Oriental Miniatures, Manuscripts and
Qajar Paintings.
      Sale: 13 and 14 April 1976, London; 91 pp.

CHRISTIE'S
      Persian and Islamic Works of Art. (Fine Persian and Turkish
Pottery, Fine Persian Lacquer, Fine Persian and Islamic Textiles
and Metalwork.)

Sale: 13 April 1976, London; 20 pp.

CHRISTIE'S
Fine Islamic Manuscripts, Miniatures, Maps and Books, and an Important Shahnameh.
Sale: 14 April 1976, London; 35 pp.

CHRISTIE'S
Important Eastern Rugs and Carpets. (Important Classical Rugs, Turkish Court Rugs, Turkish and Caucasian Village Rugs and Persian Silk Rugs and Carpets.)
Sale: 14 April 1976, London; 24 pp.

SOTHEBY'S
Catalogue of Islamic Rugs and Carpets from the 16th to the 19th Century.
Sale: 14 April 1976, London; 108 pp.

SOTHEBY'S
Catalogue of Oriental Manuscripts, Miniatures, and Qajar Paintings.
Sale: 6 July 1976, London; 53 pp.

CHRISTIE'S
Fine Persian and Islamic, Indian, Tibetan and Nepalese Works of Art.
Sale: 6 July 1976, London; 53 pp.

CHRISTIE'S
Fine Islamic and Indian Miniatures, Manuscripts and Maps.
Sale: 7 July 1976, London; 47 pp.

CHRISTIE'S
Important Eastern Rugs and Carpets, (and Fine Eastern Textiles).
Sale: 5 November 1976, London; 27 pp.

CHRISTIE'S
Islamic and Indian Manuscripts and Miniatures, and European Paintings, Prints and Maps of Islamic Interest.
Sale: 17 November 1976, London; 45 pp.

CHRISTIE'S
Seven Folios from the Houghton Shahnameh.
Sale: 17 November 1976, London; 51 pp.

SOTHEBY'S AUTUMN ISLAMIC WEEK
Catalogue of Fine Oriental Miniatures, Manuscripts and Persian Lacquer. Part One: Mughol and Indian Miniatures.
Sale: 22 November 1976, London; 40 pp.

SOTHEBY'S AUTUMN ISLAMIC WEEK
       Catalogue of Fine Oriental Miniatures, Manuscripts and
Persian Lacquer. Part Two.
       Sale: 23 November 1976, London; 40 pp.

SOTHEBY'S
       Catalogue of Important Oriental Manuscripts and Miniatures.
       Sale: 2 May 1977, London; 98 pp.

CHRISTIE'S
       Fine Islamic and Indian Manuscripts and Miniatures.
       Sale: 5 May 1977, London; 59 pp.

SOTHEBY'S
       Catalogue of Fine Oriental Miniatures and Manuscripts.
       Sale: 10 October 1977, London; 138 pp.

CHRISTIE'S
       Important Pictures, Drawings and Prints of Islamic Interest.
       Sale: 3 November 1977, London; 115 pp.

CHRISTIE'S
       Important Islamic Manuscripts and Indian Miniatures.
       Sale: 9 November 1977, London; 44 pp.

SOTHEBY'S SPRING ISLAMIC SALES
       Important Oriental Manuscripts and Miniatures.
       Sale: 3 April 1978, London; 208 pp.

SOTHEBY'S
       Catalogue of Fine Oriental Miniatures, Manuscripts and Qajar
Paintings.
       Sale: 4 April 1978, London; 156 pp.

SOTHEBY'S
       Catalogue of Fine Oriental Miniatures and Manuscripts.
       Sale: 17 and 18 July 1978, London; 114 pp.

SOTHEBY PARKE BERNET Inc.
       Fine Oriental Miniatures and Manuscripts, Islamic Works of
Art, and 19th Century Paintings.
       Sale: 15 December 1978, New York; 107 pp.

SOTHEBY PARKE BERNET Inc.
       Fine Persian Rugs and Carpets.
       Sale: 16 December 1978, New York; 181 pp.

SOTHEBY'S SPRING ISLAMIC SALES
       Catalogue of Important Oriental Manuscripts and Miniatures.
       Sale: 23 April 1979, London; 148 pp.

SOTHEBY'S SPRING ISLAMIC SALES
     Catalogue of Fine Oriental Miniatures, Manuscripts, Qajar
Paintings and Lacquer.
     Sale: 24 April 1979, London; 188 pp.

JOHN C. EDELMANN GALLERIES Inc.
     Fine Persian, Caucasian, Turkish, Turkoman, Village, Nomadic
Rugs and Carpets, Tapestries and Textiles.
     Sale: 12 and 16 June 1979, New York; 96 pp.

SOTHEBY PARKE BERNET Inc.
     Fine Oriental Miniatures, Manuscripts, Islamic Works of Art,
and 19th Century Paintings.
     Sale: 15 June 1979, New York; 144 pp.

SOTHEBY'S
     Fine Oriental Miniatures and Manuscripts.
     Sale: 9 July 1979, London; 85 pp.

SOTHEBY'S
     Important Oriental Miniatures, Manuscripts and Qajar Lacquer.
     Sale: 8 and 9 October 1979, London; 175 pp.

SOTHEBY PARKE BERNET Inc.
     Important Ancient and Islamic Glass, Classical, Egyptian, and
Near Eastern Antiquities.
     Sale: 13 December 1979, New York; 183 pp.

SOTHEBY PARKE BERNET Inc.
     Fine Oriental Miniatures, Manuscripts, Islamic Works of Art
and 19th Century Paintings.
     Sale: 14 December 1979, New York; 117 pp.

SOTHEBY PARKE BERNET Inc.
     Fine Persian Rugs and Carpets.
     Sale: 15 December 1979, New York; 139 pp.

SOTHEBY PARKE BERNET Inc.
     Fine Persian Rugs and Carpets.
     Sale: 22 March 1980, New York; 123 pp.

SOTHEBY'S SPRING ISLAMIC SALES
     Important Oriental Manuscripts and Miniatures.
     Sale: 21 April 1980, London; 167 pp.

SOTHEBY'S SPRING ISLAMIC SALES
     Fine Oriental Manuscripts, Miniatures and Qajar Lacquer.
     Sale: 22 April 1980, London; 156 pp.

SOTHEBY PARKE BERNET Inc.
     Fine Oriental Miniatures, Manuscripts and Islamic Works of

722

Art.
     Sale: 30 June 1980, New York; 95 pp.

SOTHEBY'S
     Fine Oriental Manuscripts, Miniatures and Qajar Lacquer
comprising Rashid Al-Din's "World History".
     Sale: 7 and 8 July 1980, London; 141 pp.

SOTHEBY'S
     Rashid Al-Din's "World History" (Supplement to preceding).
     Sale: 8 July 1980, London; 28 pp.

SOTHEBY'S
     Rashid Al-Din's "World History" (another separate catalogue).
     Sale: 8 July 1980, London; 8 pp.

SOTHEBY PARKE BERNET Inc.
     Catalogue of Rashid Al-Din's "World History" (special New York
catalogue).
     Sale: 8 July 1980, New York, 28 pp.

SOTHEBY'S AUTUMN ISLAMIC SALES
     Fine Oriental Manuscripts, Miniatures and Qajar Lacquer.
     Sale: 13 and 14 October 1980, London; 135 pp.

SOTHEBY PARKE BERNET Inc.
     Fine Oriental Miniatures, Manuscripts and Islamic Works of
Art.
     Sale: 9 December 1980, New York; 127 pp.

SOTHEBY'S
     Fine Oriental Manuscripts and Miniatures.
     Sale: 27 April 1981, London; 89 pp.

SOTHEBY'S SPRING ISLAMIC SALES
     Fine Oriental Miniatures, Manuscripts and Printed Books.
     Sale: 28 and 29 April 1981, London; 163 pp.

SOTHEBY PARKE BERNET (GENEVA)
     Fine Carpets.
     Sale: 8 May 1981, Geneva; 127 pp.

SOTHEBY PARKE BERNET Inc.
     Fine Oriental Miniatures, Manuscripts and Islamic Works of
Art.
     Sale: 21 May 1981, New York; 113 pp.

SOTHEBY PARKE BERNET Inc.
     Oriental Rugs and Carpets.
     Sale: 12 and 13 June 1981, New York; 119 pp.

SOTHEBY'S
     Oriental Manuscripts and Miniatures.
     Sale: 6 July 1981, London; 47 pp.

SOTHEBY'S AUTUMN ISLAMIC SALES
     Fine Oriental Miniatures, Manuscripts and Printed Books.
     Sale: 12 and 13 October 1981, London; 107 pp.

SOTHEBY'S
     The Lion Stamps of Persia.
     Sale: 6 November 1981, London; 68 pp.

SOTHEBY PARKE BERNET Inc.
     Fine Oriental Miniatures, Manuscripts, and Islamic Works of
Art.
     Sale: 10 December 1981, New York; 103 pp.

SOTHEBY PARKE BERNET Inc.
     Fine Oriental Rugs and Carpets.
     Sale: 11 December 1981, New York; 152 pp.

SOTHEBY'S
     Fine Indian Miniatures, Indian and Other Asian Works of Art,
with related material by European Artists.
     Sale: 29 and 30 March 1982, London; 250 pp.

SOTHEBY'S SPRING ISLAMIC SALES
     Fine Oriental Manuscripts.
     Sale: 26 April 1982, London; 108 pp.

SOTHEBY'S SPRING ISLAMIC SALES
     Fine Oriental Miniatures, Manuscripts and Printed Books.
     Sale: 27 April 1982, London; 140 pp.

SOTHEBY PARKE BERNET Inc.
     Fine Oriental Rugs and Carpets.
     Sale: 1 May 1982, New York; 105 pp.

SOTHEBY PARKE BERNET Inc.
     Fine Oriental Miniatures, Manuscripts and Islamic Works of
Art.
     Sale: 19 May 1982, New York; 93 pp.

SOTHEBY'S
     Oriental Miniatures, Manuscripts and Printed Books.
     Sale: 5 July 1982, London; 36 pp.

SOTHEBY'S AUTUMN ISLAMIC SALES
     Fine Oriental Manuscripts and Miniatures.
     Sale: 11 October 1982, London; 113 pp.

SOTHEBY'S
        Islamic Works of Art, Carpets and Textiles.
        Sale: 12 and 13 October 1982, London; 302 pp.

SOTHEBY'S SPRING ISLAMIC SALES
        Fine Oriental Manuscripts.
        Sale: 18 April 1983, London; 92 pp.

SOTHEBY'S SPRING ISLAMIC SALES
        Fine Oriental Manuscripts and Miniatures.
        Sale: 19 April 1983, London, 72 pp.

SOTHEBY'S SPRING ISLAMIC SALES
        Islamic Works of Art, Carpets and Textiles.
        Sale: 20 April 1983, London; 240 pp.

SOTHEBY PARKE BERNET Inc.
        Fine Oriental Rugs and Carpets.
        Sale: 30 April 1983, New York; 90 pp.

SOTHEBY'S
        Fine Oriental Miniatures, and Manuscripts including Drawings
from the Pan Asian Collection.
        Sale: 20 June 1983, London; 107 pp.

SOTHEBY PARKE BERNET MONACO S.A.
        Collection de la Villa Ispahan, Monte-Carlo.
        Sale: 28 June 1983, Monte-Carlo; 79 pp.

SOTHEBY'S AUTUMN ISLAMIC SALES
        Fine Oriental Manuscripts and Miniatures.
        Sale: 17 October 1983, London; 134 pp.

SOTHEBY'S
        Islamic Works of Art, Carpets and Textiles.
        Sale: 19 October 1983, London; 339 pp.

SOTHEBY'S SPRING ISLAMIC SALES
        Fine Oriental Manuscripts and Miniatures.
        Sale: 16 April 1984, London; 143 pp.

SOTHEBY'S
        Oriental Miniatures and Manuscripts.
        Sale: 2 July 1984, London; 47 pp.

SOTHEBY'S
        Fine Oriental Manuscripts and Miniatures.
        Sale: 15 October 1984, London; 240 pp.

SOTHEBY'S
Fine Oriental Manuscripts and Miniatures, including seven
illustrated Leaves from the Siyar-I-Nabi.
Sale: 15 and 16 April 1985, London; unpaginated; (478 items).

SOTHEBY'S
Islamic Art.
Sale: 25 June 1985, Geneva; unpaginated (500 items).

SOTHEBY'S
Indian, Himalayan, South-East Asian Art and Indian Miniatures.
Sale: 20 and 21 September 1985, New York; unpaginated; (710
items).

SOTHEBY'S
Fine Oriental Manuscripts and Miniatures.
Sale: 21 and 22 November 1985, London; unpaginated; (555
items).

SOTHEBY'S
Nineteenth Century European Drawings and Watercolors
(including drawings by Jules Laurens of Persia and the Middle
East).
Sale: 28 November 1985, London.

SOTHEBY'S
Catalogue of Fine Oriental Manuscripts and Miniatures.
Sale: 22 and 23 May 1986, London; 234 pp.

Pamphlets, Articles, Journals, Occasional Papers, Museum Catalogues, Newspaper and News Magazine Articles

ABDEL KADER, A.H.
     The Islamic Involvement in the Process of History.
     Reprinted from "Religious Pluralism and World Community";
edited by E.J. Jurji; Leiden, 1969; pp. 93-109.

ADL, CHAHRYAR M.
     Recherches Archéologique en Iran sur le Kumes Médiéval
(Rapport Preliminaire pour 1982-1983).
     Photocopy from "Academie des Inscriptions et Belles-Lettres";
France, April-June 1984; full page illustrations; pp. 271-300.

ADNANI, M.R.
     Persepolis.
     Tehran, 1972; large 8vo, soft cover; 20 pp.

     Introduction in Persian; captions to pictures in English and
Persian. Children's coloring book of designs and figures from
Persepolis.

AFNAN, SOHEIL
     The Commentary of Avicenna on Aristotle's Poetics.
     Photocopy of reprint from unknown journal, c.1948; pp. 188-
190.

ABISH, WALTER, et al
     Death in Iran.
     Letter to the editor, "New York Review of Books", 13 August
1981; signed by Walter Abish et al. ("writers and scholars from
many countries"); p. 53.

     The letter is interesting mainly for the signatories and their
past attitudes towards Iran and the Revolution.

AGA-OGLU, MEHMET
     The Fatih Mosque at Constantinople.
     Article from "The Art Bulletin", Vol.XX, No.3; New York, Sept-
ember, 1938; 4to, soft cover; pp. 179-196.

AHMAD, AZIZ
     Safawid Poets and India.
     Reprint from "Iran" IV, 1976; published by the British Instit-
ute of Persian Studies; pp. 117-132.

     The Safavid poets in Persia were at best mediocre; their
contemporaries in India were probably worse.

AHMAD, AZIZ
     Afghani's Indian Contacts.
     Article in "The Journal of the American Oriental Society",
July-September 1969; pp. 476-491 and 27 plates of letters.

Jamal e-Din Afghani (Assad-Abadi) visited India several times to further the movement of Pan Islamism in India. The author, who teaches at the University of Toronto, examines Afghani's visits, his contacts and his impact. Afghani went to India four times. His last visit, 1880-1882 was his most fruitful. The writer maintains, however, that Pan Islamism was a movement in India before Afghani became its symbol.

AHMAD, EGBAL (editor)
The Iranian Revolution.
Special issue of "Race and Class: A Journal for Black and Third World Liberation" Vol.XXI, No.1; London, Summer 1979; 8vo, soft cover; 110 pp. and map.

Contains articles on various aspects of the Iranian Revolution by Ahmad Egbal, Nikki R. Keddie, Mansour Farhang, Richard Falk, William A. Dorman, Stuart Schaar, and Fred Halliday. The contributors were all devoted supporters of the Revolution. Their rejoicing was a little premature since the Revolution did not proceed the way they had hoped and their devotion remained unrewarded.

AHSAN, SHAKOOR A.
Colloquial Elements in Modern Persian.
Photocopy of reprint from unknown journal, c.1967; 23 pp.

AHSAN, SHAKOOR A.
Western Loanwords in Modern Persian.
Photocopy of reprint of an article in unknown journal, c.1968; 22 pp.

The writer traces the origins of the importation of Western words to the turn of the 20th century when Persian contact with Europe increased. The writer points out that Western words were used even in the language of the clergy. He cites a speech by Sayyed Jamal e-Din at the Albert Hall in London in 1872 as an example. The writer concludes by saying that efforts in recent years to stem the tide of usage of foreign words would not succeed.

AJAMI, FOUAD
The Dominion of Wrath.
The New York Times Book Review; 25 August 1985; p.5.

Review of Roy Mottahedeh's "The Mantle of the Prophet".

ALAVI, BOZORG
From Modern Iranian Literature - Yadname-ye Jan Rypka.
Reprint from the "Academia" of the Czechoslovak Academy of Sciences; Prague, 1967; pp. 167-172.

The writer, who is himself one of the earliest and most notable Iranian short story writers, discusses the works of contemporary Iranian writers. Alavi teaches at (East) Berlin University.

ALAVI, BOZORG
    Review of H. Kamshad's "Modern Persian Prose".
    Article in "Mitteilungen des Instituts Fur Orientforschung"; Berlin, 1968; pp. 356-357.

ALGAR, HAMID
    The Oppositional Role of the Ulama in Twentieth Century Iran.
    Photocopy from "Scholars, Saints, and Sufis: Muslim Religious Institutions in the Middle East since 1500", edited by Nikki R. Keddie, Chap.9; Berkeley, 1972; pp. 231-255.

    An abbreviated and revised form of a paper first presented at a conference at the University of California, Los Angeles, in June 1969.

ALGAR, HAMID
    Some Notes on the Naqshbandi Tariqat in Bosnia.
    Reprint from unknown journal; c.1973; pp. 168-203.

ALGAR, HAMID
    The Naqshbandi Order: A Preliminary Survey of Its History and Significance.
    Reprint from unknown journal; c.1973; 42 pp.

ALGAR, HAMID
    Silent and Vocal Dhikr in the Naqshbandi Order.
    Paper read at unknown conference in August 1974; 13 pp.

ALLMAN, T.D.
    An American Portrait of the Iranian Revolution.
    Photocopy of "Pacific News Service Special Report"; series of 7 special reports from Iran written by the editor of "Pacific News Service"; San Francisco, c.1979.

(1)   "Iran: A Nation at Peace with Itself" 5 pp.
(2)   "Do the Moslem Mullahs Really Run Iran?" 5 pp.
(3)   "The Revolution in Tehran's Slums" 5 pp.
(4)   "Can Islam Unite Iran's Minorities?" 5 pp.
(5)   "Among Iran's Baluchis: Where the Shah Is Still Hero, and
       Khomeini Is an Atheist" 5 pp.
(6)   "Iran's Economy Works - For Iranians" 5 pp.
(7)   "The People Govern in the Land of the Thousand-and-one-
       Nights" 5 pp.

    The writer claims that he spent three weeks travelling with an interpreter some 6000 square miles through Iran, and is intent

to find in every square mile "democracy and progress" under the
rule of the clergy.

ALLWORTH, EDWARD
     The "Nationality" Idea in Czarist Central Asia.
     Offprint from "Ethnic Minorities in the Soviet Union"; New
York, 1968; pp. 229-249.

AMALSAD, D.M.
     Cotton Cloth Printing (Hand Process).
     Bombay, 1950; small 8vo, soft cover; illustrated; 42 pp.

     Text book on how to do it, as are the following six entries.

AMALSAD, D.M.
     Bleaching and Dying (Hand Process).
     Bombay, 1951; small 8vo, soft cover; one illustration; 45 pp.

AMALSAD, D.M.
     Cotton Hand Spinning.
     Bombay, 1951; small 8vo, soft cover; illustrated; 19 pp.

AMALSAD, D.M.
     Fabric Structure and Cloth Analysis.
     Bombay, 1951; small 8vo, soft cover; illustrated; 55 pp.

AMALSAD, D.M.
     Handloom Weaving.
     Bombay, 1951; small 8vo, soft cover; illustrated; 66 pp.

AMALSAD, D.M.
     Warp and Weft Preparation (Hand Process).
     Bombay, 1950; small 8vo, soft cover; illustrated; 37 pp.

AMALSAD, D.M.
     Yarn and Cloth Calculation.
     Bombay, 1951; small 8vo, soft cover; illustrated, 36 pp.

AMIET, PIERRE
     Musée du Louvre: Antiquites Iraniennes.
     Petits Guides des Grands Musees, # 39.
     Paris, 1977; illustrated; 17 pp. and map.

     In French; text by Pierre Amiet, Conservateur en Chef du
Department des Antiquites Orientales.

AMIN, S.H.
     The Iran-Iraq Conflict: Legal Implications.
     Reprinted from "The International and Corporate Law Quarterly",
Vol.31, 1982; Great Britain; pp. 167-188.

AMIN, S.H.
     The Settlement of Iran-United States Disputes.
     Reprint from "The Journal of Business Law"; London, May 1982;
pp. 248-250.

AMIN, S.H.
     Marine Pollution Regulation in the Persian Gulf.
     Photocopy of "Marine Policy Reports", Vol.5, No.1; Great
Britain, September 1982; 4 pp. including map.

AMIN, S.H.
     Iran-United States Claims Settlement.
     Reprint from "The International and Comparative Law Quarterly",
Vol.32; Great Britain, 1983; pp. 750-756.

     A brief account of the legal aspects of the "Algiers Accord"
i.e. Iran-U.S. settlement in 1981.

AMIR ARJOMAND, SAID
     Religion, Political Action and Legitimate Domination in
Shi'ite Iran: Fourteenth to the Eighteenth Centuries A.D.
     Reprint from the "European Journal of Sociology", Vol.XX;
France, 1979; pp. 59-109.

AMIR ARJOMAND, SAID
     The Shi'ite Hierocracy and the State in Pre-modern Iran:
1785-1890.
     Photocopy of reprint from "European Journal of Sociology",
Vol.XXII; France, 1981; pp. 40-78.

     In an excellent article the writer examines the years between
1785 and 1830's which, he argues, was the period that the definitive consolidation of a "Shi'ite Polity in Iran took place". As
background, the writer discusses the premise that during the first
two hundred years of Safavid rule, religion was in the hands of
the clerical state. With the ascendency of Mohammad Baqer
Majlesi (d.1699), Shi'ite orthodoxy overtook the representatives
of the clerical state. Majlesi became the chief religious figure
of the country and forced the state to take repressive measures
against Sufism, philosophical studies and virtually all else that
was at variance with his orthodoxy. Nader Shah, for political and
military (and perhaps personal) reasons, suppressed Shi'ism at
least as pronounced by Shah Esmail. The first two Qajar kings
reverted to Safavid policy. Majlesi's writings came into vogue
again, and the Mujtaheds assumed dominance in administering laws.

AMIR ARJOMAND, SAID
     A la Recherche de la Consience Collective: Durkheim's Ideo-
logical Impact in Turkey and Iran.
     Reprint from "The American Sociologist", Vol.17, No.2;
United States, May 1982; pp. 94-102.

In a well written article, the writer examines the impact of
Emile Durkheim the French sociologist (1858-1917) and Zia Golkalp,
the chief proponent of the doctrine of nationalism in Turkey
(1876-1924), on Ali Shariati (1933-1977), the major architect of
contemporary Islamic reformist ideology in Iran.

AMIR ARJOMAND, SAID
The Office of "Mullah-Bashi" in Shi'ite Iran.
Reprint from "Studia Islamica" Collegerunt, Ex Fasciculo
LVII; Paris, 1983; in English; pp. 135-146.

AMNESTY INTERNATIONAL
Annual Report, 1980.
A photocopy of pp. 329-330 of A.I.'s Annual Report for 1980.

The pages summarize the organization's activities concerning
Iran during that year. (For earlier Amnesty Reports refer to
Section A and under the names of various writers in this Section
D.)

AMNESTY INTERNATIONAL
Press Releases.
Copies of five A.I. "Urgent Action" press releases:
(1)   "Death Penalty: Iran: Executions" 4 July 1980.
(2)   "Further Information Death Penalty: Iran: Executions"
       3 September 1980.
(3)   "Further Information Iran Executions" 9 December 1980.
(4)   "Health/Legal Concern: Iran: Abolfazl Ghassemi" 15 January
       1981
(5)   "Death Penalty: Iran: Colonel Vahdat" 20 March 1981.

AMNESTY INTERNATIONAL
"Matchbox".
Amnesty International's magazine "Matchbox", November 1981.

The lead article is entitled "The Baha'is of Iran: Persecution
is government policy".

AMNESTY INTERNATIONAL
Human Rights Violations in Iran.
Photocopy of a report; London, 7 September 1982; 15 pp.

AMNESTY INTERNATIONAL
Treatment of Prisoners in Iran.
Photocopy of a report; London, 9 December 1982; 11 pp.

AMNESTY INTERNATIONAL
Press Releases.
Photocopies of five A.I. "Urgent Action" press releases:
(1)   "Health Concern/Fear of Torture: Iran: Abolfazl Ghassemi"
       15 October 1982.

(2) "Fear of Torture/Legal Concern: Iran: Taher Ahmadzadeh"
    3 December 1982.
(3) "Fear of Torture/Death Penalty/Legal Concerns: Iran: Ali Reza
    Tashayod, Mariam Tavassoli Zadeh, Abbas Tashayod, Sherafat
    Tafazoli" 10 January 1983.
(4) "Fear of Torture/Health Concern: Iran: Esmail Movasaghiyan,
    71 years old, a writer" 10 January 1983.
(5) "Death Penalty: Iran: 22 Members of the Baha'i Religion" 14
    February 1983.

AMUZEGAR, JAHANGIR
    The Oil Story: Facts, Fiction and Fair Play.
    Photocopy of reprint from "Foreign Affairs"; United States,
July 1973; pp. 676-689.

    A good article which attempts to debunk the then conventional
wisdom that the oil producing countries would inherit the wealth
of the Western world. The writer argues that supply is limited;
the Western industrialized countries are consuming ever more; and
oil had been under-priced. The writer, in a reasoned argument
suggests that the post World War II recovery of Western Europe
was primarily financed by cheap oil.

AMUZEGAR, JAHANGIR
    Ideology and Economic Growth in the Middle East.
    Photocopy of reprint from "The Middle East Journal"; United
States, Winter 1974; 9 pp.

    The article examines how the Middle Eastern countries have
fared under different political ideologies as reflected in their
economic theories.

AMUZEGAR, JAHANGIR
    The North-South Dialogue: From Conflict to Compromise.
    "Foreign Affairs"; United States, April 1976; pp. 547-562.

    A version of this paper was originally prepared for the
conference 'Alternatives to Growth' held in Houston, Texas, 19-21
October 1975. Deals particularly with the distribution and shar-
ing of the world's natural resources as it affects the economies
of the North-South countries.

ANDERSON, JON W. and STRAND, RICHARD F. (organized and edited by)
    Ethnic Process and Intergroup Relations in Contemporary
Afghanistan.
    New York, Summer 1978; 4to, soft cover; 46 pp.

    Papers presented at the Eleventh Annual Meeting of the Middle
East Studies Association at New York City, 10 November 1977.

ANKLESARIA, PESHOTAN K.
        The Direction of the Arrangement of Stones in the Barasnum
Gah in Iran and India.
        "Reprinted from I.J. Zarthoshti Madressa Centenary volume.
Bombay, 1967." pp. 162-164.

ANNAN, NOEL
        Review of Robert Bernard Martin's "With Friends Possessed:
A Life of Edward Fitzgerald."
        "New York Review of Books", 25 April 1985; pp. 3-5.

AN APPEAL IN IRAN.
        Published in "The New York Review of Books", 11 June 1981;
pp. 44-45.

        Document circulated in Iran and signed by over 100 Iranian
writers and academics. From the people who wanted the U.S. to
topple the Shah and now want the U.S. to topple Khomaini.

APOLLO: THE MAGAZINE OF THE ARTS
        London, August 1975; pp. 104-110.

        Two articles:
(1) The Palevsky-Heermaneck Collection of Islamic Art, by P. Pal.
(2) Textiles from the Islamic World, by Mary H. Kahlenberg.

ARBERRY, A.J.
        Edward Granville Browne (1862-1925).
        A Centenary address at the Iran Society; Great Britain, Feb-
ruary 1962; 20 pp.

ARMSTRONG, SCOTT
        A series of articles by Scott Armstrong appearing on
consecutive dates in "The International Herald Tribune"; 27 October,
1-2 November 1980. 1) "Carter Clung to Faith in Shah, Urged Use of
Force in Revolution, Probe Says." 27 October 1980; pp.1 and 5.
2) "Muddled U.S. Diplomacy Marked Shah's Last Days." 28 October
1980; p. 2. 3) "Aides Favoring Tough Stand by Shah Prevailed in
U.S." 29 October 1980; p. 4. 4) "U.S. Envoy Urged Contacts with
Opposition: Pessimistic Cables on Shah Angered Carter." 30 October
1980; p. unknown. 5) "Vance Was Preoccupied with SALT as Shah's
Rule Disintegrated." 31 October 1980; p. 5. 6) "Last Act in the
Tragedy of Errors of Iran's Revolution and U.S." November 1-2 1980;
p. 5.

THE ART OF THE ACHAEMENIANS, PARTHIANS and SASANIANS.
        Iran, 1977; Catalogue of the Reza Abbasi Cultural and Arts
Center, September 1977; 4to, soft cover; illustrated, some in
color; 46 pp.

ART AND ARCHITECTURE
From "Iran" Magazine: "Yesterday and Tomorrow", Nos. 18 and 19; Tehran, June-November 1973; large 4to, soft cover; full page illustrations and illustrations in text, few in color; 175 pp.

The entire issue is devoted to "Persian Architecture - Past and Present".

THE ART OF ISLAM
Broadsheet of Victoria and Albert Museum; London, c.1980.

One of the series of broadsheets relating to Victoria and Albert permanent exhibits. Large black and white illustrations of important objects with description. Brief text credits Persia with being the outstanding contributor to Islamic art.

ART NEWS
Special Issue: Persian Art; New York, 1940; illustrated in text in monochrome; 30 pp.

Magazine published monthly since 1902; special issue on the occasion of the Iranian Institute's Exhibition in New York. An interesting souvenir. The main article is by Mehmet Aga-Oglu.

THE ART OF THE PERSIAN CARPET
New York, 1960; 8vo, soft cover; 12 pp.

Re: The Fourth International Congress of Iranian Art and Archaeology held from 24 April to 2 May 1960. The pamphlet contains papers read by Beatrice Straight, Arthur Upham Pope, John Shapley and Ehsan Yarshater.

ASAD, MUHAMMAD
The Spirit of Islam.
London, 1975; 8vo, soft cover; 13 pp.

A booklet designed to promote Western understanding of aspects of Moslem beliefs and practices.

ASHJIAN, M.V. (edited by)
Album: All Saviour's Cathedral; New Julfa, Isfahan.
Iran, 1975; large booklet; illustrated, some in color; 106 pp.

A publication of the Council of the Armenians in Iran and India. Introductions in Armenian, English, French and Persian plus numerous illustrations of the art objects contained in the 17th century Armenian cathedral in Julfa.

ASMUSSEN, JES P.
Classical New Persian Literature in Jewish-Persian Versions.

        Reprint from "Studies in Bibliography and Booklore", Vol.
VIII, Nos.2-4; Cincinnati, Ohio, Spring 1968; pp. 44-53.

ASMUSSEN, JES P.
        Iranica - The Death of Cambyses.
        Reprint from "Acta Orientalia", No.XXXI; Leiden, 1968; pp.
9-20.

ASMUSSEN, JES P.
        The List of Fruits in the Bundahisn.
        Reprint from the "Asia Major Library, W.B. Henning Memorial
Volume"; London, c.1970; pp. 12-19.

AVERY, P.W.
        Developments in Modern Persian Prose.
        Photocopy of reprint from "The Muslim World", Vol.XLVI;
United States, 3 July 1956; pp. 237-252.

AVERY, P.W.
        Observations on British Policy Since the Second World War.
        Paper prepared for a seminar at Harvard University on
Problems of Contemporary Iran; April 1965; 19 pp.

        A good general survey. The writer divides the period into
two: 1946-1953 and 1953 to date of article. He basically argues
that Britain had no policy towards Iran during this entire period
other than for a brief time during the oil crisis. The writer
also dismisses the role of the two prominent British Foreign
Secretaries of the period. Ernest Bevin was not interested in
Iran at all. For Bevin there was no "Persia and the Persian
Question". Eden, on the other hand, had a Persian flair. He
considered himself a lover of Sa'di and Hafez. He had no respect,
however, for any contemporary Persian. Mosaddeq had to be brought
to his knees and humiliated before others began to entertain
similar ideas. By asserting the lack of policy on Iran by the two
Foreign Secretaries and high officials of the British government
during the period, the writer also maintains by inference that
Britain exerted no influence in Iran, which comes as news to most
knowledgeable Iranians.

AVERY, P.W. and SIMMONS, J.B.
        Persia on a Cross of Silver, 1880-1890.
        Reprint from "Middle Eastern Studies", Vol.10, No.3; London,
October 1974; pp. 259-286.

        A very good article.

AVICENNA
        Photocopy of translation into English by Ismail Dahiyat of
Avicenna's Commentary on the "Poetics" of Aristotle. Being the

Ninth part (on poetry) of the First Section (on logic) of Al
Shafa. No date.

AVRAMOVIC, DRAGOSLAV
     Industrialization of Iran: The Record, the Problems and the
Prospects.
     Typewritten manuscript of a paper prepared for the World Bank;
Tehran, 15 August 1969; 29 pp.

AZARPAY, GUITTY
     Iranian Divinities in Sogdian Paintings.
     Reprint from "Acta Iranica"; Leiden, 1975; pp. 19-29 and 9
plates.

     Author: Professor, Department of Near Eastern Studies, Univer-
sity of California, Berkeley.

AZARPAY, GUITTY and HENNING, W.B
     A Hunting Scene on an Inscribed Sassanian Silver Vessel.
     Reprint from "d'Iranica Antiques", Vol.VII; Leiden, 1967;
illustrated in text and on full page plates; pp. 145-152.

AZIM, ABDUL
     Khan-i-Arzu's Observations on the Relationship of Sanskrit
and Persian.
     Paper delivered at a seminar at Columbia University, 22 Dec-
ember 1967; 16 pp.

AZIZBEGLOU, MEHDI
     Iranian Handicrafts.
     London, 1955; small leaflet; colored full page illustration,
colored map and decorated pages; 18 pp.

     Text by Mehdi Azizbeglou; graphics by Frederick Tallberg.

738

BAILEY, MARTIN
       The Blooming of Operation Flower.
       "The Observer"; London, 2 February 1986; p. 19.

       "Arms for oil agreement (in 1977) united Israel and Iran in
secret missile project capable of launching a nuclear attack."
The article is based on documents seized at the U.S. Embassy in
Tehran.

BAKHASH, HALEH
       Veil of Fear.
       Reprint from "The New Republic"; United States, 28 October
1985; pp. 15-16.

       The writer discusses Iran's delegation to the recent United
Nations Conference in Nairobi where they created a stir by their
Islamic militancy and the clear articulation of their aims. The
writer argues that these articulate women ironically were the
beneficiaries of the women's movement during the rule of the Shah:
Their emancipation, education and social awareness. She also describes the plight of women in Iran in recent years where they have
lost almost all the benefits they had gained during the preceding
50 years. The writer believes that despite all the constraints
placed on women the Islamic regime cannot ignore or discard half
of the country's work force and will have to relax some of its
harsh measures. The writer was a prominent figure in the women's
rights movements in Iran and is presently a lecturer at Princeton
University.

BAKHASH, SHAUL
       The Evolution of Qajar Bureaucracy: 1779-1879.
       Photocopy from "Middle Eastern Studies", Vol.7, No.2; London,
May 1971; pp. 139-168.

       A survey of attempts to reform the Qajar administrative hier-
archy in the 19th century. The writer discusses how the bureau-
cracy was expanded greatly during Fath Ali Shah's rule and how it
became unmanagable during Naser e-Din Shah's reign when every
prince had his own large retinue, and in some cases a private army
(Zel ol Soltan, for example, had an army of 15000), and the chief
ministers placed every one of their relatives on the public pay-
roll. The writer discusses the role of the few chief ministers
who made a genuine attempt at reform, which invariably came to
nought because of the disinterest of the kings, the opposition of
the clergy against a strong state and the pervading indifference
and sometimes outright hostility of the governing class. One of
the writer's earliest and extremely well reasoned articles.

BAKHASH, SHAUL
       Sermons, Revolutionary Pamphleteering and Mobilization: Iran,
1978.
       Photocopy of chapter 9 of "From Nationalism to Revolutionary

Islam", edited by Said Amir Arjomand; pp. 177-194.

First written account of the "fateful" letter of 7 January 1978 attacking Khomaini, which sparked the uprising at Qom. A careful analysis of the content of revolutionary pamphleteering literature of 1978-1979.

BAKHASH, SHAUL
       Iran: A Year After.
       Photocopy from "The Economist"; London, 23 February 1980; pp. 29-35.

The writer is identified only as "a distinguished Iranian", and his name is not mentioned. He gives his view of the people and the institutions that govern post-revolutionary Iran. He suggests that those who bank their hope, or their fear, on the belief that the volatile mastery of the molla's rule must soon be overtaken by some more familiar system may be mistaken. It could, he believes, go on for quite a time.

BAKHASH, SHAUL
       Iran's Revolution.
       Review of three books from "The New York Review of Books", 26 June 1980; pp. 22-34.

Reviews of "Iran from Religious Disputes to Revolution" by M.J. Fischer, "The Rise and Fall of the Shah" by Amin Saikal and "The Fall of the Shah" by Fereydoun Hoveyda.

BAKHASH, SHAUL
       Before the Fall.
       Photocopy of book review from "The New Republic"; United States, 22 November 1980; pp. 31-34.

Review of "Paved with Good Intentions: The American Experience and Iran" by Barry Rubin.

BAKHASH, SHAUL
       Who Lost Iran?
       Book review from "The New York Review of Books", 14 May 1981; pp. 15-18.

Review of "Debacle, The American Failure in Iran" by Michael Ledeen and William Lewis. The reviewer disagrees with the view expounded in the book that the U.S. could have saved the monarchy by urging the Shah to "do whatever is necessary" to crush the opposition.

BAKHASH, SHAUL
       Reformulating Islam.

"New York Times", 22 October 1981; p. A.27.

BAKHASH, SHAUL
        The Day of the Mullahs.
        Photocopy from "The New Republic"; United States, 4 November
1981; pp. 15-18.

        Subtitled, "Iran's clerical masters tighten their grip on
chaos". An analysis of how the mollas systematically eliminated
all secular opposition and secured power.

BAKHASH, SHAUL
        Fall and Decline.
        Book reviews "The New York Review of Books", 3 December 1981;
pp. 25-30.

        Review of three books: "Roots of Revolution" by Nikki R.
Keddie; "Inside the Iranian Revolution" by John D. Stempel and
"Mission to Iran" by William H. Sullivan.

BAKHASH, SHAUL
        The Politics of Oil and Revolution in Iran: A Staff Paper.
        The Brookings Institute, Washington D.C., 1982; 37 pp.

        A well reasoned paper on Iranian oil policy since the
Revolution of 1979.

BAKHASH, SHAUL
        Against Arms Aid for Iraq.
        "The New York Times", 25 May 1982.

        The writer argues that Iran is strategically more important
than Iraq, and the West, despite the temporary insanity of the
Iranian regime, should not sever all ties with Iran. The writer,
by inference states that Iran would, sooner or later, have to
turn to the West and that time has a way of healing all enmities.

BAKHASH, SHAUL
        The Revolution Against Itself.
        Book Review from "The New York Review of Books", 18 November
1982; pp. 19-26.

        Review of three books: "Iran Since the Revolution" by Sepehr
Zabih, "Iran: the Untold Story" by Mohamed Heikal, and "Iran Between Two Revolutions" by Ervand Abrahamian.

BAKHASH, SHAUL
        The New Khomeini.
        Photocopy of article from "The New York Times", 20 February
1983.

BAKHASH, SHAUL
     The Failure of Reform: The Prime Ministership of Amin al-
Dowla, 1897-8.
     Reprint from "Qajar Iran: Political, Social and Cultural
Change 1800-1925" edited by Edmund Bosworth and Carole Willenbrand;
Edinburgh University Press, 1983; Chapter 2, pp. 14-33.

BAKHASH, SHAUL
     The Outcasts of Iran.
     Article from "The New York Review of Books", 10 May 1984;
pp. 33-36.

     The flight of writers and artists from Iran and their self
imposed exile in the West. "They wait and hope."

BALL, GEORGE W.
     What Brought Down the Shah: George Ball Reports: "The New
Peril at the Oil Crossroads".
     Photocopy of the first of a series of articles in "The
Washington Star", 14 March 1979; 4 pp.

BALL, GEORGE W.
     Iran's Revolution Isn't Over Yet: George Ball Reports: "The
New Peril at the Oil Crossroads".
     Photocopy of the second in a series of articles in "The
Washington Star", 15 March 1979; 4 pp.

BALL, GEORGE W.
     Mideast Policy Lessons from Iran: George Ball Reports: "The
New Peril at the Oil Crossroads".
     Photocopy of the last of a series of articles from "The
Washington Star", 16 March 1979; 5 pp.

     The writer with great dismay sees sad irony in the fact
that even near the turn of the 21st century religious fundamentalism and religious sectarianism are still the causes of irreconcil-
able disputes in both East and West.

BALL, GEORGE W.
     Iran's Coming Backlash.
     "The New York Times", 27 May 1979; p. E19.

     "Revolution devouring its own children." The writer sees
analogy with other revolutions and comments that the Iranian Revolution is still unfinished.

BALL, GEORGE W.
     Iran: If the Opposition Wins.
     "International Herald Tribune", 22-23 August 1981.

     Ball argues that no one could "effectively operate the hybrid institutions of a constitutional system conceived in the style of Salvador Dali". He also doubts whether the institutions created by Khomaini could function after his death.

BALTA, PAUL
     Iran: No Simple Solutions.
     Cover story from "Third World International"; Pakistan, c.early 1979; pp. 6-7.

     The magazine also includes a "Profile" of Mehdi Bazargan, the first post-revolution Prime Minister of Iran, p. 30 in the same issue.

BANANI, AMIN
     Some Notes on the Life and Works of Sadegh Hedayat: A Contemporary Reflection of Western Intellectual trends.
     Paper read at Reed College, Oregan, September 1960; 8 pp.

BANANI, AMIN
     Persian Nationalism.
     Paper read at a seminar at Columbia University, c.1965; 13 pp.

     The writer hints strongly at the incompatibility of Islam with modern nationalism but leaves the issue without resolution.

BANANI, AMIN
     Persia at the Crossroads.
     Paper "read February 3 1977 in the Iran-The Contemporary Experience Lecture Series, University of Texas at Austin", 11 pp.

     A passionate yet rational and muted exposition of the writer's theme. A beautifully written article that did not attract the attention it deserved. The writer argues that with the Persians' talent for assimilation, adaptability, change and continuity, not a great deal is too alien. Thus the writer, by inference, reasons that change and modernization can take root in Iran if it is done with prudence and without undue haste.

BANUAZIZI, ALI
     The Iranian Agony - Human Rights and the Plight of Iranian Intellectuals.
     Reprint from "Commonweal"; United States, 25 February 1983; 3 pp.

     "The fate of artists is the fate of the rest of society."

BARAHENI, REZA
     Terror in Iran.
     Article from "The New York Review of Books", 28 October 1976; illustrated plus two poems by the author; pp. 21-25. (Refer to Section A under writer's name.)

BAROYAN, O.
Discours d'Ouverture de la Conference Scientifique de Teheran.
Tehran, 1943; 8vo, soft cover; 8 pp.

In French and Persian. The Soviet Union has had a hospital in Tehran since World War II which during the 40's and early 50's also served as a center for semi political activities. The address delivered in 1943 related to 25 years of public hygiene in the U.S.S.R.

BARRETT, DOUGLAS
Persian Painting of the Fourteenth Century.
London, 1955; 4to, soft cover; illustrated in color; 24 pp.

Published by the Faber Gallery of Oriental Art, London. Introduction and notes by Douglas Barrett. From 14th century Persian manuscripts in museums in Scotland and England.

BATESON, MARY CATHERINE
At Home in Iran.
Tehran, 1976; booklet; 43 pp.

Handbook for foreigners, particularly foreign wives, living in Iran: shopping, social customs, children.

BATESON, MARY CATHERINE
"This Figure of Tinsel" : A Study of Themes of Hypocrisy and Pessimism in Iranian Culture.
Photocopy of reprint of article in "Daedalus"; United States, date unknown; pp. 127-134.

A superficial article by yet another "instant" authority on Iran, echoing Morier some 150 years later. The writer also reaches the "profound" conclusion that these characteristics produce autocratic governments.

BAUSANI, ALESSANDRO
Il "Libro della Barba" di Obeid Zakani.
Reprint from "Studi Orientali" publicati a Cura della Scuola Orientale, Universita di Roma; Rome, 1964; 19 pp.

BAYNE, E.A.
"The Bank of Tehran: A short case study of a recently founded commercial bank in a developing bank system: A letter from E.A. Bayne."
New York, 5 June 1955; illustrated, map and graphs; 18 pp.

Published by the American Universities Field Staff, Inc., New York, City. Bayne, who probably had connections with the U.S.

Government, was a thoughtful man and with his numerous contacts in Iran learned a good deal about the country. His regular audiences with the Shah in the fifties and sixties also gave him a degree of influence. Two of the bank's founders were M. Laleh, a money changer (Saraf) and M. Fateh the most senior Iranian employee of the Anglo Iranian Oil Company, both of whom had pronounced pro-British sympathies. The bank was well managed and prospered, but declined somewhat in the seventies. Fateh later wrote a useful history of the oil industry in Iran. The book, however, suffers from the writer's inflated ego and exaggeration of his own role as a primary actor in the events. The late Mohammad Reza Shah, in public pronouncements, would single out Fateh as the very epitome of British influence in Iranian domestic affairs. The Shah's invectives had their roots in the treatment he had received from the British envoy during the war years, when Fateh often acted as the messenger for the embassy. (Refer to Section A under Bullard, Sir Reader.)

BAYNE, E.A.
"How Does the Co-Op Grow?: A progress report on Iran's first rural co-operative, now nearly three years old: A letter from E.A. Bayne."
New York, 18 June 1955; illustrated and map; 18 pp.

BAYNE, E.A.
"That Spirit of 'jointness': Observation on the status of the Point IV program in Iran now that the Iranians have funds of their own for development: A letter from E.A. Bayne."
New York, 23 July 1955; 8 pp.

BAYNE, E.A.
Changing Tehran. "Persia's capital is physically in an age of change that may make for Evolution or Revolution."
Published by the American University Field Staff, Inc., Vol.X, No.2; New York, May 1961; illustrated; 14 pp.

Although the article contains some errors and does not address the question it raises; and though the writer, from the outset, has concluded that a revolution is highly unlikely, the article was nevertheless provocative in its day.

BAZIN, MARCEL
Le Trevail du Tapis dans La Région de Qom (Iran Central).
Reprinted from "Bulletin de la Societé Languedocienne de Géographie", Tom 7, Fascicule 1; France, 1978; pp. 83-92.

BEATTIE, MAY H.
The Present Position of Carpet Studies.
Article in "Apollo: The Magazine of the Arts"; London, April 1976; pp. 292-296.

BECKA, JIRI
        Jan Rypka (1886-1968).
        Photocopy of reprint from "Archiv Orientalni", No.37;
Prague, 1968; pp. 309-317.

        A short memorial biography and appreciation of the works
of the Czechoslovak scholar of Iranian and Turkish studies.

BECKWITH, JOHN
        The Influence of Islamic Art on Western Medieval Art.
        Article in "Apollo: The Magazine of the Arts"; London, April
1976; pp. 270-282.

BEESTON, RICHARD
        The Shah's Court Was Depraved Says C.I.A. Report.
        "The Daily Telegraph"; London, 3 February 1982.

BENNIGSEN, A.
        Mollah Nasreddin et la Presse Satirique Musalmane de Russie
Avant 1917.
        Reprint from "Cahiers du Monde Russe et Soviétique", Vol.III;
July-September 1962; pp. 505-520.

BENVENISTE, EMILE
        Les Noms de l'"Oiseau" en Iranien.
        Reprint of article appearing in unknown publication; Wies-
baden, July 1960; pp. 15-21.

BENVENISTE, EMILE
        Relations Lexicales Entre La Perse et La Grece Ancienne.
        Paper presented at an unnamed conference on 14 April 1965;
pp. 479-487.

BHATIA, SHYAM
        The War the World Forgot.
        Article from "The Observer"; London, c.1983; illustrated;
pp. 18-24.

        Coverage of the Iran-Iraq war some three years after the
outbreak of hostilities by a British journalist recently back
from the front.

BAILER, URI
        The Iranian Connection in Israel's Foreign Policy - 1948-
1951.
        Photocopy of reprint from "Middle East Journal", Vol.39, No.
2; United States, Spring 1985; pp. 292-315.

The writer has studied the recently released documents on the Foreign Policy of Israel as well as Israeli State Archives in connection with the preparation of the present article, and the story he recounts is indeed a sad one for Iran. After the armistice between the newly created state of Israel and the Arab countries, the Israelis were anxious to gain recognition from Turkey and Iran. Furthermore, as the government of Iraq had begun a systematic persecution of Iraqi Jews and did not allow them to leave the country, Israel sought to enlist the assistance of the Iranian government to loosen border controls to allow the "illegal" entry of Iraqi Jews into Iran for eventual immigration to Israel. Israeli intelligence agents began approaching notable Iranians to accomplish this dual purpose. Bribes were given to the then Prime Minister and several intermediaries. The Iranians reneged on the recognition issue but fulfilled their undertaking in allowing Iraqi Jews to enter the country. Writer: Member of faculty at Hebrew University, Jerusalem.

BIBLIOGRAPHY OF AFGHANISTAN.
New York, c.1974; 4to, soft cover; 19 pp.

Published as an occasional paper by the Afghanistan Council of the Asia Society, and intended as a selective, annotated bibliography, principally of books in English, which had appeared since 1968, the last year in which the more comprehensive "Annotated Bibliography of Afghanistan" by Donald N. Wilber was revised.

BIBLIOGRAPHY OF RUSSIAN WORKS ON AFGHANISTAN.
London, 1956; small 4to, soft cover; 12 pp.

Compiled by the Central Asian Research Center from bibliographies and references found in Russian publications.

BICKERMAN, ELIAS J.
The Seleucids and the Achaemenids.
Reprint from a publication by "Accademia Nazionale Dei Lincei", No.76; Rome, 1966; pp. 87-117.

A well written article dealing with the passive submission of the "Iranians" to Seleucid rule.

BICKERMAN, ELIAS J. and TADMOR, H.
Darius I, Pseudo-Smerdis, and the Magi.
Reprint from "Estratto da Athenaeua", Vol.LVI; Italy, 1978; pp. 239-261.

Writers: Bickerman; Columbia University. Tadmor; The Hebrew University.

BIENNAL DE TEHERAN:
IVéme Biennal de Teheran: Exposition de Peinture et de

Sculpture.
        Iran, 1964; 4to, soft cover; illustrated; 157 pp.

        Catalogue of an exhibition in Tehran in April and May 1964.
Introduction in Persian, captions to illustrations in Persian and
French. Contemporary Persian artists.

BIENNAL DE TEHERAN:
        Vth Tehran 'regional' Biennale.
        Iran, 1966; 4to, soft cover; illustrated; 172 pp.

        Catalogue of an exhibition of painting, graphics and
sculpture from Pakistan, Turkey and Iran held in June and July
1966 and organized by the Ministry of Culture and Arts with the
co-operation of the Cultural Committee of the Regional Cooperation
for Development (R.C.D.) Ethnographical Museum.

BILL, JAMES A.
        Iran and the Crisis of '78.
        Article in "Foreign Affairs"; United States, Winter 1978/9:
pp. 323-342.

        The writer argues that the Shah could still save the situation
"by a bold stroke designed to open the system and to introduce
political participation ...". This was written in 1978 and with
the benefit of hindsight it is obvious that it was much too late.
The article has, however, some fresh insight and an interesting
analogy to F.D.R.'s dual role as a "lion and a fox". The writer
believes the Shah played the fox from 1941 to 1972. He then played
the role of the lion and hints that he may revert to playing the
fox again. The article basically pleads and hopes for a more open
society in Iran that can accommodate the various factions.

BILL, JAMES A.
        Iran experts: Proven right but not consulted.
        Photocopy of an article from "The Christian Science Monitor",
Opinion and Commentary column; Boston, 6 May 1980; p. 19.

BILL, JAMES A.
        Five Lessons of Iran-American Imbroglio.
        Photocopy of an article from an unidentified newspaper, c.1980.

BILL, JAMES A.
        Cromwell, Napoleon and the Iranians.
        "The Christian Science Monitor", Opinion and Commentary col-
umn; Boston, 9 September 1981; p. 23.

        A study of Crane Brinton's "Anatomy of Revolution".

BILL, JAMES A.
        The Unfinished Revolution in Iran.

Article in "International Insight", Vol.II, No.I; Cleveland, Ohio, November/December 1981; illustrated; pp. 9-6.

Approaching its third anniversary, the Iranian Revolution was bogged down "in social chaos, economic uncertainty, domestic political upheavel and a costly war with neighboring Iraq". The writer argues that the Iranian Revolution has not yet run its course. When it does, then it may recover some of the attract- iveness and appeal that it held for a few short months in 1979 when millions in the Third World saw it as a "beacon for a better future". The writer was and still appears to be hopeful that some- thing sane will come out of it all.

BILL, JAMES A.
The Politics of Extremism in Iran.
Photocopy reprinted from "Peyvand", Vol.XIII, Issue 37; Arlington, Virginia, February 1982; 6 pp.

BILL, JAMES A.
The Arab World and the Challenge of Iran.
Photocopy from "Journal of Arab Affairs", Vol.2; no place of publication indicated; 1 November, Autumn 1982; pp. 29-45.

A well written article with some original observations.

BILL, JAMES A.
Power and Religion in Revolutionary Iran.
Reprint from "The Middle East Journal", Vol.36, 1 November; United Stated, Winter 1982; pp. 22-47.

BILL, JAMES A.
Islam, Politics, and Shi'ism in the Gulf.
Reprint from "Middle East Insight", Vol.3; no place of publication indicated; 1984; illustrated and map; pp. 3-12.

In a perceptive article the writer concludes that, "The most important aspect of the surge of Islam in the Gulf is that it is not something promulgated and propagated from above but rather is a massive movement bubbling up from below. It is popular Islam as opposed to establishment Islam".

BILL, JAMES A.
Resurgent Islam in the Persian Gulf.
Reprint from "Foreign Affairs"; United States, Fall 1984; pp. 108-127.

Same points as preceding.

BINDER, LEONARD.
The Proofs of Islam: Religion and Politics in Iran.

Reprint from "Arabic and Islamic Studies in Honor of Hamilton A.R. Gibb". Published by the Department of Near Eastern Languages and Literature of Harvard University, 1965; pp. 118-140.

The writer in an excellent article, written before the interest of Western observers was focused on the role of the clergy in the politics of the Islamic world, sets forth four propositions: 1) Shi'ite Islam gives greater authority to the ulama than do the Sunnis; 2) the Shi'ite clergy's authority has seldom been questioned; 3) the ulama of Iran are more organized in terms of "formal institutional roles" than their Sunni counterparts; and 4) the Shi'ite ulama have been more effective at maintaining solidarity and independance from government control.

BIRD, KAI
        Khomeini Cracks Down.
        Article in "The Nation"; United States, 19 May 1979; pp. 59-
61.

        Subtitled "making Iran safe for theocracy". One of the earliest critical magazine pieces, written only two months after the Revolution. Writer: An assistant editor of The Nation who had recently returned from Iran.

BIVAR, A.D.H.
        A Rosette Phiale Inscribed in Aramaic.
        Reprint from "BSOAS", London University, Vol.XXIV, Part 2; 1961; full page plates; pp. 190-199.

BIVAR, A.D.H. and SHAKED, S.
        The Inscriptions of Shimbar.
        Photocopy of reprint from "BSOAS", London University, Vol. XXVII, Part 2; 1964; pp. 265-291.

BIVAR, A.D.H.
        A Parthian Amulet.
        Reprint from "BSOAS", London University, Vol.XXX, Part 3; 1967; pp. 512-524.

BIVAR, A.D,H.
        Hariti and the Chronology of the Kusanas.
        Reprint from "BSOAS", London University, Vol.XXXIII, Part I; 1970; pp. 10-21.

BIVAR, A.D.H.
        Sassanians, Kushans, Kushano-Sasssanians, Hephthalites.
        Offprint from "A Survey of Numismatic Research, 1972-1977"; Berne, 1979; pp. 418-428.

BIVAR, A.D.H.
        Mithraic Images of Bactria : Are they related to Roman Mith-

750

raism?
     Reprint from "Mysteria Mithrae"; Leiden, 1979; pp. 741-751
and 8 pp. of illustrations.

BIVAR, A.D.H.
     Gondophares and the Shahnama.
     Photocopy of reprint from "Iranica Antiqua", Vol.XVI; Leiden,
1981; pp. 141-150, and one full page illustration.

BLOCHET, E.
     Catalogue of an Exhibition of Persian Paintings from the
XIIIth to the XVIIIth Cent.: formerly from the Collections of the
Shahs of Persia and of the Great Moguls.
     New York, c.1925; illustrated; 79 pp.

     Compiled by E. Blochet from the collection of Demotte.

BLUNT, WILFRID
     The Persian Garden Under Islam.
     Article in "Apollo : The Magazine of the Arts"; London, April
1976; illustrated, some in color; pp. 302-306.

BOAZMAN, MARY
     The Women of the Desert City.
     Article from "The Lady's Realm", Vol.XXIV; no place of
publication indicated; c.1910; illustrated; pp. 609-614.

     Description of the lives of Persian women in the City of
Yazd, their social life and "habits".

BOWLER, IAN J.
     Notes on Falconry in Iran.
     13 typewritten pages dated "6.5.68" together with 6 photo-
graphs.

     Writer: A British businessman associated over a long period
with Iran.

BOYCE, MARY
     Some Remarks on the Transmission of the Kayanian Heroic Cycle.
     Reprint from "Serta Cantabrigiensia"; Wiesbaden, 1954; pp. 45-
52.

     Writer: London University; one of the foremost authorities on
Zoroastrian history and culture.

BOYCE, MARY
     Zariadres and Zarer.
     Reprint from "BSOAS", London University, Vol, XVII, Part 3;
1955; pp. 463-477.

751

BOYCE, MARY
     The Indian Fables in the Letter of Tansar.
     Reprint from "Asia Major, British Journal of Far Eastern
Studies", Vol.V, Part 1; London, 1955; pp. 50-58.

     The Letter of Tansar, written in Pahlavi and translated into
Persian at the turn of the 20th century, is a moving story of the
king of Tabarestan being advised to keep a balance in his life
between fate and one's own efforts and that ultimately one's own
efforts can even affect fate.
     The letter was included in Ibn Esfandiar's "History of
Tabarestan" and was purported to have been written in Ardashir I's
reign, 226-241 A.D.. Later it was proved to have been written
during Khosrow I's reign, 557-570 A.D..

BOYCE, MARY
     Some Reflections on Zurvanism.
     Photocopy of reprint from "BSOAS", London University, Vol.XIX,
Part 2; 1957; pp. 304-316.

BOYCE, MARY
     The Parthian Gosan and Iranian Minstrel Tradition.
     Photocopy of reprint from "Journal of the Royal Asiatic
Society"; 1957; pp. 10-45.

BOYCE, MARY
     On the Sacred Fires of the Zoroastrians.
     Reprint from "BSOAS", London University; c.1960; pp. 52-68.

BOYCE, MARY
     Rapithwin, Noruz, and the Feast of Sade.
     Offprint from "Pratidanam-Indian, Iranian and Indo European
Studies" presented to Franciscus Bernardus Jacobus Kuiper on his
sixtieth birthday; London, c.1965; pp. 201-215.

BOYCE, MARY
     The Fire-Temples of Kerman.
     Reprint from "Acta Orientalia", Vol.XXX; Leiden, 1966; pp.
51-72.

BOYCE, MARY
     Bibi Shahrbanu and The Lady of Pars.
     Reprinted from "BSOAS", London University, Vol.XXX, Part 1;
1967; pp. 30-44.

     An original contribution.

BOYCE, MARY
     Obituary: Walter Bruno Henning.
     Reprint from "BSOAS", London University, Vol.XXX, Part 3;
1967; pp. 781-785.

W.B. Henning (1908-1967) was one of the leading "Orientalists" of the 20th century. His specialty was Middle Iranian studies, but he did some work on earlier periods. He was born and educated in Germany, went to England before World War II and taught at universities in England and the U.S. from 1957-1961. He was the head of S.O.A.S. and from 1961 to his death he was professor of Iranian studies at the University of California, Berkeley. In 1950 he had been invited by the Iranian Government to visit southern Iran and work on Pahlavi inscriptions.

BOYCE, MARY
The Manichaean Literature in Middle Iranian.
Photocopy of reprint from "Iranistik"; Leiden, 1968; pp. 67-76.

BOYCE, MARY
The Pious Functions of the Zoroastrians.
Reprint from "BSOAS", London University, Vol.XXXI, Part 2; 1968; pp. 270-289.

BOYCE, MARY
Middle Persian Literature.
Photocopy of reprint from "Handbuch der Orientalistik"; Leiden, 1968; pp. 31-52.

BOYCE, MARY
Some Aspects of Farming in a Zoroastrian Village of Yazd.
Reprint from "Persica"; Netherlands, 1969; two pp. of illustrations; pp. 121-140.

BOYCE, MARY
Maneckji Limj, Hataria In Iran.
Reprint from "K.R. Cama Oriental Institute Golden Jubilee", Vol.I; Bombay, 1969; pp. 19-31.

BOYCE, MARY
On the Calendars of Zoroastrian Feasts.
Reprint from "BSOAS", London University, Vol.XXXIII, Part 3; 1970; pp. 513-539.

BOYCE, MARY
Mihragan Among the Irani Zoroastrians.
Photocopy of offprint from "Mithraic Studies"; Manchester University Press; 1975; pp. 106-118.

BOYCE, MARY
Iconoclasm Among the Zoroastrians.
Reprint from "Christianity, Judaism and Other Greco-Roman Cults-Studies for Morton Smith at Sixty"; Leiden, 1975; pp. 93-111.

BOYCE, MARY
      On the Zoroastrian Temple Cult Fire.
      Reprint from "Journal of the American Oriental Society",
Vol.95, No.3; July-September 1975; pp. 456-465.

BOYCE, MARY
      On the Antiquity of the Zoroastrian Apocalyptic.
      Photocopy of reprint from "BSOAS", London University, Vol.
XLVII, Part 1; 1984; pp. 57-75.

BOYLE, JOHN ANDREW
      The Mongul Commanders in Afghanistan and India According to
the Tabaghat-Nasiri of Juzjani.
      Reprint from "Islamic Studies, Journal of the Central Instit-
ute of Islamic Research", Vol.II, No.2; Karachi, June 1963; pp.
235-247.

      Writer: Head of Department of Persian Studies at the Univers-
ity of Manchester.

BOYLE, JOHN ANDREW
      The Longer Introduction to the "Zij-i-Ilkhani" of Nasir-Edin
Tusi.
      Photocopy of extract from "Journal of Semitic Studies", Vol.8,
No.2; no place of publication indicated; Autumn 1963; pp. 244-254.

BOYLE, JOHN ANDREW
      Omar Khayyam: Astronomer, Mathematician and Poet.
      Reprinted from the "Bulletin of the John Rylands Library",
Vol.2, No.1; Manchester, Autumn 1969; pp. 30-45.

      The writer poses often-raised questions; Khayyam's date of
birth and the number of quatrains that can be safely attributed to
him. (Refer to Omar Khayyam in Section B.)

BOYLE, JOHN ANDREW
      The Significance of the Jami'Al-Tavarikh as a Source of Mongol
History.
      Reprint from "Iran Shinasi", Vol.2, No.1; no place of public-
ation indicated; 1970; 8 pp.

      A well written article by a renowned authority on Mongol Per-
sia. The writer argues that Rashid al Din could not have devoted
much time to the writing of the history. It was probably written
by a team of collaborators in the mold of Chinese dynastic histor-
ies, e.g. the official history of the Yuan or Mongol dynasty of
China.

BOYLE, JOHN ANDREW
      The Chronology of Sa'adi's Years of Travel.
      Reprint from "Islamwissenschaftliche Abhandlungen"; Wiesbaden,
1974; 8 pp.

In a well researched article, the writer uses internal text-
ual evidence in Sa'di's own writings to reconstruct the poet's
movements from the completion of his studies at Baghdad to his
return to Shiraz. The writer makes the case that the poet probably visited Syria and parts of Asia Minor during his travels.

BOYLE, JOHN ANDREW
The Alexander Romance in the East and in the West.
Reprinted from "Bulletin of the John Rylands Library", Vol.
60, No.1; Manchester, Autumn 1977; pp. 13-27.

The writer discusses an anonymous work written in Greek sometime in third century A.D. Alexandria. The tale not only includes
a great number of historical errors but at times turns into pure
fantasy and fiction. There is reason to believe the Greek text
was translated into Pahlavi sometime in the 7th century A.D. but
has not survived. The original Greek text has been translated
into many other languages.

BOYLE, JOHN ANDREW
'Believe All the Fables'.
Article from "Hemisphere Magazine"; Australia, November 1977;
illustrated, some in color; pp. 22-27.

Writer traces the history of animal fables from their origins
in India through their Persian and Arabic versions until their
eventual translation into European languages and their disseminat-
ion throughout the Western World culminating in the "Fables" of
La Fontaine.

BOZORGNIA, HOSSEIN
Iranica Suecana.
Bibliography of books by Swedish writers and other books
printed in Sweden on Iran in the collection of the compiler which
is comprised of 70 books.

BRAGINSKY, I.S.
West-East Synthesis in Goethe's Divan and Classical Persian
Poetry.
Reprint of paper presented at the XXVI International Congress
of Orientalists; Moscow, 1963; 14 pp.

The writer, a Soviet Orientalist, argues that the capitalistic
colonization of the Third World beginning in the late 15th century
led to a feeling of "bitter shame" amongst the progressive elements
of the West and that it was this feeling that created the interest
of the European intelligentsia in Eastern culture, especially
literature, and produced "apologetic literature" by Western writers
on the East.

BRAVMANN, M.M.
The Origin of the Principle of "Ismah" : Muhammad's Immunity from Sin.
Reprint from "Le Museon"; Louvain, 1975; pp. 221-225.

An interesting article in which the writer argues that the concept of immunity from sin which is ascribed to Mohammad and the Shi'ite Imams, is a pre-Islamic principle.

BREASTED, CHARLES
Exploring the Secrets of Persepolis.
From "The National Geographic Magazine"; Washington, D.C., October 1933; illustrations and photographs; pp. 381-420.

Writer: Executive Secretary, the Oriental Institute, University of Chicago.

BREGEL, YURI
The Role of Central Asia in the History of the Muslim East.
Occasional Paper Number 20, published by the Afghanistan Council of the Asia Society; New York, February 1980; large 8vo, soft cover; 19 pp.

Writer: Institute of Asian and African Affairs, Hebrew University of Jerusalem.

BRILL, STEVEN
No Gold at the Hague.
Photocopy from "The American Lawyer"; September 1982; illustrated; 6 pp.

Coverage of the Iran-U.S. Claims Tribunal at the Hague. Interview with Howard Holtzmann, one of the U.S. arbitrators.

BRITISH FOREIGN OFFICE DOCUMENTS
Correspondence between the British Foreign Office and the British Embassies in Tehran and Washington, from 31 December 1950 to 24 September 1954, recently released by the British Government; 55 pp.

The declassification has been selective. There are many documents that will not be declassified until a later date (some im the year 2050). Among the documents released the following are interesting samples:

A.   In a cable (or letter) dated 19 November 1951 from George Middleton, the British Minister in Tehran, to G.W. Furlonge, head of the Eastern Department, Foreign Office, it is stated:

"4.   The American view is that Persian nationalism is a potent and spontaneous force which will be an overriding

factor on its own account regardless of the wishes and
actions of any future government."

"5.   Our view is that Iranian nationalism certainly exists
but that its effectiveness as a political force is largely
a matter of manipulation. We think that a successor
government to Mussadiq should be capable of controlling
the feeling through propaganda and by organizing manifest-
ations of public opinion to meet its current political
requirements."

In enclosure number 2 to the above, Middleton mentions the
"emergence of two strong personalities as supplanters to Musaddiq
in the person of Sayyid Zia and Qavam-us-Saltaneh". Middleton
also states that there is widespread belief that Mosaddeq enjoys
U.S. support and he asks for steps to counter this. The power and
potential of the Tude party is exaggerated in the same cable,
mainly for the benefit of the U.S. State Department.

B.   In a dispatch dated 21 May 1953 from Sir Roger Makins, the
British Ambassador to Washington, to the Foreign Office, Makins
states that "the State Department informed us today that on an
occasion associates of the Shah have told Henderson (the U.S.
Ambassador) that His Majesty is uncertain about the British attitude towards himself. He is reported to be harping on the theme
that the British had thrown out the Qajar Dynasty, had brought in
his father and had thrown his father out. Now they could keep him
in power or remove him in turn as they saw fit. If they desired
that he should stay ... he should be informed. If on the other
hand they wished him to go he should be told immediately so that
he could leave quietly. Did the British wish to substitute another
Shah for himself or to abolish the monarchy? Were they behind the
present efforts to deprive him of his power and prestige? ..."

The Prime Minister (Winston Churchill) cables Sir Roger
Makins: "You may certainly inform the State Department that while
we do not interfere in Persian politics we should be very sorry
to see the Shah leave his post or be driven out. Perhaps Mr.
Henderson ... will convey this assurance to the Shah and say that
it comes personally from me."

C.   Several dispatches re the Shah's flight from Iran in the
aftermath of his attempt to dismiss Mosaddeq (August 1953). Cables
from Baghdad and Rome, Washington and London and dispatches re his
return following the coup that overthrew Mosaddeq.

D.   Dispatch from Sir Roger Stevens dated 24 Sept. 1954 to the
Foreign Office re his audience with the Shah and the Shah's desire
to visit Europe and the United States. Sir Roger states that until
the oil agreement is signed, he does not believe it advisable for

the Shah to travel. After a lengthy discussion, the Ambassador,
making no promises, hopes the Shah could travel in 45 days.
The Shah wishes he could leave earlier, as his Queen (Soraya) is
most anxious to see England again and especially the U.S. which
she had never seen before.

The documents speak for themselves.

BRUNNER, CHRISTOPHER J. (translated by)
     Selected texts from pre-Islamic Iran.
     Special supplement to "The Iran Council Grapevine"; published
by the Asia Society, New York, c.1970; 14 pp. and map.

     Four readings from Middle Persian literature of the
Sassanian Dynasty (224-651 A.D.):

1)   "The Babylonian Tree"
2)   "Khosraw, Son of Kawad, and a Page"
3) and 4) Two chapters from commentary on the Avesta:
     "On the Lineage of Animals" and "On the Lineage of Man".

BRUNNER, CHRISTOPHER J.
     The Chronology of the Sassanian Kusansahs.
     Photocopy of reprint from the "American Numismatic Society
Museum", Notes 19 (1974); 2 pp. of illustrations; pp. 146-164.

BRUNNER, CHRISTOPHER J.
     Middle Persian Inscriptions on Sassanian Silverware.
     Photocopy of reprint from "Metropolitan Museum Journal", Vol.
9; 1974; pp. 109-121.

BRUNNER, CHRISTOPHER J.
     The Middle Persian Explanation of Chess and Invention of
Backgammon.
     Reprint from "Journal of the Ancient Near Eastern Society of
Columbia University", Vol.10; 1978; pp. 43-51.

     Not as easy at the title suggests. Only "Middle Persians"
can understand the "Explanation".

"BULLETIN OF THE MINNEAPOLIS INSTITUTE OF ARTS"
     Vol.XXXIV, No.14; Minneapolis, Minnesota, 7 April 1945;
illustrated; pp. 45-52.

     Published weekly from October to June by the Minneapolis
Society of Fine Arts (Inc.), this issue consists of an article
entitled "Gift of Persian Miniatures" and describes the collection
of five miniatures recently donated to the Art Institute by the
late Charles C. Webber and Mrs. Webber. The miniatures date from
the late-thirteenth to mid-sixteenth century.

758

BUNDY, WILLIAM P.
        Who Lost Patagonia? Foreign Policy in the 1980 Campaign.
        Reprint from "Foreign Affairs", Vol.58, No.I; United States,
Fall 1979; 27 pp.

        An examination of two important potential foreign policy
issues in the forthcoming U.S. presidential campaign: The Carter
administration's handling of the revolutions in Nicaragua and Iran.
Writer: Former Assistant Secretary of State and former editor of
"Foreign Affairs" has had a long association with Iran. As a
lawyer at the Washington firm of Covington and Burling, he was one
of the drafters of Iran's position on Soviet withdrawal from
Azarbaijan in 1946.

BURGEL, J. CH.
        Psychosomatic Methods of Cases in the Islamic Middle Ages.
        Reprint from "Humanitoria Islamica", Vol.I; Paris, 1973; pp.
157-172.

        The writer in an interesting article maintains that Freud had
predecessors in the Islamic Middle Ages; Avicenna was an ancestor of
psychoanalytic studies and Razi was aware of the subtle and close
relationship between body and mind. The writer cites prevalent
practices for the cure of mild depression and melancholy e.g.
administering stimulants to make the patient joyous. In cases
of a lover's grief, patients were encouraged to talk of their
beloved and bring their grief out into the open. In cases of
severe depression, physicians recognized the importance of faith
on the part of the patient in the process of healing.
Treatment often included the arousing of fear, shock or shame.

BURROW, T.
        The Proto-Indoaryans.
        Photocopy of reprint from "Journal of the Royal Asiatic
Society"; Great Britain, 1973; pp. 123-140.

CALENDAR:
     1978 Appointment Calendar/Diary.
     Negarestan Museum of 18th and 19th Century Iranian Art,
Tehran; frontispiece illustrated in color; 108 pp.

     The illustrations consist of objects in the museum's own
collection.

CALENDAR:
     Wall calendar for 1980.
     Published by Jay and Sumi Gluck; Japan; illustrated in color;
6 pp.

     Illustrations are of Persian glass and taken from Gluck's
book, "A Survey of Persian Handicrafts".

CALENDAR:
     Wall calendar for 1981.
     Published by Jay and Sumi Gluck; Japan (?); illustrated in
color; 6 pp.

     Illustrations are of Persian embroideries taken from Gluck's
book, mentioned above.

CAMERON, GEORGE G.
     Darius Carved History on Ageless Rock.
     Articles from "The National Geographic Magazine"; Washington,
D.C., December 1950; illustrations; pp. 825-844.

CAMERON, GEORGE G. (with contributions by I. Gershevitch)
     New Tablets from the Persepolis Treasury.
     Reprint from "Journal of Near Eastern Studies", Vol.XXIV,
No.3; July 1965; pp. 167-192.

CAREY, JANE PERRY CLARK and CAREY, ANDREW GALBRAITH
     Iranian Agriculture and Its Development 1952-1973.
     Photocopy of reprint from "International Journal of Middle
East Studies", 7; Great Britain, 1976; pp. 359-382.

CARPET MUSEUM.
     Tehran, c.1977; large 8vo, soft cover folder containing 15
4" x 6" colored post-cards of carpets on display in the Carpet
Museum.

CATALOGUE de L'ESPOSITION ORIENTALE.
     Paris, 1925; index; advertisements; illustrations; 94 pp.

     In French. Catalogue of an exhibition at the National Library,
Paris, 19th May to 19th June 1925. Most of the objects exhibited
in this early exposition were Persian. E. Blochet played a promin-

ent part in the arrangements for the event.

CATALOGUE OF IRANIAN ART EXHIBITED IN ROME IN JUNE-AUGUST 1956.
Milan, 1956; 8vo, soft cover; 303 pp. of text and illustrations and 64 plates.

Exhibition of Iranian art from the Achaemenid period to late 17th century. An extensive exhibition with contributions by museums from Europe and the U.S.

A CATALOGUE OF THE LIBRARY OF THE LATE A.G. ELLIS.
(Part III) Comprising a fine collection of manuscripts: Arabic, Persian and Turkish; books on the Near East: mainly Arabic, Persian and Turkish texts and translations, etc..
London, 1945; 8vo, soft cover; 84 pp.

An interesting catalogue both for the number of entries, 940 books, and prices in 1945.

CATALOGUE OF ART AT NEGARESTAN MUSEUM
Tehran, 1977.

An Exhibition of lacquer mirror boxes.

CATALOGUE AND PRICE LIST OF WORKS PUBLISHED IN THE PAHLAVI COMMEMORATIVE SERIES.
Tehran, 1976; 8vo, soft cover; 40 pp.

Includes specimen reproductions of plates from various volumes in the series.

CELLI, ROSALYN
Iran in the Nineteenth and Twentieth Centuries: An Annotated Bibliography.
Photocopy of 34 typewritten pages. Edited by Nikki Keddie.

CHELKOWSKI, PETER J.
Ta'ziyeh: Indigenous Avant-Gard Theatre of Iran.
Paper read at an international symposium on Ta'ziyeh held in Shiraz in conjunction with its annual Festival of Art, 20-24 August 1976.

Indigenous it may be, but it is more primitive than avant-garde. Iran is a country that is highly unlikely to ever have "theater" for a variety of reasons, including lack of any tradition on stage and a language that sounds artificial when spoken in the vernacular. Ta'zie became popular in the late 19th century and it is interesting to note that the clergy discouraged its staging, their primary motive being that the reciter gained popularity and competed with the influence of the local cleric.

CHELKOWSKI, PETER J.
Iran: Mourning Becomes Revolution. Annual rites of self-sacrifice, atonement and revenge precipitated the toppling of the Shah and the taking of the American hostages.
Photocopy of reprint from "Asia"; United States, May-June 1980; illustrations; pp. 30-45.

The writer's interest in Ta'zie forms the basis of this article as well.

CHRISTENSEN, ARTHUR
Abasam et Tansar.
Article in French from unknown source; c.1935; pp. 43-55.

CHUBIN, SHAHRAM
Repercussions of the Crisis in Iran.
Article in "Survival", Vol.XXI, No.3; Journal published by the International Institute for Strategic Studies, London, May/June 1979; page unknown.

The writer holds the U.S. partially responsible for the Iranian Revolution and argues for a more activist policy towards Iran. He also believes the country will move gradually towards the left and hints that Marxist and neo-Marxist forces would eventually take over.

CHUBIN, SHAHRAM
The Iranian Revolution and its Consequences for the Gulf Region and the Arab World.
Reprint of article (in English) from "Iran in der Krise-Weichenstellungen für die Zukunft"; Sonderdruck, Bonn, 1980; pp. 199-206.

The writer now sees the radicalization of the Persian Gulf States.

CHUBIN, SHAHRAM
Soviet Policy Towards Iran and the Gulf.
London, Spring 1980; 8vo, soft cover; 50 pp.

Published by the International Institute for Strategic Studies, London. A recitation of traditional Soviet motives and policy.

CHUBIN, SHAHRAM
Leftist Forces in Iran.
Cover and article from "Problems of Communism", Vol.XXIX; Washington, D.C., July-August 1980; illustrated; pp. 1-25.

The writer again argues that leftist forces would eventually overthrow the clergy.

CHUBIN, SHAHRAM
      The United States (The Major Power and the Third World
Motives, Objectives and Policies).
      Photocopy of 26 pp. type-written paper for discussion in
committee of "The International Institute for Strategic Studies:
Twenty-Second Annual Conference", Stresa, Italy, 11-14 September
1980.

CHUBIN, SHAHRAM
      Regional Perceptions of the Impact of Soviet Policy in the
Middle East.
      Washington, D.C., September 1981.

      Published by "Wilson Center", Washington, D.C.

CHUBIN, SHAHRAM
      Le Guerre Irano-Irakienne: Paradoxes et Particularités.
      Cover and article from "Politique Etrangère"; Paris, February
1982; maps; pp. 381-394.

CHUBIN, SHAHRAM
      The Soviet Union and Iran.
      "Foreign Affairs", Vol.61, No.4; United States, Spring 1983;
pp. 921-949.

CLAPP, GORDON R.
      A TVA for the Khuzestan Region.
      Reprint from "The Middle East Journal", Vol.II, No.1; United
States, Winter 1957; 11 pp.

      Summary of preliminary steps towards a T.V.A. type of develop-
ment project in Khuzestan.

CLEAVES, FRANCIS WOODMAN
      SAQID=ZAH (I) D.
      Reprint from "Harvard Journal of Asiatic Studies", Vol.18,
Nos.1 and 2; June 1955; pp. 234-238.

CLIFTON, TONY
      A View from Tehran.
      Article from "Newsweek", 10 March 1986; pp. 51.

      The February 1986 offensive by Iran in the Iran-Iraq War.

CLINTON, JEROME W.
      The Madaen Qasida of Xaqani Sharvani, Part I.
      Reprint of paper originally presented in 1974 at the Middle
East Studies Association meeting, later revised by the writer;
pp. 153-170.

A discussion of the very popular poem of Khaqani (d.1202). The writer advances reasons for its popularity as the poet's other works are seldom read. Writer: Professor at Princeton University.

CLINTON, JEROME W.
     The Madaen Qasida of Xaqani Sharvani, Part II: Xaqani and Al-Buhturi.
     pp. 191-206.

A COLLECTION OF IRANIAN ARTIFACTS: FROM THE 2nd MILLENIUM TO THE 6th CENTURY B.C.
     Catalogue of the Reza Abbasi Cultural and Arts Center; Iran, 1977; 8vo, soft cover; illustrated, some in color and map; 50 pp.

     Parallel texts and captions to the illustrations in Persian and English.

A COLLECTION OF IRANIAN ISLAMIC ART: THE 9th THROUGH THE 19th CENTURY A.D.
     Catalogue of the Reza Abbasi Cultural and Arts Center; Tehran, September 1977; 8vo, soft cover; illustrated, some in color; 40 pp.

A COLLECTION OF IRANIAN MINIATURES AND CALLIGRAPHY FROM THE 14th TO THE 18th CENTURY A.D.
     Catalogue of the Reza Abbasi Cultural and Arts Center; Tehran, September 1977; 12 pp. of introductory text plus 25 plates, all but one in color.

CONFEDERATION OF IRANIAN STUDENTS REPORT.
     Vol.II, No.3; Köln, West Germany, December 1978; illustrated; 15 pp.

     In English. An account of events in Iran in 1978 by fervent supporters of the Revolution.

CONTEMPORARY PERSIAN ART: EXPRESSION OF OUR TIME.
     Pasadena, California, 1984; large booklet; illustrated, some in color; 71 pp.

     Designed to accompany an exhibition of contemporary Persian art held at the Pacific Asia Museum in Pasadena, California, 8 September to 28 October 1984, sponsored by the Foundation for Iranian Studies, Washington, D.C.

CONTENAU, G.
     L'Archeologie de La Perse des Origines à l'Epoque d'Alexandre.
     Paris, c.1930; soft cover; illustrated; 16 pp.

     In French. Lecture given at the Musée Guimet in Paris in 1930.

COOLEY, JOHN K.
    Iran, the Palestinians and the Gulf.
    An article from "Foreign Affairs"; United States, Summer
1979; pp. 1017-1034.

    In a hasty conclusion, the writer maintains that the new
Iranian regime allied with the PLO has altered the balance of power
in the region. Writer: Correspondent for the Christian Science
Monitor.

COOPER, ROGER
    Riot and 'Quake: Iran's Week of Agony.
    Cover Story, "Sunday Times Magazine"; London, 12 November
1978; illustrated; pp. 24-40.

COOPER, ROGER
    Civil War in Iran.
    An article from "The Spectator"; Great Britain, 5 September
1981; p. 7.

COOPER, ROGER
    Khomeini's Crumbling empire.
    Article from "The Observer" color supplement; London. c.1981;
illustrated; pp. 14-28.

    The writer maintains the war, the Mojahedeen and loss of oil
revenues will cause Khomaini's downfall. He recently travelled to
Iran and was imprisoned for unknown reasons.

COOPERMAN, STANLEY
    Iran's False Front.
    Article from "The Nation"; New York, 24 September 1960; pp.
176-178.

    The writer was a Fulbright Scholar in Iran at the time of
writing. A well written article, even though most of his assumpt-
ions did not come about as envisaged.

COTTAM, RICHARD
    Political Party Development in Iran.
    Copy of typewritten paper prepared for a seminar at Harvard
University on problems of contemporary Iran, held in April 1965;
18 pp.

    The writer was one of the few Westerners at the time who
thought liberal democratic institutions could be viable in a country
such as Iran. He maintains that, "It is an irony of the first
order that had it not been for the intervention of the liberal
democratic West liberal democratic institutions might have established root in Iran". The writer sees no viability for the Shah's
regime and predicts that the Iran Novin party, formed in 1964, would

fail as had other artificial political parties instituted by the
Shah. (Refer to Cottam, Richard in Section A.)

COWEN, JILL SANCHIA
     Drama and Morality in Two Early Mongol Illustrated Sequences
from the "Kalilla Wa Dimna".
     Article in "Oriental Art", Vol.XXX, No.2; London, Summer 1984;
illustrated; pp. 167-177.

     Detailed examination of 17 Iranian paintings of animal fables
contained in a late 13th century album in the library of the
Topkapi Serayi Museum in Istanbul.

COX, GENERAL SIR PERCY
     The Death of Herr Wassmuss.
     Article in the "Journal of the Royal Central Asian Society",
Vol.XIX, Part I; London, January 1932; 8vo; pp. 151-155.

     An obituary account of the activities of the famous German
spy in Persia during World War I. (Refer to Sykes, Christopher in
Section A.)

COYAJEE, SIR J.C.
     The Supposed Sculpture of Zoroaster on the Tak-i-Bostan.
     Photocopy of reprint from "Journal and Proceedings, Asiatic
Society of Bengal", Vol.XXII, No.6, issued 12 March 1928; pp. 391-
409.

COYAJEE, SIR J.C.
     The Shahnameh and the Feng-Shen-Yen-I.
     Photocopy of reprint from "Journal and Proceedings, Asiatic
Society of Bengal", Vol.XXVI, NO.4, 1930; pp. 491-511.

COYNE, MICHAEL
     Inside Iran.
     "The Observer"; London, 6 October 1985; pp. 40-45.

     A collection of photographs by an Australian journalist of
the devastating effects of the five year Iran-Iraq war.

CRAWFORD, VAUGHN EMERSON; HARPER, PRUDENCE OLIVER; MUSCARELLA,
OSCAR WHITE; and BODENSTEIN, BEATRICE ELIZABETH
     Ancient Near Eastern Art Guide to Collections.
     Photocopy of publication by the Metropolitan Museum of Art;
New York, 1966; map and illustrations in text; 41 pp.

CRESSON, REBECCA SHANNON
     We Lived in Turbulent Tehran.
     Article in the "National Geographic Magazine", Vol.CIV, No.5;
Washington, D.C., November 1953; map and illustrations; pp. 707-720

Wife of an American teacher who was in Tehran for two years tells of her experiences during the Mosaddeq era.

CROWE, YOLANDE
Islamic Pottery and China.
Article in "Apollo: The Magazine of the Arts"; London, April 1976; illustrations; pp. 296-302.

THE CROWN JEWELS
Tehran, 1964; booklet; full page color illustrations; 45 pp.

A guide book to the Crown Jewels of Iran, published by Bank Markazi Iran (The Central Bank of Iran) where the jewels are on deposit and were on view to the general public.

THE CROWN JEWELS OF IRAN
Tehran, 1970; small 8vo, soft cover; illustrated in color; 50 pp.

Published also by the Bank Markazi Iran. More informative than the preceding.

DAFTARY, FARHAD
W. Ivanow: A Biographical Notice.
Reprint from "Middle Eastern Studies"; London, May 1972;
pp. 241-244.

A tribute to a distinguished Orientalist, Waldimar Ivanow
(1886-1970). Ivanow was the greatest authority on Ismaili Studies.
Born in Russia, he learned Persian and Arabic in St. Petersburg,
and served as a consular official in Iran, 1912-1914. He subsequently became a British citizen, and in 1920 went to India where
he lived for almost 40 years. In 1959 he returned to Iran and
remained until his death. Ivanow was one of the great authorities on the Persian poet Naser Khosrow.

DAILY EXPRESS
Special Edition: The Day of the S.A.S.: "The Inside Story of
How Britain Ended the Siege of Princess Gate." (Iranian Embassy
seizure in London.)
London, 1980; illustrated special issue in color supplement
format; 64 pp.

THE DAILY TELEGRAPH
Iranians Offer Only Token Resistance.
London, 27 August 1941; three full columns on p. 1 and
separate article on p. 6 (back page).

The Invasion of Iran by the Allies.

THE DAILY TELEGRAPH
R.A.F. Bomb Fortified Pass in Iran.
London, 28 August 1941; two articles on p. 1 and separate
article on p. 6.

THE DAILY TELEGRAPH
Resistance Ends in Iran.
London, 29 August 1941; four articles on p. 1 and separate
article on p. 6.

THE DAILY TELEGRAPH
Anglo-Russian Advance in Iran To Go On.
London, 30 August 1941; one article on p. 1 and separate
article on p. 6.

THE DAILY TELEGRAPH
Wavell's 'Well Done' on Iran.
London, 1 September 1941; one article on p. 1 and another on
p. 5.

THE DAILY TELEGRAPH
British and Russian Link in Iran.

768

London, 2 September 1941; p. 1.

THE DAILY TELEGRAPH
Third British Force Links with Russian.
London, 3 September 1941; one article on p. 1 and continued
on p. 6.

THE DAILY TELEGRPAH
Indians Fine Showing in Iran Advance.
London, 5 September 1941; two articles on p. 1 and continued
on p. 6.

THE DAILY TELEGRAPH
How Nazis Plotted Coup in Iran.
London, 15 September 1941; one article on p. 1 and continued
on P. 6.

THE DAILY TELEGRAPH
New Shah Promises Constitutional Rule.
London, 18 September 1941; one article on p. 1 and continued
on p. 6.

THE DAILY TELEGRAPH
New Shah Discloses His Plans for Iran.
London, 29 September 1941; one article on p. 1 and continued
on p. 6.

DALLAL, AHMAD
Al-Biruni on Climates.
Photocopy of reprint from "Archives Internationales d'Histoire
des Sciences", Vol.34, No.112; Rome, June 1984; 18 pp.

DANDAMAYEV, M.
Foreign Slaves on the Estates of the Achaemenid Kings and
Their Nobles.
Paper presented by the U.S.S.R. delegation at the 25th Inter-
national Congress of Orientalists, Moscow; 1960.

An interesting article, discussing a seldom explored subject
in some detail.

DANNESHJOO
"Organ of the Iranian Students' Association."
Vol.I, No.3; Lawrence, Kansas; November 1953; 10 pp.;
Vol.I, No.4; April 1954; 12 pp.;
Vol.I, No.5; June 1954; 8 pp.;
Vol.II, No.1; New York City, December 1954; 8 pp;
Vol.II, No.2; January 1955; 8 pp.;
Vol.II, No.3; March 1955; 8 pp.;

Vol.II, No.4; May 1955; 8 pp.;
Vol.II, No.5; June 1955; 8 pp.;
Vol.II, No.6; August 1955; 4 pp.;
Vol.III, No.1; November 1955; 6 pp.;
Vol.III, No.2; February 1956; 8 pp.;
Vol.III, No.3; April 1956; 12 pp.;
Vol.III, No.4; June 1956; 16 pp.;
Vol.IV, No.1; November 1956; 16 pp.;
Vol.IV, NO.2; February 1957; 16 pp.;
Vol.V, No.3; April 1957; 16 pp.;
Vol.V, No.4; June 1957; 20 pp.;
Vol.VI, No.1; Fall 1957; 20 pp.;
Vol.VI, No.2; Spring 1958; 20 pp.;
Vol.VI, No.3; Summer 1958; 24 pp.

See "Iranian Students Association Bulletin" for first two
issues. Edited from 1953 to December 1954 by Cyrus Samii; from
December 1954 to February 1956 by Javad Vafa; from February 1956
to summer of 1958 by Cyrus Ghani.

DARIUS' PRAYER.
Reproduction of the text of a prayer by Darius the Great at
Persepolis; in Cunieform, with translations in Persian, English
and French: "God protect this country from foe, famine and false-
hood."

DARSH, S.M.
An Outline of Islamic Family Law.
London, 1980; 8vo, soft cover; 20 pp.

A booklet summarizing the provisions of the Islamic code as
they affect marriage, divorce, custody of children, inheritance,
wills, property rights, etc..

DAVIS, WELLESLEY REID
Notes on the Musee de Bosphore.
New York, 1898; booklet; monochrome full page illustrations;
34 pp.

"Notes on selected items from the collection of Dikran G.
Kelekian of Eastern Art Treasures, published for Mr. Kelekian of
303 Fifth Avenue, N.Y.C." The collection of a prominent Islamic
Art dealer.

DAWALIBI, MA'RUF
Islam Versus Capitalism and Marxism.
Qom, Iran, 1969; booklet; 26 pp.

Published by the Department of Publication of "Darut Tablighe
Islami of Qom, Iran, an Islamic educational center". The writer
is an ex-Prime Minister of Syria.

DAWISHA, ADEED
        Iran's Mullahs and the Arab Masses.
        Article in "The Washington Quarterly"; published by the
Center for Strategic and International Studies, Georgetown
University, Washington, D.C., Summer 1983; pp. 162-168.

        Writer: Deputy director of studies at the Royal Institute
of International Affairs, London.

DEBUSMANN, BERND
        Iran Learns to Live With Ruins of Hated Reigns.
        "The Los Angeles Times", News Feature section; 21 May 1981;
pp. 1-3.

        The writer reports on a plot by Moslem fundamentalists to des-
troy monuments in Persepolis and how it had been narrowly averted
by the authorities. Also includes article by Leslie Seldin
entitled "Western Archaeologists in Dark on possible Return to
Iran".

DE JONQUIERES, GUY
        U.S. Company Denies $28m. Iran Refund.
        "The Financial Times"; London, 11 February 1976; p. unknown.

        The article reports on the Iranian government's order for 80
F-14 "Tomcat" aircraft from the Grumman Company. The Grumman trans-
action was one of the shabbiest in the 70's involving bribery and
kick-backs.

DE LACOUPERIE, A.TERRIEN
        The Onomastic Similarity of Nai Hwang-Ti of China and Nakhunte
of Susiana.
        London, 1890; 8vo, soft cover; 10 pp.

DE MORGAN, JACQUES
        Feudalism in Persia: Its Origins, Development and Present
Condition.
        Reprint from the "Smithsonian Report" for 1913; Washington,
D.C., 1914; pp. 579-606.

        An interesting article by a noted French archaeologist (1857-
1924) working in western Iran at about the turn of the century.
(See separate entries in Section C.)

DENNY, WALTER B.
        The Image and the World: Islamic Painting and Calligraphy.
        Springfield, Mass., 1976; 8vo, soft cover; illustrated; 55 pp.

        Catalogue of an exhibition held at the Museum of Fine Arts,
Springfield, Mass., 29 February to 11 April 1976.

DESAUNOIS, JEAN
     The Shah and His Empress Talk about Their Life in Exile,
His Illness and Her Dreams.
     Article from "People Weekly"; United States, c.January 1980;
pp. 18-23.

     An interview in Contadora.

DESAUNOIS, JEAN
     My Life in Exile: Empress Farah.
     Article possibly from "Sunday Telegraph" color supplement;
London, c.January 1980; illustrated; pp. 14-25.

     An interview with the former Queen in exile. Includes also
an interview with the Shah entitled "Let Them Eat Grass? Never
In My Day".

DESMET-GREGOIRE, HELENE
     Les Objets Concernant le Pain dans les Collections du Musee
de l'Homme.
     Reprint from "Objets et Mondes" Tome 20, Fasc.1; Paris,
Spring 1980; illustrated; pp. 33-44.

DIBA, FARHAD
     Catalogue of Books on Persia in the Diba Collection.
     Tehran, 1976; 8vo, soft cover; 251 pp.

DIMAND, M.S. (edited by)
     The Metropolitan Museum of Art Persian Miniatures - A Picture
Book.
     New York, 1944; 8vo, soft cover; 2 pp. of text and twenty
plates.

DIMAND, M.S.
     An Unpublished 17th Century Compartment Vase Carpet.
     Photocopy of reprint from "Forschungen Zur Kunst Asiens; In
Memoriam Kurt Erdman"; Istanbul, 1970; illustrated; pp. 190-193.

DIMAND, MAURICE S.
     The Seventeenth Century Isphahan School of Carpet Weaving.
     Reprint of article from "Islamic Art", a publication of the
Metropolitan Museum of Art; New York, 1972; illustrated in text;
pp. 255-266.

DISCOVERING ANTIQUES.
     Turkey in the Sixteenth and Seventeenth Centuries: Part 21 of
"Discovering Antiques: The Story of World Antiques".
     Published weekly by Purnell; London, c.1970; illustrated,
largely in color; pp. 481-504.

Articles include: "The Ottoman Empire" by Malcolm Davidson, "Turkish Miniatures" by David Talbot Rice, "Eastern Fashions in Dress" by Madge Garland, "Turkish Ceramics" by John Carswell, "Ottoman Rugs of the 16th and 17th Centuries" by May Beattie, and "Bookbindings of the Moslem World" by Daria Jones.

DISCOVERING ANTIQUES.
The Arts and Crafts of India: Part 65 of "Discovering Antiques: The Story of World Antiques".
Published weekly by Purnell; London, c.1970; illustrated, largely in color; pp. 1537-1560.

Articles include: "India and the Raj" by Giles Eyre, "Furniture in India" by Veronica Murphy, "Skills of the Indian Craftsmen" by Robert Skelton, "Paintings for the East India Company" by Mildred Archer, "Swords and Daggers" by Vesey Norman, "Embroidery of India" by Christopher Cooke.

DOCUMENTS RELATING TO FOREIGN SALES AND OPERATIONS OF THE NORTHROP CORPORATION.
c. 1976; photocopy of 530 typewritten folio size pages.

Investigation carried out by the auditing firm of Ernst and Ernst on behalf of the U.S. Securities and Exchange Commission.

"Table of Contents"
Part A: Section IV of the 'Report on Special Investigation of Northrop Corporation and Subsidiaries' by Ernst and Ernst.

Part B: Select Ernst and Ernst Notes of Interviews and Supporting Documents Provided by Northrop Corporation in the Course of the Special Investigation.

1. General Discussion of the Role of Agents and Consultants Serving Northrop Abroad.
2. Material Relating to Northrop Agents in Europe.
    a.   Frank De Francis
    b.   Economic and Development Corporation (EDC).
    c.   Other agents in Europe.
3. Material Relating to Kermit Roosevelt and Associates, Inc.
4. Material Relating to Northrop Agents in Iran.
    a.   Management and Technical Consultants (MTC).
    b.   Page Communications/GNPS Consortium.
5. Material Relating to Agents in Saudi Arabia, Adnan Khashoggi and Triad Financial Establishment.
6. Material Relating to Agents in Latin America.

A revealing guide to the intricate web of arms sales, bribery and corruption. Northrop was one of the serious offenders in Iran and its Iranian "agents" are named in the documents.

DOWDEN, RICHARD
     In the Terror of Tehran.
     Article from "The New York Review of Books", 2 February 1984; pp. 8-11.

     An account of the writer's recent visit to Tehran, including inside Evin Prison, Behesht e-Zahra Cemetery, etc.

DRESDEN, MARK J.
     "An Introductory Note" to Guitty Azarpay's discussion of Sogdian Painting; The Pictorial Epic in Oriental Art.
     Paper presented at a seminar held at the University of California at Berkeley, 1981; 10 pp.

     Writer: Professor at University of Pennsylvania.

DUCHESNE, GUILLEMIN J.
     L'Homme dans la Religion Iranienne.
     Reprint from "Anthropologie Religieuse"; Leiden, 1955.

     Writer: Professor at the University of Liege, Belgium.

DUCHESNE, GUILLEMIN J.
     Notes on Zervanism in the Light of Zaehner's Zurvan, with Additional References.
     Photocopy of reprint from "Journal of Near Eastern Studies", Vol.XV, No.2; United States, April 1956; pp. 108-112.

DUCHESNE, GUILLEMIN JAQUES
     Heraclitus and Iran.
     Photocopy of reprint from "Numen", Vol.3, No.1; Leiden, Summer 1963; pp. 34-49.

     An interesting article on Iranian origins of certain schools of Greek philosophy.

DYSON, ROBERT H. Jr.
     The Archaeological Evidence of the Second Milennium B.C. on the Persian Plateau.
     Reprint of chapter XVI, Vol.II, of Cambridge University "History of Iran"; 1968; 37 pp.

     Writer: Professor of Anthropology, University of Pennsylvania.

E

EARLY ARABIC PRINTING (FROM THE LATE 15th TO THE Mid-19th CENTURY):
An Exhibition in the British Library, 27 August to December 1979.
        London, 1979; 4 pp.

EBTEHAJ, ABOL HASSAN
        A Program of Economic Growth.
        Photocopy of article from unidentified journal; pencilled-in
date "Sept. 1961"; pp. 234-243.

        Writer: Head of Bank Melli, ambassador to France and Head of
Plan Organization 1955-1959 where he laid the groundwork for some
of the most ambitious projects completed over the next 15 years.
An outspoken critic of arms spending, he was forced out of
office and was imprisoned for some nine months on totally false
and politically motivated charges. He was never tried and international pressure led to his release. He retired from public life
and founded a private bank (Iranian's Bank). Ebtehaj possessed
immense energy and great ability and is a man of principle and
integrity.

THE ECHO OF IRAN "A SERIOUS STUDY OF IRANIAN AFFAIRS".
        Vol.I, No.2; Tehran, 28 February 1963; 67 pp.

        A monthly review. This issue contains articles on foreign
affairs, oil, politics, the economy, sociology, plus an interview
with A. Khosravani, Minister of Labor and Social Services. Inter
alia, articles on the "Single Party System for Iran?" by Richard
Pfaff of the University of Colorado, "The Rights of Women" by
Margaret Shaida, and "The Qashqai Tribe", unattributed.

THE ECONOMIST
        All Fall Down.
        Cover and editorial; London, 16 December 1978; pp. 9-10.

        An important article on the course of events in 1978, referr-
ing to the Tasua and Ashura demonstrations in December 1978.
Also includes an article headed: "Iran: Voting with their stamping
feet" from The Economist's Tehran correspondent; pp. 51-52 of same
issue.

EDULJEE, H.E.
        The Date of Zoroaster.
        Reprint from "Journal of the K.R. Cama Oriental Institute"
No. 48; Bombay, 1980; map; pp. 103-160.

        The generally accepted date of Zoroaster is some time in mid-
6th century B.C. There have been attempts by Zoroastrians and
some scholars to place the birth of Zoroaster at about 1500 B.C.
(some have even suggested 6000 B.C.), thus establishing that Zoroaster is the first person to have preached monotheism, i.e. before

Moses and Akhenatun. The writer here settles on the second
millenieum B.C. (some time between 1700 and 1400 B.C.).

EDULJEE, H.E.
     The Legend of Kerespaspa.
     Reprint from "Journal of the K.R. Cama Oriental Institute",
No. 50; Bombay, 1983; pp. 32-86.

EL AZHARY, M.S.
     The Attitudes of the Superpowers Towards the Gulf War.
     Article in "International Affairs", Vol.59, No.4; London,
Autumn 1983; pp. 609-621.

     The writer clearly sides with Iraq in the Gulf War, brushing
aside the fact that Iraq invaded Iran. He labels the invasion as
"defensive". Writer: Research fellow at the University of Exeter.

ELGOOD, CYRIL
     Persian Gynaecology.
     Reprint from "Medical History", Vol.XII; 4 October 1968;
pp. 408-412.

     The writer argues that many Persian manuscripts which were
considered as "erotic" or even "indecent" were, in fact, serious
medical treatises which represent the development of gynaecology.
(Refer to writer in Section B.)

ELWELL-SUTTON, L.P.
     Scaldheads and Thinbeards in Persian Folk-Tale Literature.
     Reprint of lecture at the IVth International Congress for
Folk-Narrative Research in Athens, 4-6 September 1964; Athens,
1965; pp. 105-108.

     Scaldheads: The cheaters or tricksters. Thinbeards: The dupes.

ELWELL-SUTTON, L.P.
     Family Relationship in Persian Folk-Literature.
     Photocopy of reprint of a lecture delivered at Athens Congress
(same as preceding); Athens, 1965; pp. 160-166.

ELWELL-SUTTON, L.P.
     The Unfortunate Heroine in Persian Folk Literature.
     Photocopy of reprint from "Yad Name-Ye Irani Ye Minorski";
Tehran, 1969; 14 pp.

     The writer in an amusing article discusses the fate of the
heroine in Persian folk tales. He shows that the heroine, whether
"despised" or "beloved", is more fortunate than the male characters
and she invariably achieves "good fortune" at the end of the tale.

ELWELL-SUTTON, L.P.
The Rubaiyat Revisited.
Review of "The Original Rubaiyyat of Omar Khayam in a New
Translation with Commentaries by Robert Graves and Omar Ali Shah".
Reprint from "Delos", No.3; Austin, Texas, 1969; pp. 170-191.

A brilliant article that put to rest the authenticity of the
alleged 1153 edition of Khayyam in possession of the Afghan
General Omar Ali Shah. (The manuscript was supposed to have been
written some 30 years after Khayyam's death.) The writer shows
Omar Ali Shah's ignorance of Persian literature and language,
and the naiveté of poor Robert Graves who was "used" in the
charade. The alleged manuscript was a copy of Edward Heron Allen's
note book (published in 1899) in which Allen attempted to collate
Fitzgerald's translations with their originals, the so-called
"Bodleian" and "Calcutta" manuscripts of Khayyam's poems. Furthermore, the writer exposes the entire effort as "crude Propaganda
for contemporary Pseudo Sufism". (Refer to Omar Khayyam of Robert
Graves and Omar Ali Shah in Section B.)

ELWELL-SUTTON, L.P.
The Omar Khayyam Puzzle.
Photocopy of reprint of article in unknown journal, with no
date (c.1970); pp. 167-179.

The writer discusses the number of quatrains that can be
correctly attributed to Omar Khayyam and the number of suspect
"Original" Khayyam manuscripts. The writer makes a brave effort,
but the puzzle remains with us because of the difficulty in dating
Persian manuscripts and the advanced "art" of forgery.

ELWELL-SUTTON, L.P.
The Foundation of Persian Prosody and Metrics.
Reprint from "Iran" XIII; published by the British Institute
of Persian Studies; London, 1975; pp. 75-97.

ELWELL-SUTTON, L.P.
No Place for Poets.
Photocopy of a review of the book "God's Shadow" by Reza
Baraheni, which appeared in "The Times Literary Supplement";
London, 18 March 1977; p. 295.

The writer deflates the alleged literary merits of Baraheni,
the erstwhile pet of certain radical chic circles in the U.S.

ELWELL SUTTON, L.P.
Fundamentalism in Flood.
Review of two books: "The Political Economy of Modern Iran"
by Homa Katouzian and "Paved with Good Intentions" by Barry Rubin
from "The Times Literary Supplement"; London, 28 August 1981;
p. 987.

One of the best short pieces by the reviewer. He is, however, too harsh in his treatment of "The Political Economy of Modern Iran", and sees almost no merit in the work.

ENGLE, JOHANNES
The New Power of Oil: An Interview with the Shah of Iran.
"The Washington Post"; 3 February 1974; pp. C1 and C5.

AN ERA OF PROGRESS
U.S.I.S. publication; c.1968/9; large 8vo, soft cover; illustrated; 39 pp.

Forward by Armin H. Meyer, U.S. Ambassador to Iran. "The Story of 15 Years of Progress in Iran"; with frequent references to USAID and American-Iranian co-operation in the development of Iran.

EPSTEIN, EDWARD JAY
The Secret Deals of the Oil Cartels: An Illustrated History: Part I.
Cover story, "New York Times Magazine"; 23 June 1975; illustrated in color.

"Part I: How seven companies carved up the world."

EPSTEIN, EDWARD JAY
The Secret Deals of the Oil Cartels: An Illustrated History: Part II.
"New York Times Magazine"; 30 June 1975; illustrated in color; pp. 40-57.

"Part II: The Resistable Rise of OPEC." The writer is best remembered for his book "Inquest" which cast doubts on the thoroughness of the work of the Warren Commission in investigating the assassination of John F. Kennedy.

ERDMAN, PAUL
The Oil War of 1976: How the Shah Won The World: A Scenario.
Photocopy from "New York Times Magazine"; c.1975/6; illustrated; pp. 39-51.

The writer was one of the first "novelists" to discover the commercial value of writing on Iran, and benefited accordingly.

ESFANDIARY, FEREIDOUN
Is It the Mysterious or Neurotic East?
Article from the "New York Times Magazine"; 24 March 1957; illustrated; pp. 13 and 70-72.

In a much too facile manner the writer reaches the conclusion

that "The primitive life, so romantic in prospect, is in reality
filled with tension and anxiety. These emotions ... are a
direct cause of bloodshed in Asia and Africa today". Tensions
in patriarchal societies are the main cause of revolutions, and
extended therapy is recommended.

ESHRAGHI, F.
        Anglo-Soviet Occupation of Iran in August, 1941.
        Photocopy from "Journal of Middle Eastern Studies", Vol.20,
No.1; Great Britain, January 1984; pp. 27-52.

        A subject which has not been adequately probed in the West.
The writer also shies away from examining the effects of the
occupation on the Persian psyche and whether Iranian history would
have taken a different course in the absence of the invasion and
occupation. The writer gives only a straight narrative account.

ESHRAGHI, F.
        The Immediate Aftermath of the Anglo-Soviet Occupation of
Iran in August 1941.
        Photocopy from "Journal of Middle Eastern Studies", Vol.20,
No.3; Great Britain, 1984; pp. 324-351.

        Same criticism as above.

ESIN, E.
        The Contribution of Jalaleddin Rumi to the Development of
Turkish Culture.
        Photocopy of lecture delivered at Columbia University, 13
February 1959; 10 pp.

        Sheer nonsense! Since Mowlana was born in Balkh (which the
writer refers to as Turkestan) and died in Konya, the writer
concludes that he was a Turk and should be regarded as the national
poet of modern Turkey. Mowlana Jalal e-Din was born in Balkh (then
part of greater Khorasan) and as a child accompanied his father on
a Hajj Pilgrimage. Thereafter, due to the instability of Khorasan,
Jalal e-Din came to Konya at the age of 14. The writer does not
bother to explain why the poet never wrote one single verse in
Turkish, nor does she identify the Turkish "literary tradition"
that the Mowlana is supposed to have stemmed from.

ESSEM
        Mieux Vaut ... en Pleurer.
        1981/2; large 8vo, soft cover; illustrated; 51 pp.

        Book of anti-Khomaini cartoon drawings by "ESSEM".

ETTINGHAUSEN, RICHARD
        Important Pieces of Persian Pottery in London Collections.

Reprint from "Ars Islamica", Vol.II, Part I; Reprint series No.5 Published by the American Institute for Persian Art and Archaeology; New York, 1935; illustrated; pp. 45-64.

Probably the earliest article in English by the writer, who had studied under the great German specialists of Islamic art, and had recently emigrated to the U.S.

ETTINGHAUSEN, RICHARD; LUKENS, MARIE; JENKINS, MARILYN; and KEENE, MANUEL.
Islamic Art.
New York, c.1965; small 4to, soft cover; full page illustrations and illustrations in text, some in color; map; 48 pp.

Published by the Metropolitan Museum of Art; objects are from the museum's own collection.

ETTINGHAUSEN, RICHARD
The Immanent Features of Persian Art.
Reprint from "The Connoisseur"; London, July 1966; Reprint series no.1 published by the Iran-American Society, Washington, D.C.; illustrated; 8 pp.

ETTINGHAUSEN, RICHARD
Decorative Arts and Paintings: Their Character and Scope.
Photocopy of reprint from "Arts and Architecture"; United States, c.1967; pp. 274-292.

Writer discusses the diversity of the roots of Islamic Art.

ETTINGHAUSEN, RICHARD
The Impact of Muslim Decorative Arts and Painting on the Arts of Europe.
Reprint from "Art and Architecture"; United States, c.1967; pp. 292-320.

ETTINGHAUSEN, RICHARD
Islamic Carpets: The Joseph V. McMullan Collection.
"The Metropolitan Museum of Art Bulletin", Vol.XXVIII, No.10; New York, June 1970; small 4to, soft cover; illustrated, some in color and map; pp. 401-432.

The McMullan Collection, now in possession of the Metropolitan, was probably the best private collection in the world. The quality and sheer number of 16th and 17th century carpets are staggering.

ETTINGHAUSEN, RICHARD, et al.
Notes on Islamic Art in Its Historical Setting.
New York, 1975; small 4to, soft cover; maps; 44 pp.

A booklet prepared by the Metropolitan Museum of Art to
accompany the exhibits in the Museum's Islamic Galleries. Articles
on various aspects of Islamic art: calligraphy, miniatures, pottery, metal work, etc., and on the successive dynastic periods
during which these arts flourished; written by Carol Bier, Richard
Ettinghausen, Madeline Hart, Marilyn Jenkins, Carolyn Kane,
Manuel Keene and Marie Lukens Swietochowski, all members and
associates of the Islamic Department of the museum.

"ETUDES SUR LA PERSE MODERNE": A FACSIMILE EDITION.
Photocopy of a 5 page typescript announcing the publication
in 1976 of a facsimile edition of Eugène Flandin's book and illustrations, to mark the 100th anniversary of his death.

THE EVOLUTION OF THE U.S.-IRANIAN RELATIONSHIP: PARTS A and B.
Photocopy of declassified U.S. Department of State documents,
obtained under the Freedom of Information Act.

Two documents: Part A, marked Secret, is sub-titled "A Brief
Overview of the U.S.-Iranian Relationship, 1941-1979"; 37 pp.
Part B, marked Top Secret, is sub-titled "A Survey of U.S.-Iranian
Relations, 1941-1979". Portions of these documents, particularly
Part B, have been blacked out. Even with alleged sensitive sect-
ions obliterated, some hitherto unknown facts or confirmation of
facts emerge.

EXCAVATIONS IN IRAN: THE BRITISH CONTRIBUTION.
Oxford, 1972; booklet; illustrated in text and map; 48 pp.

"Published by the Organizing Committee of the Sixth Inter-
national Congress of Iranian Art and Archaeology, Oxford, 1972."
There was an accompanying exhibition at the Ashmolean Museum,
Oxford, under the same title for the duration of the congress.
A series of short accounts of work at various sites in Iran
written by the relevant excavators.

AN EXHIBITION OF COFFEE-HOUSE PAINTINGS.
Tehran, 1967; pamphlet; illustrated, some in color; 36 pp.

Published by the Iran-America Society to accompany an
exhibition of "Coffee-House Paintings" from the private collection
of an Iranian held in the autumn of 1967 in Tehran. The introduction and descriptions of the works are in both English and
Persian. Absolute rubbish that became fashionable in Tehran in
the 60's through promotion and "hype". "Coffee-House Paintings"
were crude semi-religious paintings that hung on the walls of tea
shops from the turn of the 20th century through the 50's. In
order to enhance their value, promoters even began calling them
"Pahlavi Paintings" as distinguished from Qajar paintings, and
the Iran-America Society fell for the hype. They were later

purchased by the office of Queen Farah. This even led to the collection and exhibition of Iranian cinema billboards, which at their best, have nowhere ever been regarded as even low art.

EXHIBITION OF PAINTINGS FROM THE 14th-19th CENTURY.
London, 1975; 4to; 122 pp.

Tehran, 12-18 May 1975 at the Hilton Hotel, exhibition presented by the Alexander Gallery, London, in association with B. Cohen and Sons; M. Newman and Sons; The Trafalgar Galleries; and Williams and Son. Catalogue prepared by Sotheby Parke Bernet, London. This was hucksterism at its worst. The paintings (all European) were fourth rate at best. Sponsors of the sale were Persians as well as Europeans.

EXPOSITION D'UNE SERIE D'ART MODERNE IRANIEN PRESENTEE PAR MANOU MARTIN.
Cairo, 1939; 8vo, soft cover; illustrated; 8 pp.

Catalogue of objects d'arts displayed in an exhibition held in the Continental-Savoy Hotel, Cairo, 11 to 31 March 1939.

FALLACI, ORIANA
        An Oriana Fallaci Interview: The Shah of Iran.
        Photocopy of article in "The New Republic"; United States,
1 December 1973; pp. 16-21.

        The interview took place in 1973. Fallaci elicited a great
deal from the Shah who seems to have been caught off guard (as
were Kissinger before him and Khomaini after him). Probably the
most revealing interview during the last ten eyars of his rule.

FALLACI, ORIANA
        An Interview with Khomeini.
        "The New York Times Magazine", 7 October 1979; one illustrat-
ion; pp. 29-31.

        No one had hitherto elicited such direct replies from the
Ayatollah. How she obtained the interview and how Khomaini
consented are more intriguing.

FALLACI, ORIANA
        Interview with Ayatollah Khomeini 7 October 1979.
        Together with about 40 articles on Iran from various U.S.
newspapers, covering the period from March 1979 to November 1979;
46 pp.

        A condensed review of events in Iran during the above mention-
ed period as reported by U.S. correspondents from various newspapers.

FALLACI, ORIANA
        Everybody Wants to Be Boss: An Interview with Mehdi Bazargan,
Prime Minister of Iran.
        "The New York Times Magazine"; 26 October 1979; pp. 20-23,
30-37, 63-71.

        How a man of such meagre talents became one of the main
leaders of the opposition inside Iran will require more intuition
than scholarship to fathom. The interviewee is totally out of his
depth; he did not believe that the Shah would be so quickly toppled;
he could not see that the clergy would assert itself so strongly
and that one form of autocratic rule would be replaced by another.
One thing which stands out is the sincerity of Bazargan's answers.

FARLEY, CHRIS; COATES, KEN; ALLAUM, FRANK; KINNOCK, NEIL, M.P.;
et al.
        Iran - Time for Protest.
        Letter to the editor, "The Guardian"; London, 31 January 1976;
p. 12.

        A letter signed by a group of British Labour M.P.'s and others protesting against political repression in Iran.

FARMAN, HAFEZ F.
      Iran: A Selected and Annotated Bibliography.
      Washington, D.C., 1951; 4to; 36 pp.

      Typewritten manuscript produced by the Iranian Embassy. The
text is divided into three parts: (a) General Reference, (b) Pre-
Islamic, and (c) Islamic Period. Writer: University of Texas at
Austin. The present article and the one below by Farmayan, Hafez F.
are all by the same individual. The following five articles are all
by members of the same family who spell their names differently or
have adopted variations of the same family name.

FARMAN, HAFEZ F.
      Iran: A Selected and Annotated Bibliography.
      Washington, 1951; large 8vo, soft cover; 100 pp.

      Issued by the Library of Congress General Reference and
Bibliography Division. A bibliography of publications in European
languages including a few basic official Iranian government
publications and important recent works in Persian. One of a
series of country-bibliographies published by the Library of
Congress and designed principally as an aid to U.S. Federal agencies and libraries. A selected general list, the emphasis placed
on 19th and 20th century works. Brief, essentially descriptive
annotations. Divided into three parts: General, the pre-Islamic
Period and the Islamic Period.

FARMAYAN, HAFEZ F.
      The Forces of Modernization in Nineteenth Century Iran: A
Historical Survey.
      Photocopy of article in "Beginnings of Modernization in the
Middle East; The Nineteenth Century", Edited by William R. Polk
and Richard L. Chambers, University of Chicago Press; Chicago,
c.1966/7; Chapter 6; pp. 119-151.

      A paper given at a conference at the Center for Middle Eastern
Studies, University of Chicago, 1966. The writer discusses the
political figures, innovations introduced by them in the administration of the country and writers who exercised varying degrees
of influence. The political figures are Abbas Mirza, Qaem-Maqam,
Amir Kabir and Mirza Hossein Khan Sepahsalar. The writer credits
Amir Kabir, and correctly so, with the introduction of certain
innovations that enabled the country to function for the next 50
years. Some of the pamphleteers discussed are Akhundov, Talebov
and Malkum.

FARMANFARMA, ABOLBASHAR
      Constitutional Law of Iran.

Reprint from "The American Journal of Comparative Law", Vol. 3, No.2; United States, April 1954; pp. 241-247.

A general discussion. Writer: A prominent lawyer in Tehran now residing in the U.S.

FARMANFARMAIAN, KHODADAD
Why and How Should the Near and Middle East Countries be Organized to Check Further Expansion of Soviet Russia.
Typewritten manuscript; Colorado, 1948; 58 pp.

Senior year term paper, discussing the countries of the Near and Middle East one at a time, outlining their current positions and problems, and proposing steps to be taken both internally and by Western powers to prevent further spread of Communism. The writer, a noted Iranian economist was prominent in the political and economic life of Iran from 1956 to 1978. In 1969 he became Governor of the Central Bank and later head of the Plan Organiz- ation. He was instrumental in recruiting some of the ablest Iranian economists to work at various government agencies.

FARMANFARMAIAN, KHODADAD
Social Change and Economic Behavior in Iran.
Reprint from "Explorations in Enterpreneurial History", Harvard University; Cambridge, Mass., c.1955; pp. 178-183.

FARMANFARMAIAN, KHODADAD; GUTOWSKI, ARMIN; OKITA, SABURO; ROSSA, ROBERT V.; WILSON, CARROLL L.
How Can the World Afford OPEC Oil?
Photocopy of reprint from "Foreign Affairs", Vol.53, No.2; New York, January 1975; pp. 201-222.

This was when it was thought that OPEC would bankrupt the West and plans were put forward to recycle oil revenues.

FARMANFARMAIAN, KHODADAD (translated by)
Biographies of: (1) "Firouz Mirza Nosrat ed-Dowleh: Father of Abdul-Hussein Mirza Farmanfarma" (d.1883) and (2) "Abdul-Hussein Mirza Farmanfarma" (1858-1939).
Translated from the original Persian; 10 March 1984; 5 type- written pp.

Abdul-Hossein Mirza Farmanfarma was a leading political figure from the 1890's to 1925. He dominated most cabinets of which he was a member and served as Prime Minister during World War I. He was one of the most interesting and important political personages of the latter part of Qajar rule and deserves a full length biography.

FARZAD, MASUUD (arranged and translated by)
"Mowlavi-Rumi's The Schoolmaster's Headache."

Photocopy of reprint from unknown journal, dated 1967; illustrations; 8 pp.

Farzad was a scholar of some note. He translated Hamlet into
Persian, not entirely successfully but much better than translations of Shakespeare plays by other Iranians. His translation
of a poem by Edna St. Vincent Millay, "My Candle Burns at Both
Ends", however, is probably the single best translation of a poem
from English to Persian. It is regretable that he did not pursue
that endeavor. The writer in the last 30 years of his life was
obsessed with producing the difinitive and annotated text of the
Divan of Hafez. The resulting work was not successful.

FARZAD, MASUUD
        Whitman and Sufism: Towards "A Persian Lesson".
        Reprint from "American Literature", Vol.47, No.4; January,
1976; pp. 572-582.

The writer examines Walt Whitman's mystical visions and
messages and believes Whitman, like his contemporaries Emerson and
Thoreau, had read Hafez, Sa'di and Mowlavi. The writer examines
the Persian mystic influences in "Leaves of Grass" and Whitman's
last work "The Persian Lesson", which Whitman had originally
titled "A Sufi Lesson". The writer also examines the scholarship
of the sixties which focused on a fragment in "Leaves of Grass"
titled "Song of Myself", which also indicates Whitman's debts to
the Persian mystic poets.

FIFTH INTERNATIONAL CONGRESS OF IRANIAN ART AND ARCHAEOLOGY.
        Tehran, 1968; 8vo, soft cover; 62 pp. in English and 20 pp.
in Persian.

Held in Tehran, Esfahan and Shiraz, April 1968. Includes the
program, subjects to be discussed, and the list of delegates.

THE FINANCIAL TIMES
        Financial Times Survey: Iran.
        London, 20 August 1973; illustrated and map; pp. 11-23.

THE FINANCIAL TIMES
        Financial Times Survey: Iran.
        London, 25 July 1977; illustrated; pp. 11-20.

THE FINANCIAL TIMES SURVEY OF IRAN
        London, 1 April 1985; 20 pp.

The best survey by any publication since the Revolution.
Includes profiles of the current leadership.

FIROOZI, FERYDOON
        Tehran - A Demographic and Economic Analysis.

786

Reprint from "Middle Eastern Studies", Vol.10, No.1; London, January 1974; map; pp. 60-76.

The writer traces the expansion and economy of Tehran from its designation as the capital in c.1786 to 1966. He notes that in the first census in 1869 Tehran had a population of 155,000, which by 1966 had grown to 2,700,000. The current population estimate is about 5,500,000.

FISCHEL, WALTER J.
The Jews of Kurdistan a Hundred Years Ago.
Paper presented at a "Conference on Jewish Relations", New York, 1944; reprinted from "Jewish Social Studies", Vol.VI, No.3; pp. 195-226; and maps.

There is historical evidence that Jews lived in Persia from the time of Cyrus the Great. The three identifiable areas which had early Jewish communities are Mashhad, Esfahan and the western part of Persia, including Kurdestan. The writer states that the Kurdestan region gave a false prophet "David Alroy" in 12th century A.D. Not much more is known until the early 19th century when European visitors undertook further studies. In Persian Kurdestan and surrounding areas in 1827 the number of Jews was about 30,000. The writer discusses their status and activity during the first third of the 19th century. Despite some errors of Persian history and names, an extremely useful article.

FISCHEL, WALTER J.
Isfahan, The Story of a Jewish Community in Persia.
Reprint from "Joshua Starr Memorial Volume"; New York, 1953; pp. 111-128.

The Jewish community in Esfahan dates from at least 310 A.D.. From the time of the Mongol invasion (1258) to the beginning of the Safavid Dynasty in early 16th century not much is known of the community. Under Shah Abbas I, the Jews prospered and engaged in crafts and commerce. Chardin (c.1670) maintains that there were about 35,000 Jews in Persia. Esfahan, as the center of Persian Jews, had a large share of this population. The later Safavids were not tolerant and forced Jews to convert to Islam, especially under Shah Abbas II. In early Qajar times (1830's) the number of Jews in Esfahan probably numbered about 1,000. It is estimated that there were 60,000 to 70,000 Jews in Iran at the outset of the 1979 Revolution, at least a third of whom have emigrated.

FISK, ROBERT
Dead Hand of the Patriarch - The New Calm of Tehran is a Sign of Stagnation Rather than Change.
Article from "The Times"; London, 10 June 1985.

FISK, ROBERT
>   Nation with a Death Wish.
>   "The Times"; London, 7 March 1986; page unknown.

"How the Gulf War is affecting the people of Iran."

FITZGERALD, FRANCES
>   Giving the Shah Everything He Wants.
>   Cover Story, "Harpers Magazine"; New York, November 1974;
illustrated; pp. 55-82.

One of the most important anti-Shah articles written up to that time in adding fuel to the American intelligentsia's opposition to the Shah's regime. While containing some factual errors it is effectively presented and well written in a matter-of-fact style. The writer sets the tone of her argument in her opening paragraphs by retelling a story an influential Iranian official had told her. One night when he had had too much to drink he had crashed his car into the gates of the Shah's palace. He is not sure whether he had done this solely as a result of his intoxication or as an unconscious act of protest. The writer cites this story as indicating the ambivalent attitude of even those close to the Court and she concludes that with such supporters there is no future for the Shah. The writer, however, fails to appreciate, or at least does not comment upon the fact that many Iranians in high positions played both sides of the game with Westerners of certain sensibilities, while having no commitment to either side. The official quoted here by the writer rose to an even more prominent position as envoy to one of the most important countries in Western Europe. The title of the article refers to the Nixon-Kissinger commitment of May 1972. The writer's interest in Iran waned considerably when the Revolution did not live up to her expectations.

FITZGERALD, FRANCES
>   The Shah Discovers His People.
>   Article from unidentified journal; c.December 1978.

The writer refers to the mass marches of late 1978 and believes it is too late for the Shah to salvage anything. The article is almost gleeful about the course of events.

FOROUGHI, ABOL HASSAN KHAN
>   Le Soufisme.
>   Iran, 1920; in French; Printed copy of a lecture delivered by A.H. Foroughi, director of L'Ecole Normale in Tehran, to the Alliance Francaise in Darol Fonoun School on 25 November 1919; 20 pp.

Introduction by M. Bonin, French Minister in Tehran. Abol Hassan Khan Foroughi was the brother of the noted Persian scholar and statesman Mohammad Ali Foroughi.

FRANK, R.M.
Review of Fathollah Kholeif's book: "A Study on Fakhr al-Din-al-Razi and His Controversies in Transoxiana", published in Beirut in 1966.
Reprinted from "Bibliotheca Orientalis", Vol.XXV, Nos.3 and 4; Chicago, May and July 1968; pp. 229-233.

FREEMASONRY IN IRAN
Copy of typewritten broadsheet, marked "For Your Information", No.663-4; 10 March 1969; 17 pp.

An anonymous review of a three-volume work on Iranian Freemasonry by Esmail Raeen which had recently been published. The review includes a ten page list of "Freemasons in Iran (1968)" taken, in an edited form, from volume III of that work. The publication of the three volumes by the late Raeen caused a sensation in Iran in the late sixties. Masonry in Iran dates back to the early 19th century and has been a force in Iranian politics, especially since the beginning of the 20th century. It was commonly believed that the rank and file members in Iran had a special relationship with Britain. In the light of the very tight official control over all publications, there were questions as to why these books had been allowed to appear, especially since Masons occupied some of the most powerful and sensitive political and economic posts in the country. The motives behind the publication of the books are still a mystery. The only plausible explanation appears to have been an attempt by the Shah to discredit the "old Anglophile Persians".

FRIENDLY, ALFRED
Liberal-Minded Shah Runs Tight Ship.
Typewritten manuscript of five articles datelined Tehran, by Alfred Friendly of the 'Washington Post', 5 July 1966; 10 pp.

Friendly had his doubts about the viability of the Shah in the early sixties. By 1966 he appears to believe the country is on the right path with a bright future.

FRYE, RICHARD NELSON
Notes on the Early Sassanian State and Church.
Reprinted from a publication by Instituto Per L'Oriente; Rome, 1956; 22 pp.

FRYE, RICHARD NELSON
Treasures of the Hermitage Museum.
Reprinted from "Archaeology", Vol.II, No.2; no place of publication indicated; Summer 1958; pp. 105-110.

Short discussion of, inter alia, the Pazyryk Carpet.

FRYE, RICHARD NELSON
        Development of Persian Literature under the Samanids and
Qarakhanids.
        Reprint from "Yadname-ye Jan Rypka"; Czechoslovak Academy
of Sciences, 1967; pp. 69-74.

FRYE, RICHARD NELSON
        Problems in the Study of Iranian Religions.
        Reprint from "Religions in Antiquity", edited by Jacob
Neusner; Leiden, 1968; pp. 583-589.

FRYE, RICHARD NELSON
        Iran to Persia, Continuity of Traditions.
        Reprinted from "K.R. Cama Oriental Institute Golden Jubilee
Volume"; Bombay, 1969; pp. 139-146.

FRYE, RICHARD NELSON
        The Institutions. Persian Institutions under the Achaemenids.
        Photocopy of reprint from "Historia"; Wiesbaden, c.1969; pp.
83-93.

FRYE, RICHARD NELSON
        History and Sassanian Inscriptions.
        Reprint from the "Academia Nazionale Dei Lincei", No.160;
Rome, 1971; pp. 215-223.

FRYE, RICHARD NELSON
        The Sassanian System of Walls for Defense.
        Reprinted from "Studies in Memory of Gaston Wiet", Institute
of Asian and African Studies, The Hebrew University of Jerusalem;
Jerusalem, 1977; pp. 7-15.

GHAFFARY, FAROKH
     Le Cinema en Iran.
     Published by the High Council of Culture and Art; Tehran,
c.1968; illustrated; 23 pp.

     Writer: A man of considerable erudition and well versed in
the arts; also a gifted film maker and actor.

GAGE, NICHOLAS
     Shah of Iran Is Facing Challenge from Foes Led by Moslem
Clergy.
     "The New York Times", 4 June 1978; pp. 1 and 10.

     Soon thereafter the New York Times was shut down by a labor
dispute, not resuming publication until the end of November 1978.

GAGE, NICHOLAS
     Iran: Making of a Revolution.
     Article from "The New York Times Magazine", 17 December 1978;
illustrated; pp. 24-28, 115, and 132-139.

GAGE, NICHOLAS; APPLE, R.W.; PACE, ERIC; et al.
     Shah Leaves Iran for Indefinite Stay; Crowds Exult, Many
Expect Long Exile.
     "The New York Times", 17 January 1979; pp. 1 and 8-10.

     Series of articles on the Shah's departure from Iran and its
repercussions, plus a review of his reign.

GAGE, NICHOLAS; IBRAHIM, YOUSSEF M.; APPLE, R.W. Jr.; MARKHAM,
JAMES; et al.
     "Army Withdraws Its Support from Bakhtiar; Iranian Prime
Minister Reported to Resign."
     "The New York Times", 12 February 1979; pp. 1 and 8.

     Series of articles on state of affairs inside Iran and its
repercussions abroad.

GALLOWAY, DAVID
     Looking Back at Pop.
     Iran, c.1976/7; pamphlet on colored paper; 56 pp.

     Text in English in front half of booklet, and in Persian in
back half. The rise of the Pop Art movement principally in the
U.S. and an exhibition of same in Tehran during the period when it
was officially deemed the fashion and policy to collect Rauschen-
bergs and Warhols.

GANDJEI, TOURKHAN
     The Genesis and Definition of a Literary Composition: The Dah-
Nama "Ten Love Letters".

Reprint from "Der Islam", Issue No.47; Berlin, 1971; pp. 59-66.

The Manteq ol-Ushaq of early 14th century. Writer: Professor at SOAS, London University.

GARTHWAITE, G.R.
The Bakhtiyari Ilkhan, an Historical View.
Paper delivered at the American Anthropological Association Annual Meeting, New York, 17-21 November 1971; 18 pp.

Writer: Leading authority on the Bakhtiari tribe. The material in this article was later incorporated in a book. (See separate entry under Section A.)

GELB, LESLIE H.
U.S. Reportedly Aids Anti-Khomeini Exiles: CIA Is Said To Finance Propaganda Broadcasts, Paramilitary Units.
"International Herald Tribune", 8 March 1982; pp. 1 and 2.

Later retracted as "inaccurate".

GERSHEVITCH, ILYA
Zoroaster's Own Contributions.
Reprint of revised text of lecture delivered at the Oriental Institute of the University of Chicago on 18 May 1961; later published by the Institute; pp. 12-38.

GERSHEVITCH, ILYA
Old Iranian Literature.
Reprint from "Handbuch der Orientalistik"; Leiden, 1968; 30 pp.

GERTH, JEFF
Chase's Lawsuit Against Iran: Case Illustrates Legal Tangle in Hostage Crisis.
"The New York Times" Business Section, 11 November 1980; pp. D1 and D13.

GHADIMI, HOSSEIN (M.D.)
Child Care in Iran.
Reprint from the "Journal of Paediatrics"; United States, c.1955; illustrated in text; pp. 620-628.

Writer: Chief of Paediatric Department, Shiraz Medical Faculty, has been practicing medicine in the U.S. since the late sixties.

GHANI, CYRUS
The New Constitution of Iran.
An analysis of the Islamic Republic Constitution. Written in

October 1979 and privately circulated; 11 pp.

The present Constitution, formally ratified 3 December 1979, was circulated from September 1979. The writer believes the document is unique among constitutions in that the governed are not guaranteed any "civil rights", and in the light of the host of institutional checks and controls woven into it, he questions its viability or strict adherence after Khomaini's death.

GHANI, CYRUS
An Outline of Crane Brinton's "The Anatomy of Revolution" (1938) and Its Applicability to the Persian Revolution of 1979.
November 1979; Privately circulated; 18 pp.

GHANI, CYRUS and CAROLINE
The Alien and United States Laws with Particular Reference to Foreign Students.
New York, 1958; 8vo, soft cover; 51 pp.

Pamphlet published by the Iranian Students Organization.

GHARABEGIAN, MARKAR
Catalogue des Peintures du Chahnameh de Ferdowsi par Darviche Parvardeye Iran.
Exposition: Ecole Normal De Teheran; 28 April 1934; 8vo; 17 pp. in French and 15 pp. in Persian.

'Darviche' is the nom de plume of a 20th century Persian miniaturist, Andre Souryogian.

GHASSEMZADEH, G.; SAFINIA, S.E.M.; and NAVA'I, M.
Evolution du Probleme des Droits de l'Homme en Iran.
Geneva, c.1950; 8vo; illustrated; 26 pp.

In French. Three papers prepared for and published by UNESCO-IRAN tracing the history of human rights and its abuses in Iran. Ghassemzadeh: Well known and respected Iranian jurist, Professor at Tehran University and the foremost authority on Iranian Constitutional Law.

GHIRSHMAN, ROMAN
The Island of Kharg.
Published by the Iranian Oil Operating Companies, Tehran, c.1961; illustrated in text and on full page; 11 pp.

A history of the island written after the decision to make it the main oil terminal.

GHIRSHMAN, ROMAN M.
Les Sanctuaires de Masjed-i-Solaiman (Iran).

Reprint published by the "Académie des Inscriptions et Belles-lettres"; Paris, 1972; pp. 30-40.

GHIRSHMAN, ROMAN
Les Scènes d'Investiture Royale dans l'Art Rupestre des Sassanides et Leur Origine.
Extrait de "La Revue Syria", Tom LII, 1975, Fascicules 1-2; Paris, 1975; illustrated; pp. 119-129.

GHULAM, YOUSIF
The Islamic Artist Used the Art of Arabic Calligraphy as a Medium of Art Expression.
Reprint from unknown publication; c.1965; illustrated in text and on separate plates; 15 pp.

GIBB, FRANCES
Peacock Throne May Fall to the Gavel.
"The Times"; London, 9 March 1982; p.1.

False report that Crown Jewels were to go on sale.

GIBB, SIR HAMILTON A.R.
Problems of Middle East Studies.
Reprint from "Middle East Studies", Vol.IV, No.2; London, Spring 1963; 16 pp.

Writer: A distinguished Professor of Islamic studies at Harvard University.

GILBAR, GAD G.
Demographic Development in Late Qajar Persia (1870-1906).
Reprint from "BOAAS", London University, Vol.II; 1976-1977; pp. 125-156.

The writer's main thesis is that demographic changes had a great affect on the economy which in turn affected the political situation, culminating in the demand for constitutional reform. Writer: Professor at University of Haifa.

GILBAR, GAD G.
The Big Merchants (Tujjar) and the Persian Constitutional Revolution of 1906.
Reprint from "BOAAS", Vol.11; Great Britain, 1976-1977; pp. 275-303.

GILBAR, GAD G.
Persian Agriculture in the Late Qajar Period 1860-1906: Some Economic and Social Aspects.
Reprint from "BOAAS", Vol.12, No.3; Great Britain, 1978; pp. 312-365.

GILBAR, GAD G.
The Persian Economy in the Mid 19th Century.
Reprint from "Die Welt Des Islams", Vol.19; no place of
publication indicated, 1979; pp. 177-211.

GIUZALIAN, L.T.
The Bronze Qalamdan (Pen-Case).
Reprint from "Ars Orientalis", VIII; Moscow, 1968; pp. 95-
119 and 6 pp. of illustrations.

The object discussed is amongst the earliest Islamic bronze
works, made in eastern Khorasan and now in the Hermitage collection. The writer maintains that there are no more than ten bronze
objects that could be dated to the mid 12th century.

GODARD, ANDRÉ (edited by)
Athar-e-Iran.
Paris, 1936-1938; "Annales du Service Archeologique de
L'Iran"; five issues; large 8vo; illustrations on full plates;
Tome I, Fascicule II; pp. 187-387. Tome II, Fascicule I; pp. 1-
176. Tome II, Fascicule II; pp. 176-355. Tome III, Fascicule I;
pp. 1-173. Tome III, Fascicule II; pp. 173-329.

An invaluable publication in its day for Iranian archaeologists and scholars. The articles were mostly written by Godard
and his wife, Yedda Godard, but also included lengthy articles by
other scholars in the field. The periods covered were both pre-
Islamic and Islamic.

GOITEIN, S.D.
Interfaith Relations in Medieval Islam.
Reprint of lecture delivered at Columbia University; New
York, 22 October 1973; Prefaced by Isaiah Berlin; 13 pp.

Writer: Professor at the Institute for Advanced Studies,
Princeton, New Jersey. The subject of the lecture was the status
of Jews in the Medieval Arab world.

GOLD, MILTON
Tonybee on the Turks in the Near and Middle East.
Reprint from the "Journal of the Royal Asiatic Society";
Great Britain, October 1961; pp. 77-99.

The writer dismisses Tonybee's argument that since the Turks'
origins are nomadic and as they continued to be nomads, they remained a people without a history or a civilization. Tonybee had
further argued that the Turks became civilized only so far as they
became Persianized and it was the Persian influence that revitalized
their culture. The writer states that Tonybee was always fascinated
by the history and origin of the Turks. In his later works Tonybee

toned down his polemics, came to share Turkish national aspirat-
ions and had praise for Attaturk's efforts at modernization.

GOODMAN, LENN EVAN
Ghazali's Argument from Creation (1).
Reprint from the "International Journal of Middle Eastern
Studies" 2; Great Britain, 1971; pp. 67-85.

Writer: Professor at University of Hawaii.

GOODMAN, LEN EVAN
The Epicurian Ethic of Muhammad Ibn Zakariya Al-Razi.
Reprint from "Studia Islamica", Fasciculo XXXIV; Paris, 1971;
pp. 5-26.

GOODMAN, LENN EVAN
Razi's Psychology.
Reprint from "Philosophical Forum", No.4; no place of public-
ation indicated, 1972; pp. 26-48.

The writer discusses Razi's (c.865-925) theories of percept-
ion and sensation, pleasure and desire.

GOODMAN, LENN EVAN
Razi's Myth of the Fall of Soul: Its Function in His Philos-
ophy.
Reprint from "Essays on Islamic Philosophy and Science";
Albany, 1975; pp. 25-40.

GOODMAN, LEN EVAN
Did Al Ghazali Deny Causality?
Reprint from "Studia Islamica", Ex fasciculo XLVII; Paris,
1978; pp. 83-120.

GRABAR, OLEG
Reprint of review from "Ars Orientalis" II, 1957, of A.M.
Pribytkova's book in Russian dealing with a series of monuments of
the early Saljuq Period (11th century) in the southern part of
Central Asia; Moscow, 1955; pp. 545-547.

Pages 547-560 contain a review of another book in Russian on
Islamic art by the same author. Reviews are in English.

GRAHAM, ROBERT
Iran: Suffering from the Embarrassments of Riches.
"The Financial Times"; London, 27 August 1975; p. unknown.

There was no embarrassment. The riches were flaunted.

GRAY, BASIL
The Essence of Islamic Art.

Article in "Apollo: The Magazine of the Arts"; Lonodn, April
1976; pp. 262-270.

GREENFIELD, JONAS S. and SHAKED, SHAUL
Three Iranian Words in the Targum of Job from Qumran.
Photocopy of reprint from "Zeitschrift Der Deutschen Morgen-
landischen Geseuschaft", Band 122; Wiesbaden, 1972; pp. 37-45.

GRIGGS, LEE
Oil and Water Rebuild an Ancient Land: The Riches of Khuzestan Unlock the Future for Descendants of Darius the Great.
Pages from "Fortune Magazine"; United States, November 1970;
illustrated and map; pp. 88-97.

GROPP, GERD and NADJMABADI, SAIFEDDIN
Ein Gedicht Von Hafez in Einem Safavidenpalast.
Reprint from "Archaeologische Mitteilungen Aus Iran", Vol.2;
Berlin, 1969; illustrated; pp. 193-196.

GROPP, GERD
Die Funktion Des Feuertempels Der Zoroastrier.
Reprint from "Archaeologische Mitteilungen Aus Iran";
Berlin, 1969; illustrated in text and separate plates, 69 illus-
trations in all; pp. 147-175.

GROP, GERD
Der Gurtel Mit Riemenzungen Auf Den Sasanischen Reliefs In
Der Grossen Grotte Des Taq-e Bostan.
Reprint from "Archaeologische Mitteilungen Aus Iran", Vol.3;
Berlin, 1970; pp. 273-287 and 10 full page plates.

GROSVENOR, GILBERT M.
When the President Goes Abroad.
From "National Geographic", Vol.117, No.5; United States,
May 1960; pp. 588-649.

"A Pictorial record" of Eisenhower's 11 nation tour in
December 1959, including Iran.

GROUSET, RENE
L'Iran Exterieur: Son Art.
Paris, 1932; 8vo, soft cover; illustrated; 18 pp.

In French. Lecture given at the Musée Guimet in Paris, 1930.

GROUSSET, RENE and GODARD, ANDRE
"Pièces du Musée de Teheran, du Musée du Louvre et de
Collections Particulaires."
Paris, c.1937; 8vo, soft cover; 83 pp.

Illustrated catalogue of an exhibition of Persian art held in Paris c.1937.

GRUBE, E.
Herat, Tabriz, Istanbul: The Development of Pictorial Styles.
Reprint from unknown journal; c.1970; illustrated; pp. 85-109.

The writer argues that "The history of Moslem painting is closely related to the political history of the Moslem world and the fates of dynasties, courts and cities" ... hence "A particular style was not always the creation of one school but rather the result ... [of the] shift of political power involving the transplantation of artists from one city to another ...". The writer by way of illustrating his thesis examines schools of painting in various cities in the Moslem world.

A GUIDE TO BUSINESS IN IRAN: MARCH, 1976.
Large 8vo, soft cover; 60 pp. plus tables and appendices.

Probably published by the chartered accountants Coopers and Lybrand in Tehran.

GWERTZMAN, BERNARD; APPLE, R.W. Jr.; et al.
Worst Week.
"The New York Times"; Sunday, 11 November 1979; Section 4, p. 1E.

Series of articles on the current situation in Iran and the taking of "60" American hostages in Tehran.

GWERTZMAN, BERNARD; SULZBERGER, A.O. Jr.; PACE, ERIC; et al.
Deposed Shah Dies in Egypt at 60.
"The New York Times"; 28 July 1980; pp. 1 and 9-11.

Front page and inside page series of articles on the death of the Shah, a review of his reign, and speculation on the effect of his death on the fate of the American hostages in Iran.

HABIB ANAVIAN GALLERIES, NEW YORK.
New York, 1979; catalogue; illustrated in color; 62 pp.

The catalogue "Presents 59 art works selected from the collection of ancient and Islamic art" and offered for sale.

HAERI, MEHDI
Islam and the State in Iran.
Copy of typewritten paper prepared for a seminar at Harvard University on problems of contemporary Iran held in April 1965; 18 pp.

Writer: A noted theologian. Ayatollah Khomaini had been a pupil of his father who was the leading ayatollah of the time. The writer later became a student of Khomaini. He discusses the political nature of Islam and states that Mohammad was a prophet of faith and government. The writer questions the exclusion of the clergy from the political scene of Iran and maintains that their participation, along with secular groups would have a salutory effect.

HAFIZ
Some Odes of Hafiz.
Tehran, c.1974.

Folder of 30 postcards of some of Hafiz's odes written by celebrated calligraphers, inter alia, Darvish, Saba and Mir Emad; there is also identification of the styles of the calligraphy in both Persian and English.

HALLIDAY, FRED
The Revolution Turns to Repression.
Article from "The New Statesman"; London, 24 August 1979; pp. 262-264.

The writer, a believer in the Revolution of 1979 would have probably preferred a more orthodox Marxist direction.

HALOUN, G. and HENNING, W.B.
The Compendium of the Doctrines and Styles of the Teaching of Mani, the Buddah of Light.
Photocopy of reprint from "Asia Major", New Series, Vol.III, part II; London, 1952; pp. 184-212, and separate plates.

HAMBLY, G.R.G.
Aqa Mohammad Khan and the Establishment of the Qajar Dynasty.
Photocopy of reprint from the "Royal Central Asian Society"; London, 1955; pp. 161-174.

An interesting article wherein the writer argues that Aqa

Mohammad Khan was an extraordinary leader and the last of the great conquerors of Central Asia basing his power on tribal manpower and loyalty in the mold of Genghis Khan, Teimur and Nader Shah. In 1794 he established a dynasty which was to rule until 1925. The dynasty and the country managed to survive into the 20th century as an independent monarchy, free of at least a colonial status. The writer further argues that his cruelty was required to bring about stability, peace and a strong central government.

HAMID, ALHAJ MAULVI MUHAMMAD
A Short Guide to Lahore Fort.
Karachi, 1965; small 8vo, soft cover; folding map; 20 pp.

A guide book to the Royal Building Museum in the Fort at Lahore built by the Moghol King Akbar c.1566.

HANAWAY, WILLIAM L. Jr.
Hunting as a Theme in Persian Literature.
Reprint from unknown publication; c.1963; 32 pp.

HANAWAY, WILLIAM L. Jr.
Persian Literature.
Reprint of a chapter from "The Study of the Middle East", edited by Leonard Binder; United States, 1976; pp. 399-478.

HANSMAN, JOHN and STRONACH, DAVID
A Sassanian Repository at Shahr-i-Qumis.
Reprint from "Journal of the Royal Asiatic Society"; London, 1970; full page illustrations; pp. 142-155.

HARNEY, DESMOND
Some Explanations for the Iranian Revolution.
Photocopy of an article from an unidentified journal; Great Britain, 1980; pp. 134-143.

"Based on a lecture given to the gathering on the 19th February 1980." A frank and perceptive article by a former member of various British services who first served in Iran in 1958 and had spent a total of 11 years in Iran at different periods.

HARNEY, DESMOND
The Mind and Heart of an Ambassador: Sir Anthony Parsons on the Fall of the Shah.
Review of the book "The Pride and the Fall" by Sir Anthony Parsons; "Journal of the Society of Asian Affairs"; London, mid 1984; pp. 33-37.

HARPER, PRUDENCE OLIVER
Sources of Certain Female Representations in Sassanian Art.
Reprint from "Accedemia Nazionale Dei Lincei", Vol.160; Rome,

1971; pp. 503-515 and five full page plates.

HARPER, PRUDENCE OLIVER
       An Eighth Century Silver Plate from Iran with a Mythological
Scene.
       Reprint from "Islamic Art in the Metropolitan Museum of Art";
New York, 1972; illustrated in text; pp. 153-168.

       There are few works of art in the transitional period from
pre-Islamic to the Islamic era, i.e. 8th century A.D.. A detailed
study by the writer both as to the subject and the date of the
plate.

HARPER, PRUDENCE OLIVER
       Thrones and Enthronment Scene in Sassanian Art.
       Photocopy of reprint from "Iran" XVII, published by the
British Institute of Persian Studies; London, 1979; pp. 49-64 and
8 full page plates.

HARTSHORN, LT. COL. E.S.
       The Mesopotamia Expedition.
       Reprint from "The Coast Artillery Journal" for the Command
Course at the Army War College, Washington D.C., 1922/3; maps,
one folding; 24 pp.

       Great Britain vs. Turkey; campaign in the Near East during
World War I, 1914-1917. Outline account of theatre of operations,
political and military situation, the conduct of the campaign and
an analysis of the strategy of the combatants.

HARVEY, JOHN H.
       Turkey as a Source of Garden Plants.
       Article in "Garden History: The Journal of the Garden History
Society", Vol.IV, No.3; London, Autumn 1976; 7 pp.

       An interesting article which includes an appendix of "plants
cultivated in Iran and Turkey by c.1600" with a glossary of their
names in English, Arabic, Persian, Turkish as well as their
scientific names.

HASKELL, MOLLY
       Feminism Is a Mirage in the Shah's Iran.
       Photocopy from "The Village Voice"; New York, 21 June 1976;
pp. 13-17.

       Views of a U.S. film critic invited to Iran. Officials in
Iran expected a glowing report from their guest. The result was
a hostile account of her visit and of a festival of films directed
by women.

HASSON, RACHEL
        Early Islamic Glass.
        Jerusalem, 1979; booklet; illustrated; 38 pp.

        A lecture delivered at the L.A. Mayer Memorial Institute
for Islamic Art in Jerusalem on 13 December 1977.

HATAMI, ABBAS; BURNETT, DAVID; and RIBOUND, MARC
        Iran: les Temoins.
        Pages from an unidentified French journal; c.1980; pp. 30-54.

        Photo-journalism; a selection of the work of four press
photographers, two Iranian, one American, and one French. Scenes
in Tehran during the winter of 1978/79. In black and white, except
for Burnett's work which is in color. The emphasis is on a grue-
some depiction of those killed, maimed and executed during and
after the Revolution. Prepared by the "early supporters" of the
Revolution.

HATAMI, AZIZ
        Persepolis, Pasargade and Naghsh-e-Rustam.
        Tehran, c.1971; booklet; illustrated, mostly in color, plus
separate folding map in color; 72 pp.

        Published by the General Department of Publications and
Broadcasting, Government of Iran, on the occasion of the 2,500th
anniversary of the founding of the Achaemenid dynasty. History
and archaeology of these ancient sites.

HATIF ESFAHANI
        The Tarji-band.
        Translated by Edward G. Browne; Oakland, California, 1983;
8vo, soft cover; 26 pp.

        In Persian and English. Hatef was the only good poet of 18th
century Persia His fame rests almost entirely on the Tarji-band:
"In the heart of each atom which thou cleavest thou will behold
a sun in its midst."

HAWKES, NIGEL
        Article from "The Observer"; London, 26 May 1985; illustrated
with photographs of Mosaddeq, Eden and the three Rashidian brothers.

        In anticipation of the broadcasting by Granada Television of
the "Iran" segment of its series on "End of Empire", the writer
reveals many of the "murkier" aspects of how Britain and the U.S.
collaborated in the plot to overthrow the Government of Mosaddeq
in August of 1953. The most important parts of the article are
based on an interview with a former British MI6 agent which reveal
the following: It was agents acting for the British who kidnapped

the chief of police , General Afshartous, and murdered him; the
British spent some £700,000 to pay street mobs to begin the
uprising against Mosaddeq; the money was channelled through the
Rashidian brothers who acted as British agents throughout the
period. The writer concludes that the successful plot that overthrew Mosaddeq encouraged Eden in 1956 to attempt the same ploy
against Nasser which led to the Suez disaster.

HAYES, ALFRED
     Emerging Arrangements in International Payments: Public
and Private.
     Washington, 1975; 8vo, soft cover; 46 pp.

     Reprint of lecture delivered at the International Monetary
Fund headquarters, 31 August 1975. Includes pages of commentary
and report of questions and answers by Khodadad Farmanfarmaian.

HEAD, SIMON
     The Monarchs of the Persian Gulf.
     Article from "The New York Review of Books"; 21 March 1974;
pp. 29-36.

     A good article, even though the writer's alarm was premature.
The oil price rise of 1973 did not destroy the economy of the
Western industrialized nations and the "Monarchs of the Gulf" did
not end up buying General Motors or General Electric as was widely
predicted.

HEHN, ROLAND
     "Persian vor 100 Jahren."
     Article in "Du" magazine; Zurich, February 1969; illustrated;
pp. 86-99.

     The photography of Ernst Holtzer in Persia in the late 19th
century.

HEKMAT, ALI ASGHAR
     Nauruz Greetings.
     Tehran, 1947; 16mo, soft cover; 7 pp.

     Poems (quatrains) written by the author in Persian and trans-
lated into Arabic, French and English, to celebrate the Iranian
New Year and sent as greetings. The Iranian Now Ruz (new day) is
celebrated in March at the vernal equinox. The Christian Copts in
Egypt also celebrate Nay Ruz. In their calendar, however, the New
Year falls on either 10th or 11th September.
     Writer: Minister of Education under Reza Shah and Minister
of Foreign Affairs under Mohammad Reza Shah. He held other high
positions in the Persian government and was important in the
development of modern secular education under Reza Shah.

<u>HEKMAT, A.A. and AMIRAN, A.</u>
     Activites Educatives en Iran.
     Tehran, c.1948; 8vo, soft cover; illustrated.

     In French. Published under the auspices of UNESCO-IRAN.
Hekmat's contribution is a summary of the pre-war and wartime
education programs in Iran. The article by Amiran is a short
survey.

<u>HELINE, THEODORE</u>
     Iran, Lebanon and the Land of Araby.
     Reprint of two articles appearing in "New Age Interpreter";
Los Angeles, California, January and February 1944.

     An examination of the Palestine questions and of the 1943
Tehran Conference in the light of Biblical prophecy and the
"cosmic forces which direct world history". The thoughts of a
Christian fundamentalist before the area became permeated with
Islamic and Jewish fundamentalism.

<u>HELMS, RICHARD and MEYER, ARMIN H.</u>
     Contacts with the Opposition; A Symposium.
     A Symposium held at the School of Foreign Service, Georgetown
University, in which 19 diplomats took part; booklet edited by
Martin F. Herz; Washington, D.C., c.1981.

     Two former U.S. ambassadors to Iran:
     Helms: News agency correspondent before World War II until
1942; C.I.A., 1947-1973; Director of C.I.A. 1966-1973; Ambassador
to Iran 1973-1976. Helms' paper basically argues that since U.S.
policy was to support the Shah, contact with the opposition would
have "encouraged" the opposition and "enraged" the Shah. Helms
further argues that among the dissatisfied elements (not those in
outright opposition to the government) who were in contact with
the U.S. Embassy, no one ever suggested that "corruption or
inflation would topple the regime and the monarchy. The clergy
was not even in the running then."
     Meyer: Career diplomat, served at U.S. Embassies in Baghdad,
1946-1948; Beirut, 1952-1954; Kabul, 1955-1957; Ambassador to
Lebanon, 1961-1965; Ambassador to Iran, 1965-1969; Ambassador to
Japan, 1969-1972. Meyer argues that no one at the embassy in
Tehran was under orders not to contact opposition elements and,
in fact, the embassy did have contact with a wide spectrum of
Iranian society. Meyer's main point is that in Iran the issue
became academic because no one, including Khomaini, ever thought
that within a mere six month period the Shah would be toppled.
     A most interesting topic selected by Martin Herz, even though
the participants do not appear to have responded to the issue

directly. The booklet also contains former U.S. Ambassador (1966-1970) to Afghanistan, Robert G. Neuman's comments on the subject, with several references to Iran.

HENNING, WALTER BRUNO
     Mani's Last Journey.
     Reprint from "BSOAS", London University, Vol.X; 1942; pp. 941-953.

HENNING, W.B.
     Bibliography of Important Studies on Old Iranian Subjects.
     Tehran, 1950; 8vo; 53 pp.

     Re: Pre-Islamic Iran.

HENNING, W.B.
     A Pahlavi Poem.
     Reprint from "BSOAS", London University, Vol.XIII, Part 3; 1950; pp. 641-648.

HENNING, W.B.
     The Monuments and Inscriptions of Tang-i-Sarvak.
     Photocopy of reprint from "Asia Major", New Series, Vol.II, Part 2; London, 1952; pp. 151-178, with 20 plates.

     An account of a visit and study of the Parthian remains in a valley near the town of Behbahan.

HENNING, W.B.
     A New Parthian Inscription.
     Reprint from the "Journal of the Royal Asiatic Society"; London, October 1953; illustrations; pp. 132-136.

HENNING, W.B.
     The Inscription of Firuzabad.
     Photocopy of reprint from "Asia Major", New Series, Vol.IV, Part 1; London, 1954; illustrations in text and in full page plates; pp. 98-102.

HENNING, W.B.
     The Ancient Language of Azerbaijan.
     Reprint from "Transactions of the Philological Society"; Great Britain, 1954; pp. 157-178.

HENNING, W.B.
     The Structure of the Khwarezmian Verb.
     Photocopy of reprint from "Asia Major", New Series, Vol.V, Part 1; London, 1955; pp. 43-49.

HENNING, W.B.

The Great Inscriptions of Sapur 1.
Reprint from "BSOAS", London University, Vol.IX, Part 4; c.1955.

The Pahlavi inscription at Naqsh Rustam, dating from the reign of Shapur I, 241-272 A.D., is considered the most important commentary on the Sassanian empire. The writer re-examines the findings and deciphering of the 1936 expedition by the Oriental Institute of Chicago.

HENNING, W.B.
     Surkh Kotal, Notes and Communications.
     Reprint from "BSOAS", London University, Vol.XVIII, Part 2; 1956; pp. 366-367.

HENNING, W.B. (edited by)
     The Inscription of Naqs-i-Rustam.
     London, 1957; folio; 2 pp. of text and 48 monochrome plates.

HENNING, W.B.
     The Inscription of Tang-i-Azao.
     Reprint from "BSOAS", London University, Vol.XX; 1957; pp. 335-342 and one plate.

HENNING, W.B.
     New Pahlavi Inscriptions on Silver Vessels.
     Reprint from "BSOAS", London University, Vol.XXII, Part 1; 1959; pp. 132-134.

HENNING, W.B.
     The Bactrian Inscription.
     Reprint from "BSOAS", London University, Vol.XXIII, Part 1; 1960; pp. 47-55.

HENNING, W.B.
     The Kurdish Elm.
     Reprint of an article from an unknown journal, c.1962; pp. 68-72.

An interesting article on the origin of the word Narvan (Elm) in Middle Persian.

HENNING, W.B.
     In Memorium - 1908-1967.
     Bibliography of the works of W.B. Henning; London, 1969; 34 pp.

HERALD TRIBUNE
     Trend of Iranian Economy - 1957.
     Special section of the "New York Herald Tribune", Section 13; 8 September 1957; pp. 1-12.

Entire section devoted to articles on Iran.

HERALD TRIBUNE
Major Mosque in Iran Was Shelled.
"International Herald Tribune"; 9 April 1985.

An account of aerial bombing by Iraq of what is probably the most artistically important mosque in the world, the Friday Mosque in Esfahan.

HERON ALLEN, EDWARD
"The Ruba'i in Persian Poetry and the Ruba'iyyat of Omar Khayyam."
Article in "The Poetry Review", Vol.II, No.5; London, May 1913; pp. 205-220.

From a lecture delivered before the Poetry Society, March-April 1913. Heron-Allen himself published a literal prose translation of Omar Khayyam's "Rubaiyat" in 1898. A manuscript letter from the writer is also inserted. Subsequently bound in marbled-paper covers.

HERZ, MARTIN F.
A View From Tehran: A Diplomat Looks at the Shah's Regime in June 1964.
Washington, D.C., c.1979; 8vo, soft cover; 11 pp.

A declassified dispatch from the American Embassy in Tehran to the U.S. State Department, dated 15 June 1964, published 15 years later by the Institute for the Study of Diplomacy, Georgetown University, Washington, D.C. Drafting Officer: Martin F. Hertz, Counsellor for Political Affairs, U.S. Embassy, Tehran. Subject: "Some Intangible Factors in Iranian Politics". The dispatch is remarkably prescient in anticipating the events of 1978/79. Brilliant analysis by a distinguished Foreign Service officer. Unfortunately diplomats with the insight of Herz were rare. The writer discusses the hollowness of the recently formed "Iran Novin" party and how the very founders of the new political party told U.S. officials that it was a sham. Herz hints strongly that unless some steps are taken towards political reform, the future of the country would be bleak.
It should be mentioned that the report was written as part of a group effort of the Political Section of the U.S. Embassy which was then staffed with some of the ablest U.S. Foreign Service officers to serve in Iran. Herz was more sanguine than his assistants and it was the junior officers who won him over to their point of view.

HERZFELD, ERNST E.
A New Inscription of Xerxes from Persepolis.

Chicago, 1932; 8vo, soft cover; full page illustrations;
14 pp.

Published by the Oriental Institute of the University of
Chicago. Includes a translation of a transliteration and a
commentary on a "foundation" document of Xerxes discovered during
excavations carried out by the writer under the auspices of the
Institute.

HICKMAN, WILLIAM F.
Ravaged and Reborn: The Iranian Army 1982.
Washington, D.C., 1982; "Staff Paper" prepared for the
Brooking Institute, Washington, D.C.; 8vo, soft cover; 33 pp.

One of the better political papers written on Iran since the
Revolution. The writer, a Lt. Commander in the U.S. Navy, in a
short space, gives the history of the Iranian Army under Mohammad
Reza Shah, its attitude during the Revolution, the purges, its
emerging popularity since the Iran-Iraq war and its future.

HILLMAN, MICHAEL CRAIG
Hafez and Poetic Unity Through Verse Rhythms.
Reprint from "Journal of Near Eastern Studies", Vol.31;
United States, January 1972; 10 pp.

In an excellent article the writer argues that the fact
that very few attempts have been made to translate Hafez into
English, and those few have not succeeded, is less due to the
fact that able poets such as Edward Fitzgerald and Matthew Arnold
never tried their hand at it than "the fact that there is
inherent in the verse form employed by Hafez an emphasis on the
musical potentiality of words, phrases and verse lines that
resist translation. In fact in some of Hafez's poems, the
patterns of verbal rhythm seems to be a basic organizing
principle, the plain sense of the poetic statement complementing
the verbal music." He further quotes T.S. Eliot's observation
that "the music of verses is not a line by line matter but a
question of the whole poem".

HILLMAN, MICHAEL C.
Furugh Farrukzad - Modern Iranian Poet.
Photocopy from "Middle Eastern Muslim Women Speak", Univer-
sity of Texas Press; Austin, Texas, 1977; pp. 291-317.

A biographical sketch of the Iranian poet whose career was
cut short in a tragic accident in 1966. The article includes an
English translation of some of her poems.

HINNELLS, JOHN R.
Reflection on the Lion-Head Figure in Mithraism.
Reprint from "Acta Iranica"; Leiden, 1975; pp. 333-369 and

full page plates.

HINNELLS, JOHN R.
Zoroastrian Influence on the Judaeo-Christian Tradition.
Photocopy of reprint from "Journal of the K.R. Cama Oriental Institute", No.45; Bombay, 1976; p. 23

HINNELLS, JOHN R.
The Parsis: A Bibliographical Survey.
Photocopy of reprint from "Journal of Mithraic Studies", Vol.III, Nos.1 and 2; 1980; pp. 98-149.

HITTI, PHILIP
America and the Arab Heritage.
Reprint from "The Arab Heritage", Princeton University Press; Princeton, 1944; 8vo, soft cover; 24 pp.

An essay on Western cultural heritage derived from the Islamic world and the opportunities that exist for the study of both Arabic and that cultural heritage in Europe and in the United States.

HITTI, PHILIP
Arab Philosophy, Arabic Language, Arabic Literature.
Reprint from "The Encyclopaedia Americana", 1948 edition; 8vo, soft cover; pp. 115a to 129.

HOFFMAN, STANLEY
Review of Gary Sick's book, All Fall Down.
"New York Times" Book Review Section; 16 June 1985; pp. 1, 32-33.

An excellent review of an excellent book.

HOLDSWORTH, MARY
Turkestan in the Nineteenth Century.
Oxford, 1959; small 4to, soft cover; map; 81 pp.

"A Brief History of the Khanates of Bukhara, Kokand and Khiva." An occasional paper issued by the Central Asian Research Center. An outline study of three distinct Central Asian communities in the 19th century whose fate it was to be swallowed up by Russian imperialism.

HOMAYOUN, DARIUSH
Political Development of Iran.
Paper prepared for a seminar at Harvard University on Problems of Contemporary Iran held in April, 1965; 51 pp.

One of the few papers at the above seminar that was favorable towards the Pahlavi regime and exuded confidence and optimism. The writer argues that Reza Shah was an administrative reformer in the mold of Abbas Mirza and Amir Kabir whose principle aim was to establish a secular regime that could withstand foreign pressure. Reza Shah's hopes were smashed with the Allies' invasion of Iran in 1941. The writer makes the interesting point that the Mosaddeq movement had nothing to do with reform or modernization. Its sole purpose was to eradicate foreign influence. He then argues that the time is propitious for certain fundamental reforms and yet the government has done little. The government can co-opt the opposition by adopting certain measures towards liberalization of the political system. The writer also pleads the cause of the clergy which he maintains is a nationalist force to reckon with. Their energy must be utilized and attempts should be made to reconcile them with modernization. The writer sees no threat from the communists and believes they will discredit themselves in the long run. It is the secular intellectuals and the clergy that must be courted. "Shi'ism is waiting for its Pope John XXIII." The writer was in the opposition movements in his youth before he himself was "co-opted" by the system. He was a successful journalist who began his career as a columnist and later founded the daily newspaper "Ayandegan". He served as Minister of Information during a crucial period from August 1977 to the end of August 1978.

HOVEYDA, AMIR ABBAS
      The Landscape of Iranian Culture.
      c. 1968; 18 pp.

An excellent speech by the then Prime Minister. The speech contained certain autobiographical elements with references to his past and his career.

HOVEYDA, AMIR ABBAS
      Text of address by the then Prime Minister, at the Aspen-Persepolis Symposium on "Iran: Past, Present and Future"; 19 September 1975; 38 pp.

The symposium was not a great success as the Iranian participants over-stated their case and some of the invitees from the West also went overboard. Hoveyda's speech dealt with the determination of Iran to keep its identity intact in the face of modernization. Hoveyda, who served longer than any Prime Minister in the post-Constitutional period, was a man of infinite charm and steadfast friendship. He served as a moderating influence on the "hard liners" and to a small extent he was able to ameliorate the growing discontent. A well educated man in the humanist tradition, he maintained for many years that corruption, which he equated with injustice, would be the Achilles' heel of the Iranian regime. On at least two occasions he seriously attempted to eliminate or at least limit the activities of the influence peddlers. He received only half-hearted support and the campaigns were aborted. His arrest and imprisonment in

November 1978 was wholly unwarranted and he became the "sacrificial
lamb". Although he had the opportunity to leave Iran, he chose
to remain behind and answer for his service in the Shah's regime.
His wanton murder will serve as a constant reminder of the
barbarity of the revolutionary regime.

HOVEYDA, FEREYDOUN
        Not All Clocks for Human Rights Are the Same.
        Article from the "New York Times"; 8 May 1977; p. 35.

HOVEYDA, FEREYDOUN
        L'Architecte de l'Invisible.
        Photocopy from "La Nouvelle Revue Francaise"; Paris, January
1979; in French; pp. 30-47.

        A discussion of Henry Corbin's views on Persian Sufism.

HOVEYDA, FEREYDOUN
        The Fall of the Shah: Part I.
        Article from "The Sunday Telegraph"; London, 21 October 1979;
pp. 8-9.

        Excerpts from his forthcoming book.

HOVEYDA, FEREYDOUN
        The Fall of the Shah: Part II.
        Article from "The Sunday Telegraph"; London, 28 October 1979;
pp. 8 and 9.

HOVEYDA, FEREYDOUN
        Iran: Mythologie de la Révolution.
        Photocopy of article in "Scarabée International" Nos.5/6;
Paris, Printemps-Eté 1983; in French; pp. 22-50.

        The role of pre-Islamic myths (especially that of the father
killing his son) in the events of 1978-1979. The writer finds
similarities between legend and reality.

HUMBACH, HELMUT M.
        Sir Henry Rawlinson's Copies of the Paikuli Inscription.
        Reprint from "Fondation Culturelle Iranienne"; Louvin, 1974;
pp. 199-204 and 9 plates.

HUMBACH, HELMUT M.
        Aramaeo-Iranian and Pahlavi.
        Reprint from "Acta Iranica"; Leiden, 1974; pp. 238-243.

HUMBACH, HELMUT M.
        Mithra in the Kusana Period.
        Offprint from "Mithraic Studies", edited by John R. Hinnells;
Manchester University Press, 1975; pp. 135-141.

HUMMER, W.B.
Report from Tehran: Iran's Boom Spurs Bank Development.
Photocopy from "Bankers Monthly Magazine"; Chicago, 15 March
1977; pp. 34-40.

Ebullient in its praise. Writer: An investment banker in
Chicago who wrote the article after a brief visit.

HUNTER, SHIREEN T.
The Future Is at Stake in Iran.
Article from "The New York Times"; c.August 1984.

A well argued article. The writer basically pleads for some
reconciliation between Iran and the U.S. as the key to a moderate
post Khomaini regime.

HUREWITZ, J.C.
Ottoman Diplomacy and the European State System.
Reprint from "Middle East Journal"; United States, Spring
1961; pp. 141-152.

The writer's main thesis: "The Ottoman Empire was the first
non-Christian country to participate in the European State System
and the first unconditionally to accept its form of diplomacy."
The writer traces the development of the diplomatic exchanges.

HUREWITZ, J.C.
The Beginning of Military Modernization in the Middle East:
A Comparative Analysis.
Reprint from "Middle East Journal"; Spring 1968; pp. 144-158.

A seldom explored subject but the article is too general and
the sources are too familiar.

HUREWITZ, J.C.
Military Politics in the Muslim Dynastic States 1400-1750.
Reprint of a chapter in a "forthcoming book" by the "Journal
of the American Oriental Society", Vol.88; January-March 1968;
pp. 96-104.

HUREWITZ, J.C.
The Persian Gulf Prospects for Stability.
Reprint from "Headline Series" published by the Foreign
Policy Association; United States, April 1974; illustrations in
text and maps; 63 pp.

Nothing original and dated.

HUSAINI, AMIRA
Religious Power in Iran: Pre-Islamic Origins.
Photocopy from "Dissent"; no place of publication indicated;

Winter 1981; pp. 218-220 and 235.

<u>HUSSAIN, TAHA</u>
La Rhétorique Arabe de Djahiz à 'Abd al-Kahir.
Leiden, c.1931; 8vo, soft cover; 24 pp.

A paper presented at the 18th Congress of Orientalists in
Leiden 11 September 1931, by the great 20th century Egyptian
writer.

IBRAHIM, YOUSSEF M.
     Inside Iran's Cultural Revolution.
     Article from "The New York Times Magazine"; 14 October 1979;
pp. 36-39, 76-80 and 84.

IBRAHIM, YOUSSEF M.
     Piety and Power: Iran's Clerics Tighten Grip by Instilling
Islam in Every Detail of Life.
     "Wall Street Journal"; 1 December 1982; pp. 1 and 22.

IGNATIUS, DAVID and KESSLER, FELIX
     The Plotters: Khomeini Foes in Exile Hope to Emulate Him by
Winning from Afar.
     Photocopy from "Wall Street Journel"; 23 September 1981; pp.
1 and 24.

ILYNISKY, G.
     Agrarian Relations in Iran at the End of the XIX and the
Beginning of the XX Centuries.
     Reprint of an article in both English and Russian in unknown
Russian journal; c.1960; pp. 7-29.

IMAM
     Vol.I, No.9; London, 27 August 1980; illustrated; 50 pp.

     A monthly periodical published by the Embassy of the Islamic
Republic of Iran, London. This issue features "the Quds Liberation Congress in Tehran" among other articles.

IMAM
     Vol.I, No.12; London, 28 February 1981; illustrated; 50 pp.

     Another issue of the preceding. This issue "published on
the occasion of the second anniversary of the Islamic Revolution
in Iran" includes a lengthy article reviewing the days that led
to Khomaini's return.

IMPERIAL ORGANIZATION FOR SOCIAL SERVICES 1947-1967.
     Tehran, 1967; booklet; illustrated, folding map and charts
in text; 76 pp.

     "A Record of Twenty Years of Services to People by the
Imperial Organization for Social Services 1947 to 1967."
Coronation commemorative issue.

IMPERIAL ORGANIZATION FOR SOCIAL SERVICES 1947-1967.
     Tehran, 1967; booklet; 77 pp.

     French edition of preceding.

814

INDIAN MANUSCRIPTS: AN INTRODUCTION TO THE PERMANENT EXHIBITION.
     London, 1977; 12 pp.

     Published by the British Library, Department of Oriental
Manuscripts and Printed Books.

THE INDUSTRIAL AND MINING DEVELOPMENT BANK OF IRAN (IMDBI).
     Report prepared by the International Finance Corporation
(IFC), 25 July 1968; 11 pp. and two appendices.

     A summary of the history, funding and financial activities
of the IMDBI, established in 1959. IMDBI was one of the best
managed institutions in Iran and played an important part in the
economic development of the country in the sixties and seventies.
The report was prepared when IFC decided to invest in Iranian
industry through IMDBI.

INTERNATIONAL BIBLIOGRAPHY OF MODERN LANGUAGE ASSOCIATION (MLA).
     Extract from Vol.III, Iranian Linguistics; 1970, 3 pp.

INTERNATIONAL COMMITTEE FOR THE DEFENCE OF HUMAN RIGHTS IN IRAN.
     New York, 1981; 4 pp.

     Copy of typewritten press release from the Committee announc-
ing its formation; marked for release 14 December 1981. Includes
a list of founding members. An honorable effort but wrong
composition of founders. An abortive attempt.

AN INTRODUCTION TO THE ART OF BLACK AFRICA.
     Tehran, 1977; 4to soft cover; illustrated; 21 pp.

     Basically a catalogue of an exhibition of Black African Art
held in Tehran from 1 November to 16 December 1977. An attempt
at solidarity by the former regime.

INVESTMENT GUIDE TO IRAN.
     Tehran, c.1977; 4to, soft cover; 48 pp.

     Prepared by Citibank of New York. Superficial, some errors,
and not useful even in its day.

IRAN
     London, 1956; booklet; illustrated; 52 pp.

     Published by the Iranian Oil Participants, Limited. Geog-
raphy, history, religion, culture, economy, inhabitants. One of
the better efforts of its kind.

IRAN
     New York, 1957; small 4to, soft cover; illustrated and cover

map; 23 pp.

Reprint of a Special Supplement which appeared in the "New York Herald Tribune"; 8 September 1957. Prepared by the Iranian Information Center, New York.

IRAN
United States, March 1969; large 8vo, soft cover; illustrated in color and map; 16 pp.

Prepared by the Economic Research Division of the Chase Manhattan Bank, N.A. Economic review, with sections on natural resources, agriculture, industry and trade. Better than similar publications by other U.S. banks but still mediocre.

IRAN - INTERNATIONAL ECONOMIC SURVEY.
Prepared by Chemical Bank, April 1975; map and illustrated; 21 pp.

IRAN AND THE HISTORY OF MEDICINE.
67 page computer print-out of articles from medical journals, principally from 1965 on, of authors and titles on medical subjects relating to the above field from the 19th century onward.

IRAN AT A GLANCE, THE LAND OF CONTRASTS.
New York, August 1956; 8vo, soft cover; illustrated; 32 pp.

Published by the Iranian Students' Association of New York. Better than anything the Iranian Embassy or the Iranian Information Center had put out.

IRAN COMMITTEE FOR DEMOCRATIC ACTION AND HUMAN RIGHTS.
Illinois, c.1979; three typewritten pages: An introduction plus two pages of "Excerpts from the 'Bill of Vengence'", a proposed "Justice bill submitted to the Islamic Parliament in Iran for final approval."

THE IRAN COUNCIL GRAPEVINE.
Five issues of a newsletter issued by the Iran Council of the Asia Society of New York; Vol.I, No.1; October 1977; 4 pp.. Vol.I, No.2; January 1978; 4 pp.. Vol.I, No.3; May 1978; 6 pp. Vol.II, No.2; January 1979; 6 pp.. Vol.II, No.4; October 1979; 45 pp.

Includes an edited transcript of the interview of Ayatollah Khomaini by Oriana Fallaci on 12 September 1979 originally having appeared in "The New York Times Magazine", of 7 October 1979.

IRAN: FACTS AND FIGURES.
No.6: Women of Iran.

Tehran, October 1969; small 8vo, soft cover; 10 pp.

Published by the Iranian Ministry of Information. This booklet traces the history of the status of women in Iran, and the benefits gradually gained in the fields of economics, education and employment, beginning with Reza Shah's proclamation unveiling Iranian women in 1935, and culminating in "full equality" under Mohammad Reza Shah's "White Revolution" begun in 1963.

IRAN: "JOURNAL OF THE BRITISH INSTITUTE OF PERSIAN STUDIES", VOLS. I, II and III.
London; Vol.I, 1963; Vol.II, 1964; Vol.III, 1965; 4to, soft cover; illustrated, maps and diagrams, including back cover map; Vol.I, 101 pp.; Vol.II, 103 pp.; Vol.III, 132 pp.

Published annually by the British Institute of Persian Studies in Tehran. Each volume has about ten articles on Iranian culture, literature, art and history.

IRAN: PAST AND PRESENT.
Tehran, March 1950; 8vo, soft cover; illustrated; 65 pp.

"Introduction by A. Vahid." A brief sketch of the history, geography and administrative organization of the country, as well as some "essential hints" on its cultural and economic aspects; specially prepared on the occasion of a State visit to Pakistan (1-16th March 1960) by the late Shah.

IRAN (PERSIA).
New York, c.1975; 8vo, soft cover; illustrated in color plus map; 16 pp.

Booklet on history, culture and tourism in Iran published for the "Iran Information and Tourism Year" of 1975.

IRAN - PERSIA: AZARBAIJAN.
Tehran, 1975; 8vo, soft cover; illustrated in color plus map; 12 pp.

Illustrated tourist guide to Azarbaijan Province published by the Iranian Ministry of Information and Tourism, as part of the "South Asia Tourism Year" of 1975.

IRAN-PERSIA: HAMADAN, KERMANSHAH - A GUIDE.
Tehran, 1975; 8vo, soft cover; illustrated in color plus folding map; 14 pp.

Tourist brochure and guide to Hamadan and Kermanshah. Same as above.

IRAN: PERSIAN MINIATURES, IMPERIAL LIBRARY.
Tehran, 1960's; 1 pp. of text plus 31 color plates.

Plates of the illustrated manuscript, the Shahnama Bysonghori and some later work.

IRAN REVIEW.
Vol.I, No.I; Washington, D.C., July 1960; 4to, soft cover; illustrated; 16 pp.

Issued by the Iranian Embassy, Washington, D.C.; magazine format with articles on economics and current affairs in Iran.

IRAN 75: IRAN TRADE AND INDUSTRY.
An Independent Survey of the Iranian Economy.
Vol.IX, No.7; Tehran, September 1975; large 8vo, soft cover; 96 pp.

Journal containing articles on economy, finance, mining, forestry, petroleum, transport, the Fifth Plan, aviation, tourism, housing, etc. in the year 1975. Published by "Echo of Iran".

IRAN TODAY.
Vol.I, No.I; Tehran, c.1957; illustrated, some in color; 47 pp.

"A Quarterly Review Published by the Department of Information and Broadcasting, Tehran, Iran." Articles on art, culture, and social welfare in contemporary Iran, including an article on and some good photographs of Iranian medalists in the 1956 Olympics at Melbourne.

IRAN TRADE AND INDUSTRY.
Iran, August 1975; large 8vo, soft cover; 42 pp.

Contains, inter alia, surveys of agriculture and of housing, and construction "problems".

IRANIAN CALLIGRAPHY: A SELECTION OF WORKS FROM 15th TO 20th CENTURY.
Tehran, 1975; small 4to, soft cover; illustrated, some in color; 66 pp.

Catalogue of exhibition of the Aydin Aghdashloo Collection held at the Negarestan Museum, 23 April to 24 May 1975. Captions to illustrations in both Persian and English. The collection was one of the best of Persian calligraphy in Iran.

IRANIAN MINIATURES OF THE FIFTEENTH AND SIXTEENTH CENTURIES.
Leningrad, 1973; folder containing 16 large postcard size color reproductions; 4 pp. insert of text.

818

From library collections in Leningrad; in Russian and English.

IRANIAN STUDENTS ASSOCIATION BULLETIN.
Easton, Pennsylvania; No.I, May 1953; illustrated; 4 pp.; No.2, August 1953; illustrated; 4 pp.

First 2 issues of the Iranian Students Association newsletter, published in English for Iranians studying in the U.S.A. (See also "Daneshjoo", the title of all subsequent issues of the newsletter.)

IRANIAN STUDIES: JOURNAL OF THE SOCIETY FOR IRANIAN CULTURAL AND SOCIAL STUDIES.
New York; 8vo, soft cover;

Vol.I, No.I, Winter 1968.
Vol.I, No.2, Spring 1968;
Vol.I, No.3, Summer 1968;
Vol.I, No.4, Autumn 1968;
Vol.II, No.I, Winter 1969;
Vol.II, No.2-3, Spring and Summer 1969;
Vol.II, No.4, Autumn, 1969;
Vol.III, No.I, Winter 1970;
Vol.III, No.2, Spring 1970;
Vol.III, No.3-4, Summer and Autumn 1970;
Vol.IV, No.I, Winter 1971;
Vol.IV, No.2-3, Spring and Summer 1971;
Vol.IV, No.4, Autumn 1971;
Vol.V, No.I, Winter 1972;
Vol.V, No.2-3, Spring and Summer 1972;
Vol.V, No.4, Autumn 1972;
Vol.VI, No.I, Winter 1973;
Vol.VI, No.2-3, Spring and Summer 1973;
Vol.VI, No.4, Autumn 1973;
Vol.VII, No.1-2, Winter and Spring 1974;
Vol.VII, No.3-4, Summer and Autumn 1974;
Vol.VIII, No.1-2, Winter and Spring 1975;
Vol.VIII, No.3, Summer 1975;
Vol.VIII, No.4, Autumn 1975;
Vol.IX, No.I, Winter 1976;
Vol.IX, No.2-3, Spring and Summer 1976;
Vol.IX, No.4, Autumn 1976;
Vol.X, No.1-2, Winter and Spring 1977;
Vol.X, No.3, Summer 1977;
Vol.X, No.4, Autumn 1977;
Vol.XI, 1978;
Vol.XII, No.1-2, Winter and Spring 1979;
Vol.XII, No.3-4, Summer and Autumn 1979;
Vol.XIII, No.1-4, 1980;
Vol.XIV, No.1-2, Winter and Spring 1981;

Vol.IXV, No.3-4, Summer and Autumn 1981;
Vol.XV, No.1-4, 1982;
Vol.XVI, No.1-2, Winter and Spring 1983;
Vol.XVI, No.3-4, Summer and Autumn 1983;
Vol.XVII, No.1, Winter 1984;
Vol.XVII, No.2-3, Spring and Summer 1984;
Vol.XVII, No.4, Autumn 1984;
Vol.XVIII, No.I, Winter 1985.

Editor: From inception in Winter of 1968 to Winter of 1981, Ali Banuazizi; from 1982 to present, Ervand Abrahamian and Farhad Kazemi. Presently the best publication on Iranian culture, literature and arts in a language other than Persian.

IRANIAN STUDIES: JOURNAL OF THE SOCIETY FOR IRANIAN CULTURAL AND SOCIAL STUDIES.
Cumulative Index Vol.1-15, 1968-1982.
New York; 8vo, soft cover; 33 pp.

Note: Some articles from the above journal which were in reprint form have been entered in this section D under the name of the writer.

IRANIAN WOMEN: THE STRUGGLE SINCE THE REVOLUTION.
London, Spring 1980; 8vo, soft cover; illustrated and map; 32 pp.

Published by the Iranian Women's Liberation Group. Charts the set-backs to women's rights in Iran since the Revolution, and lists some of the groups working inside Iran to achieve women's liberation. Written during the euphoria after the Revolution and still optimistic on prospects for women.

IRANICA ANTIQUA.
Vol.I; Leiden, 1961; 8vo, soft cover; illustrated, folding maps and illustrations in text; 204 pp.

Contains articles in English, French and German. Under the general editorship of R. Ghirshman and L. Vanden Berghe.

IRANICA ANTIQUA.
Vol.II, Fasc.I; Leiden, 1962; 8vo, soft cover; illustrated and illustrations in text; 95 pp. plus 6 black and white plates.

IRANICA ANTIQUA.
Vol.III, Fasc.2; Leiden, 1963; 8vo, soft cover; illustrated, map, and illustrations in text; pp. 85-173.

IRANICA ANTIQUA.
Vol.IV, Fasc.2; Leiden, 1964; 8vo, soft cover, illustrated

820

and illustrations in text; pp. 85-174.

IRANICA ANTIQUA.
     Vol.V, Fasc.I, Leiden, 1965; 8vo, soft cover; illustrated
and folding map; 82 pp.

IRANICA ANTIQUA.
     Vol.V, Fasc.2, Leiden, 1965; 8vo, soft cover; illustrated,
folding maps and diagrams in text; pp. 83-160.

IRANSCHAHR, H.K.
     La Vérité et les Fondements de la Vraie Mystique.
Lausanne, September 1937; 4 pp.

     Forty two easy steps to "enlightenment".

IRONS, WILLIAM
     Nomadism as a Political Adaptation: The Case of the Yomut
Turkmen.
     Photocopy of reprint from the "American Ethnologist", Vol.I,
No.4; November 1974; pp. 635-658.

     The writer, a Professor at Pennsylvania University, puts forth
the argument that the Turkeman Tribe of northern Persia adapted
nomadism not for economic reasons but for military purposes.
Their nomadism gave them increased mobility and agility and hence
greater military prowess.

ISLAMIC ART.
     Ohio, 1956; 8vo, soft cover; illustrations in full page; 9
pp. of text and 16 plates.

     An Exhibition of Islamic Art at the Ohio State Museum, July-
August 1956. Most of the items exhibited were on loan.

ISLAMIC ART FROM THE COLLECTION OF EDWIN BINNEY 3rd.
     Washington, D.C., 1966; small 4to, soft cover; illustrated,
some in color; 100 pp.

     Catalogue of a Smithsonian Institution Travelling Exhibition
of the "Islamic Art of the Book" from the early 14th through 19th
centuries; 1966-1968. Binney did not begin his collection until
the late 50's and yet he amassed one of the best private collections of Moghol art. He sold most of his collection in the
seventies.

ISLAMIC CALLIGRAPHY AND ILLUMINATION.
     London, 1970; folder containing 18 photographic slides plus
8 pp. of introduction by Martin Lings and commentary on the slides.
Published by the British Museum.

ISLAMIC INSIGHTS: AN INTRODUCTION TO ISLAMIC ART.
Katonah, New York, 1980; booklet; illustrated; 20 pp.

Designed to accompany a loan exhibition of textiles, miniatures, metalwork, calligraphy, pottery, etc. held 16 March to 25
May 1980 at the Katonah Gallery, Katonah, New York and sponsored
by the National Endowment for the Humanities and the New York
State Council on the Arts.

ISLAMIC POTTERY, 800-1400 A.D.
London, 1969; large booklet/catalogue; illustrated; 50 pp.

Catalogue of "an Exhibition arranged by the Islamic Art
Circle and held at the Victoria and Albert Museum 1 October to 30
November 1969".

ISLAMIC REVOLUTION.
Vol.I, No.10; Falls Church, Virginia, January 1980; illustrated and maps; 24 pp.

Published monthly by Research and Publication Inc. "Dimensions of the Movement in Iran": pro-Khomaini articles on contemporary Iran and events in the Middle East.

ISLAMIC REVOLUTION.
Vol.II, No.3; Falls Church, Virginia, June 1980; illustrated
and maps; 26 pp.

ISSAWI, CHARLES
The Christian-Muslim Frontier in the Mediterranean, a History
of Two Peninsulas.
Reprint from "Political Science Quarterly", Vol.LXXVI, No.4;
United States, December 1961; pp. 544-554.

An excellent and thought provoking article that discusses the
penetration and arrest of Islam in Europe and conversely the failure of Christianity to make inroads in the Eastern Mediterranean.
The frontier ended at the straits of Gibralter at one end, beyond
which Islam could not overcome deep rooted Christianity; and the
Dardanelles at the other end, where Christianity was halted by
well established Islam. Issawi briefly mentions a variety of
reasons, namely that Islam penetrated for the most part through
overland routes; Indonesia and parts of East Africa being the exceptions. The high mountains of Europe were an obstacle, as were the
forests in Eastern Europe. Furthermore, schisms within both relig-
ions also impeded their expansion, i.e. Protestantism and Shi'ism.

ISSAWI, CHARLES
Iran's Economic Upsurge.
Reprint from "Middle East Journal", Vol.21, No.4; no place

822

of publication indicated; Autumn 1967; pp. 447-461.

     Issawi in another interesting and well written essay main-
tains that Iran's rapid economic growth in the period 1963-1966
was chiefly due to the quality of the civil servants; the cumulative effects of the Second and Third Plans which vastly increased
roads, railroads and communication networks.

ITO, GIKYO
     Gathica.
     Photocopy of reprint from "Orient", Vol.VI; no place of
publication indicated; 1970; pp. 15-33.

     Writer: Reader of Iranian Studies, Kyoto University.

IVANOW, WALDIMAR
     List of Publications by W. Ivanow up to 1 July 1939.
     Four printed pages plus small typewritten insert of "Later
additions" covering the period 1940-1948.

     The list contains the titles of research works by the author.

IVERSON, KENNETH R.
     Report on Iran: Report No.7.
     Iran, 24 August 1953; 8 pp.

     Copy of a report made for the Near East Foundation following
a visit to Tehran by the writer beginning 13 August. He describes
events of the week of Mosaddeq's overthrow. Also outlines some
of the projects being undertaken in villages under the auspices
of the Near East Foundation, the Ford Foundation, and the Point
IV Program.

JACKSON, A.V. WILLIAMS
____
     The Ancient Persian Doctrine of a Future Life.
     Photocopy from "The Biblical World"; Chicago, August 1896;
pp. 149-163.

JACKSON, A.V. WILLIAMS
____
     Ormazd or the Ancient Persian Idea of God.
     Photocopy of reprint from "The Monist", Vol.IX; Chicago,
January 1899; pp. 161-178.

JACKSON, A.V. WILLIAMS
____
     On Sanskrit; Notes of a Journey to Persia.
     Photocopy of reprint of two articles from the "Journal of the
American Oriental Society", Vol.XXV; United States, 1904; pp.175-
184.

JACKSON, A.V. WILLIAMS
____
     The Etymology of Some Words in the Old Persian Inscriptions.
     Photocopy of reprint from the "Journal of the American Orien-
tal Society", Vol.38; United States, 1918; pp. 121-124.

JAZAYERY, MOHAMMAD ALI
____
     Western Influence in Contemporary Persian: A General View.
     Photocopy of reprint from "BSOAS", London University, Vol.
XXIX, Part I; London, 1966; pp. 79-96.

     The article deals not with Western loan words but with words
made up by Persians as a result of Western influence. Writer:
University of Texas at Austin, presently at work on a biography
of Ahmad Kasravi.

JAZAYERY, MOHAMMAD ALI
____
     Western Loan Words in Persian, with Reference to Western-
ization.
     Photocopy of reprint of article in two parts from "Islamic
Culture", Vol.XL; no place of publication indicated; 1967; pp.
207-220; Vol.XLI, pp. 1-19.

JAZAYERY, MOHAMMAD ALI
____
     Observations on Loanwords as an Index to Cultural Borrowing.
     Photocopy of reprint from "Studies in Language, Literature,
and Culture in the Middle Ages and Later"; University of Texas
at Austin, 1969; pp. 80-96.

     Probably the writer's most significant article in a series
of articles on the evolution of modern Persian under the influence
of the West.

JAZAYERI, MOHAMMAD ALI
____
     Review of "A Modern Persian Prose Reader", by Hassan Kamshad.
     Reprint from the "Journal of the American Oriental Society";

824

1969; pp. 460-465.

JAZAYERY, MOHAMMAD ALI
        Persian Verbs Derivable from Other Parts of Speech.
        Photocopy of reprint from a publication by the University of
Indiana Press; 1969; pp. 111-126.

        An interesting article dealing with the increasing tendancy
of modern Persian writers and the public to produce compound
verbs. The writer is not optimistic that the trend can be
reversed.

JAZAYERY, MOHAMMAD ALI
        Modern Persian Prose Literature.
        Photocopy of reprint from the "Journal of the American
Oriental Society", Vol.9, No.2; April-June 1970; pp. 257-265.

        A review of H. Kamshad's "Modern Persian Prose Literature".

JAZAYERY, MOHAMMAD ALI
        The Arabic Element in Persian Grammar: A Preliminary Report.
        Photocopy of reprint from "Iran, Journal of the British
Institute of Persian Studies", Vol.VIII; 1970; pp. 115-124.

JEFFERY, ARTHUR
        The Present Status of Quranic Studies.
        Photocopy of reprint from "Report on Current Research";
United States, 1957; 16 pp.

JEFFERY, ARTHUR
        Ibn Al-Arabi's Shajarat Al-Kawn (Part I).
        Photocopy of reprint from "Studia-Islamica", Ex Fasciculo X;
Paris, 1959; pp. 43-77.

        Writer: Professor of Semitic Languages at Columbia University.

JEFFERY, ARTHUR
        Ibn Al-Arabi's Shajarat Al-Kawn (Part II).
        Photocopy of reprint from "Studia Islamica", Ex Fasciculo XI;
Paris, 1959; pp. 113-160.

JENKINS, MARILYN
        Islamic Pottery: A Brief History.
        Reprint from the "Metropolitan Museum of Art Bulletin"; New
York, Spring 1983; booklet; illustrated mainly in color and map;
52 pp.

        Illustrations are taken from the museum's own collection of
Islamic pottery.

JOHNS, RICHARD
Pageantry - and Politics.
"The Financial Times"; London, 12 October 1971; p. unknown.

Persepolis celebrations of the 2,500th anniversary of the
Iranian monarchy.

LES JOYAUX DE LA COURONNE.
Tehran, 1973; booklet; full page color illustrations; 54 pp.

In French. Published by Bank Markazi Iran. Description of
the Crown Jewels on display at Bank Markazi. Prepared along the
lines of the 1970 booklet, with additional material and superior
to previous work.

K

KANTOR, HELEN J.
        Luristan Bronze.
        Photocopy of reprint from "The Cincinnati Art Museum Bull-
etin", Vol.5, No.2; October 1957; illustrated in text, illustrations on full page plates and map; 20 pp.

        Writer: Oriental Institute of the University of Chicago.

KARIMI - HAKKOK, AHMAD
        A Well Amid the Waste: An Introduction to the Poetry of
Ahmad Shamlu.
        Reprint from "World Literature Today", a literary quarterly
of the University of Oklahoma; Spring 1977; pp. 201-206.

        An introduction to the poetry and thoughts of one of the
most prominent contemporary Iranian poets. Shamlu's neo-Marxist
polemical poetry as well as excellent poetry readings attracted
a large following amongst the opposition prior to the Revolution
of 1979. Since the Revolution, no known work of his has been
published. Writer: Rutgers University.

KASRA, PARICHEHR
        Fitzgerald's Recasting of the Rubaiyat (First Edition).
        Photocopy of reprint from "Zeits Schrift Der Deutschen
Morgen Lanischen", Vol.130, No.3; Wiesbaden, 1980; pp. 458-489.

        The writer maintains that Edward Heron Allen's and Arberry's
identification of certain ruba'is as the root of Fitzgerald's
quatrains are too "simplistic" and that Fitzgerald's selection
of parts of the ruba'is and blending them into a new quatrain
was much more complex. The writer further discusses how Fitzgerald utilized the Ouseley (Bodleian) and the Calcutta manuscripts in his formulation of the translation.

KATOUZIAN, HOMA (HOMAYOUN)
        The Hallmarks of Science and Scholasticism: A Historical
Analysis.
        Photocopy of article from unidentified journal; c.1970; pp.
89-109.

        A study of the views of science and the scientific
communities held in earlier ages and other (including non-Western)
traditions.

KATOUZIAN, HOMAYOUN
        Nationalist Trends in Iran.
        Reprint from "International Journal of Middle East Studies,
10 (1979)"; Great Britain; pp. 533-551.

        Paper presented to the Middle East Center when, in 1975-76,

the writer was a visiting fellow of St. Anthony's College, Oxford.

KATOUZIAN, HOMAYOUN
     The Political Economy of Oil Exporting Countries.
     Photocopy from "Mediterranean Peoples"; France, September
1979; 20 pp.

KATOUZIAN, HOMAYOUN
     Riba and an Interest in an Islamic Political Economy.
     Reprint from "Mediterranean Peoples" No.14; France, Janvier-
Mars 1981; pp. 97-109.

     The prohibition of "riba" is a fundamental tenet of Islamic
Law. The writer argues that "riba" should not be defined as all
forms of interest, and that in the modern economic world with a
surplus of funds in some oil-rich Arab states, a rigid interpret-
ation of the definition of "riba" can lead to "social injustice
and economic dislocation". Some forms of lending and borrowing
are outside the original intentions of the Law Giver. The writer
discusses two specific areas where exceptions should be made:
a) An interest equivalent to the rate of inflation should be
allowed, otherwise "principles of Islamic Justice would be
violated"; and, b) since the origins of "riba" refer to the
rental charges on loans to the poor, hence interest charged on
loans to any business enterprise should be allowed.
     There is some merit in the writer's interpretation of Islamic
Law. The present regime in Iran has found a less complex approach
whereby interest accrues to one's deposit in an Iranian bank but
it is effected through other names: Return on investment, non-
regular but recurring bonuses and prizes in forms of household
goods and other amenities.

KATOUZIAN, HOMA (HOMAYOUN)
     The Agrarian Question in Iran.
     Geneva, May 1981; 8vo, soft cover; 46 pp.

     A World Employment Programme Research Paper published by the
I.L.O. as part of its Rural Employment policy statement.

KATOUZIAN, HOMA (HOMAYOUN)
     The Arisdisolatic Society; A Model of Long-term Social and
Economic Development in Iran.
     Reprint from "International Journal of Eastern Studies 15
(1983)"; Cambridge University Press; United States; pp. 259-281.

KATOUZIAN, M.A.
     Land Reform in Iran: A Case Study in the Political Economy
of Social Engineering.
     Photocopy from "The Journal of Peasant Studies"; Great
Britain, January 1974; pp. 220-239.

KATOUZIAN, M.A.
    Oil Versus Agriculture; A Case of Dual Resource Depletion
in Iran.
    Reprint from "The Journal of Peasant Studies", Vol.5, No.3;
Great Britain, April 1978; pp. 347-369.

KAZEMZADEH, FIRUZ
    The Muslim Clergy and the Peacock Throne.
    Reprint from "World Order"; A Bahai Magazine; United States,
Summer 1971; pp. 45-52.

    A review of Hamid Algar's "Religion and the State in Iran
1785-1906: The Role of the Ulama in the Qajar Period".

KEDDIE, NIKKI R., et al.
    Historical Obstacles to Agrarian Change in Iran.
    "Claremont Asian Studies", No.8; Claremont, California,
September 1960; 8vo, soft cover; 24 pp.

KEDDIE, NIKKI R.
    Religion and Irreligion in Early Iranian Nationalism.
    Photocopy of reprint from "Comparative Studies in Society
and History", Vol.IV, No.3; United States, April 1962; pp. 265-
295.

    The writer maintains that "early Iranian nationalists" may
not have been devout Moslems. The three persons she cites are:
Jamal e-Din Afghani, Mirza Aqa Khan Kermani and Shaikh Ahmad
Rouhi. The writer also emphasizes the influence of the Babi
reformers and the liberal thinkers of Transcaucasus. That the
Islamic religious beliefs of the three persons named are suspect
has been the subject of other studies, and Keddie is probably
correct. The writer, however, draws no convincing conclusions
from her premise.

KEDDIE, NIKKI R.
    Symbol and Sincerity in Islam.
    Photocopy of reprint from "Studia Islamica", ex fasc. XIX;
Paris, 1963.

    The writer makes the point that Moslem political leaders
often preach tenets that they do not really believe in. The on-
rush of modernism has made it all the more imperative that they
maintain the fiction that every concept, regardless of how alien,
has some root in Qoranic teaching.

KEDDIE, NIKKI R.
    The Origin of Religious-Radical Alliance in Iran.
    Reprint from "Past and Present", No.34; United States, 1966;
pp. 70-80.

A revised version of a paper delivered before the Iranian Students Association Conference on contemporary Iran, Harvard, 1965. An excellent article in which the writer for the first time sets forth her thesis, which has also been explored by other writers. She traces the root of the alliance from the period of the opposition to the Reuter's Concession of 1872 and the Tobacco Protest of 1891-1892 and the firmer alliances of 1905-1911.

KEDDIE, NIKKI R.
British Policy and the Iranian Opposition: 1901-1907.
Photocopy of reprint from "Journal of Modern History", Vol. 39, No.3; September 1967; pp. 266-282.

The writer argues that the British were slow to realize the power of the clergy in Iran. It is only after the Tobacco protests that they began to explore such contacts and it was not until 1900 and later that serious contacts were established with the clergy. The British used the clergy effectively up to 1907 but thereafter, 1907-1909, the British were more interested in reaching an accord with the Russians and contacts with the clergy were curtailed. The writer, by referring to diplomatic dispatches of the period, makes the point that the Foreign Office under Grey was lukewarm to such contacts and entanglements.

KEDDIE, NIKKI R.
The Roots of the Ulama's Power in Modern Iran.
Text of paper delivered before "Middle East Studies Association"; Chicago, December 1967; 14 pp.

Nothing original and some errors of fact.

KEDDIE, NIKKI R.
The Iranian Power Structure and Social Change 1800-1969; An overview.
Reprint from the "International Journal of Middle East Studies", No.2; Great Britain, 1971; pp. 3-20.

There is nothing original in the first part of the article. In the second part, dealing with the sixties, the writer generally praises the economic and social progress of the era, and her criticism is muted in the light of her subsequent views. The article contains a few errors of fact and names.

KEDOURIE, ELIE
Faith and Fanaticism.
Book review of: "Among the Believers: An Islamic Journey" by V.A. Naipal, from the "New Republic"; New York, 4 November 1981; pp. 31-34.

KELEKIAN, DIKRAN KHAN (compiled by)
The Potteries of Persia.

Paris, 1909; booklet; illustrated and illustrations in text;
38 pp.

Kelekian, an art dealer, was also an honorary Iranian consul
in New York and Iran's Commissioner General at the St. Louis
Exposition. Several of the works illustrated are from his
private collection.

KENNEDY, EDWARD M.
The Persian Gulf; Arms Race or Arms Control?
"Foreign Affairs", Vol.54, No.1; United States, October 1975;
includes map; pp. 14-35.

Kennedy basically criticizes the Nixon-Kissinger policy
initiated in May 1972 to make the Shah the custodian of Western
interests in the Persian Gulf and guaranteeing the supply of any
arms (short of nuclear weapons) requested by him.

KENNION, COLONEL R.L.
Note on the Preservation of Persian Fauna.
Article in the "Journal of the Royal Central Asian Society",
Vol.XIX, Part I; London, January 1932; maps; pp. 86-88.

Also an article by Sir Percy Cox on the death of
Wassmuss, pp. 151-156; and another article titled, Islam in North-
west China Today, by Rev. G. Findlay Andrew, pp. 89-101.

KESSLER, MELVIN M.
Ivan Victorovitch Vitkevich.
Washington, D.C., 1960; 8vo; 26 pp.

Vitkevich (1806-1839) was a Russian agent in Central Asia
and Afghanistan who died under mysterious circumstances, but
officially recorded as suicide.

KHADEM, ALI
The Law and the Foreign Nationals in Iran.
Tehran, 1971; 4to, soft cover; 149 pp.

Prepared almost entirely from already existing material.
Writer: A practising attorney in Tehran.

KHAN, MUHAMMAD WALI ULLAH
Lahore and Its Important Monuments.
Karachi, 1964; 4to, soft cover; full page illustrations,
some in color; maps and illustrations in text, some in color;
91 pp.

A guide to the monuments of Lahore, principally dating from
the Moghol period (1521 to mid 18th cent.). Akbar Shah,
Jahangir, Shah Jahan and Aurangzeeb all contributed extensive new

palaces, mosques and gardens to the city.

KHOMEINI, ROUHOLLAH
	Islamic Government.
	Arlington, Virginia, 19 January 1979; 8vo, soft cover; 74 pp.

	Number 1897 in the "Translations on Near East and North
Africa: Islamic Government" published by the Joint Publications
Research Center, Arlington, Virginia, for the National Technical
Information Service of the U.S. Department of Commerce.

KHOMEINI, ROUHOLLAH
	Ayatollah Khomeini Defines His Stance in Respect to Embassy
Occupation.
	Full page advertisement in "The New York Times"; 18 November
1979; p. 63.

KHORASAN
	Tehran, 1975; 8vo, soft cover; illustrated in color plus map;
16 pp.

	Illustrated tourist guide to the province of Khorasan in
eastern Iran and its cities, including Mashhad. Published by the
Iranian Ministry of Information and Tourism.

KIFNER, JOHN
	Documents Show Shah Sought U.S. Lobby.
	"The New York Times"; 30 May, 1979; p. A6.

	Iranian Government files reveal the particulars of Mrs. Jacob
Javits' contract for public relations work for Iran Air and
disclosure of the role of Iranian intermediaries. The writer is
presently the most knowledgeable and thoughtful U.S. reporter
covering the Middle East, Iran and Iraq in particular.

KIFNER, JOHN
	Iran's Council Is Divided – And Ruling.
	"The New York Times"; 6 April 1980; p. 1E.

	Page also includes brief article entitled "One More Hope for
the Hostages Rises and Falls".

KIFNER, JOHN
	Khomeini Faction Challenged by More Conservative Group.
	"New York Times"; 13 April 1982; pp. 17.

KIFNER, JOHN
	Iran: Obsessed with Martyrdom.
	Cover story, "New York Times Magazine"; 16 December 1984;
illustrated; pp. 36-54.

832

KIFNER, JOHN
        Experts Link Iraqi Losses to Lack of Fighting Spirit.
        "International Herald Tribune"; Paris, 1-2 March 1986;
p. 2.

        "Some military experts in Baghdad traced the lack of
enthusiasm among the Iraqi soldiers to two major political factors:
What they viewed as a lack of a strong, clear sense of Iraqi
national identity ... The nation exists within lines that
were drawn on a map by European Powers", and "lack of fighting
spirit."

KILPATRICK, GEORGE D.
        Dura-Europos: The Parchments and The Papyri.
        Photocopy from "Greek, Roman and Byzantine Studies", Vol.5,
No.3; Great Britain, Autumn 1964; pp. 215-225.

KISSINGER, HENRY A.
        U.S. Must Beware Shortsighted Gulf Policy.
        "The International Herald Tribune"; 4 February 1985; p. 4.

        Subtitled: "It is in Western interest to cushion OPEC
countries against the shock of collapsing oil prices, and to
prevent either side in the Iran-Iraq war from attaining uncondit-
ional victory."

KORN, DAVID
        The Muslims of Central Asia.
        Reprint from "Mid East; A Middle East – North Africa Review";
United States, December 1966; pp. 5-12.

KRAFT, JOSEPH
        Letter from Iran.
        Article from the "New Yorker" magazine; 18 December 1978;
letter is dated 11 December from Tehran; pp. 134-168.

        An article which, by the date it was published, had been
overtaken by events and had lost its significance. The writer,
an American columnist, knew most of the people in the Iranian
power structure, but they were not the main players during the
course of 1978. The article was hastily written and contains
errors of fact and names.

KUBICKOVA, VERA
        Qaani: Le Poète Persan du XIXe Siècle.
        Prague, 1954; 8vo, soft cover; 81 pp.

        Published by the Czechoslovakian Academy of Sciences.
Contains a series of essays on Qaani, his life and work; a summary
of critical studies of his writings; a comparison between his

poem "Kitab-i Parisan" and Sa'di's Golestan; and an examination
of the picture of contemporary society given in "Kitab-i Parisan".

KURDISTAN NEWS AND COMMENT: NUMBER 5.
    London, March 1981; 8vo, soft cover; illustrated and maps;
36 pp.

    Small journal published by the Kurdestan Solidarity Committee
(U.K.) and the Kurdestan Komitee (Holland). Contains an article
on "Iranian Kurdistan since the war" (with Iraq) which includes
extracts from two articles by French journalist Eric Rouleau
which had appeared in "Le Monde" on 12 and 13 December 1980.

LADJEVARDI, HABIB
       The Origin of U.S. Support for Autocratic Iran.
       Article from the "International Journal of Middle East
Studies, 15 (1983)"; United States; pp. 225-239.

       An original and thought provoking article. The writer dis-
cusses the origin of U.S. support for autocratic rule in Iran
(1945-1947), and argues that the U.S. actually encouraged and
guided the Shah to act more "firmly" and thus planted the seeds
of the conduct of his later rule. However, the article is too
brief and the evidence presented is scanty. Writer: Middle East
Center, Harvard.

LAMB, HAROLD
       The Road of the Crusaders.
       Article in "The National Geographic Magazine"; Washington,
D.C., December 1933; illustrations and photographs; pp. 645-693.

       The writer wrote popular histories of Omar Khayyam, Cyrus
the Great, Genghis Khan and Tamerlane.

LAMB, HAROLD
       Mountain Tribes of Iran and Iraq.
       Article in "The National Geographic Magazine"; Washington,
D.C., March 1946; illustrated in color, including double-page map;
pp. 385-408.

LAMBTON, ANN K.S.
       Islamic Society in Persia.
       London, 1954; small 8vo, soft cover; 32 pp.

       "An Inaugural Lecture delivered on 9 March, 1954."

LAMBTON, ANN K.S.
       The Persian Ulama and Constitutional Reform.
       Photocopy from "Le Shi'isme Imamite"; Paris, 1970; pp. 245-
269.

       Paper delivered at the University of Strasbourg, 6-9 May 1968.

LAQUEUR, WALTER
       Trouble for the Shah.
       Photocopy from "The New Republic"; United States, 23 Septem-
ber 1978; pp. 18-21.

       Subtitled: "The next regime - or the one after next - is
bound to be worse." Writer: Editor of "The Washington Quarterly".

LARKIN, PHILIP
       Review of Robert Bernard Martin's With Friends Possessed: A
Life of Edward Fitzgerald.
       "Observer"; London, March 1985; p. 66.

Writer: A major post World War II English poet.

LAWRENCE, BRUCE B.
     Al-Biruni's Approach to the Comparative Study of Indian
Culture.
     Reprinted from the "Biruni Symposium", Persian Studies,
Series No.7; Columbia University, 1976; pp. 27-47.

     Writer: Duke University.

LAZARD, GILBERT
     Le Dialectologie du Judéo-Persan.
     Photocopy of reprint from "Bibliography and Booklore", Vol.
VIII, No.2-4; Cincinnati, Ohio, Spring 1968; pp. 77-98.

LAZARD, GILBERT
     Henri Massé (1886-1969).
     Photocopy of reprint from "Journal Asiatique", 1969; Paris,
1970; pp. 205-210.

LAZARD, GILBERT
     Les Origines de la Poésie Persane.
     Reprint from "Cahiers de Civilisation Mediévale", VIV Année,
No.4, October-December 1971; Poitiers, 1971; pp. 305-317.

LAZARD, GILBERT
     Emile Benveniste (1902-1976).
     Photocopy from "Journal Asiatique"; Paris, 1977; 7 pp.

LAZARD, GILBERT
     Le Langage Symbolique du Ghazal.
     Photocopy from "Accademia Nazionale dei Lincei"; Rome, 1978;
pp. 59-71.

LAZARD, GILBERT
     Notes sur le Jargon des Juifs d'Iran.
     Photocopy from "Journal Asiatique"; Paris, 1978; pp. 251-255.

LAZARD, GILBERT
     Le Dialecte Talesi de Masule (Gilan).
     Photocopy of reprint from "Studia Iranica", Tome 7, fascicule
2; Leiden, 1978; pp. 251-268.

LEDEEN, MICHAEL A. and LEWIS, WILLIAM H.
     Carter and the Fall of the Shah: The Inside Story.
     Photocopy from "The Washington Quarterly"; Spring 1980; pp.
3-40.

     The article contains the heart of the book "Debacle", later
published by the authors. (Refer to Section A.)

LEIGH, DAVID
     Britain's Role in Mosaddegh's Downfall.
     "The Guardian"; London, 28 July 1980; p. 11.

     Article on Great Britain's role in restoring Mohammad Reza
Shah to the throne in 1953; and an obituary printed the day after
the Shah's death.

LENCZOWSKI, GEORGE
     The Arc of Crisis: Its Central Sector.
     Article in "Foreign Affairs", Vol.57; No.4; United States,
Spring 1979; pp. 796-820.

     The article concentrates on external and internal pressures
on the foreign policies of the U.S. and Iran since World War II.

LENTZ, WOLFGANG
     What is the Manichaean Nous?
     Photocopy of article from "Ural - Altaische Jahrbucher", Vol.
XXXIII, issue 1-2; Wiesbaden, 1961; pp. 101-106.

LENTZ, WOLFGANG
     The "Social Functions" of the Old Iranian Mithra.
     Reprint of the revised version of a paper read at the XXVII
International Congress of Orientalists, Ann Arbor, Michigan, 1967;
published in "Asia Major's W.B. Henning Memorial Volume"; c.1968;
pp. 245-255.

LENTZ, WOLFGANG
     Yima and Khvarenah in the Avestan Gathas.
     Photocopy of reprint from "A Locust's Leg", Studies in honor
of S.H. Taqizadeh; Great Britain, c.1970.

LETTER FROM IRANIAN FREEMASONRY GROUPS.
     Three page typewritten carbon-copy of a letter from Iranian
Freemasonry Groups in reply to the publication in Rome of Volume
III of Esmail Rai'en's "Freemasonry in Iran" in March 1969.

     The writer/s of the letter allege/s that the book was C.I.A.
inspired and financed and lists a "large number of Iranians who
are in contact with the C.I.A. or who are its officials or agents".
How the book was published is still a mystery and equally mystify-
ing is how this counter attack was circulated. The assumption
that Raeen's book was published in Rome is dubious and it appears
that the book was in fact published in Tehran with some degree of
official blessing for yet unknown purposes. The alleged C.I.A.
list was published in Tehran and is patently absurd.

LEVEY, MICHAEL
     The Very Rich Hours of the Shah: The Houghton Shahnameh.

Book review of The Houghton Shahnama, by Martin Bernard
Dickson and Stuart Carey Welch from "New York Review of Books";
7 October 1982; pp. 13-16.

The reviewer states that "the present edition, reproducing
every miniature is not only a monument, but also a memorial to
something that has been destroyed and can no longer be completely
studied and appreciated in any other form".

LEWIS, BERNARD
Register on Iran and Adharbayajan in the Ottoman Deter-i-
Khagani.
Photocopy from "Mélanges Massé"; Tehran, 1963; 5 pp.

LEWIS, BERNARD
The Regnal Titles of the First Abbasid Caliphs.
Photocopy of reprint from "Dr. Zakir Husain Presentation
Volume"; c.1965; pp. 13-22.

The practice initiated by the Abbasid Caliphs or designated
heirs to adopt a special personal title or epithet usually
indicating a relationship to God.

LEWIS, BERNARD
Kamal-al-Din's Biography of Rashid-al-Din Sinan.
Photocopy of reprint from "Arabica - Revue d'Etudes Arabes",
Tome XIII, Fas.3; 1966; pp. 225-267.

Re the grand master of the Assasins in Syria.

LEWIS, BERNARD
The Mongols, the Turks and the Muslim Polity.
Reprint of a lecture delivered on 11 March 1967 and subsequently published in "Transactions of the Royal Historical Society",
5th series, Vol.18; 1968; pp. 49-68.

The writer, in a provocative article, argues that the Mongol
invasion did not have a permanently devastating effect on the
invaded nations. He further argues that the invasion was inevitable since Persia was in a state of disarray, the Caliphate in
Baghdad was in a state of disintegration, and the Islamic world
in general was in a state of decline having been checked in the
West. While conceding that the depopulation of the major cities,
the murder of several millions of people, the burning of cities,
centers of learning and libraries were catastrophic, the writer
states that the invaded nations quickly recovered and did not re-
trogress into a dark age, the net effect being that by the beginning of the 16th century there were two major nations, the Ottomans
and the Persians. The writer's reasoning may be valid in part
in an over-all view of history, but to consider the invasion as
beneficial is debatable. Furthermore, the emergence of the two
"major nations" led to wars between them that were to last for

250 years, and both nations fell into a state of decay from which neither ever fully recovered. At least the writer spares us the enthusiasm of the art experts who rejoice in the Mongol invasion for the bond that was created between Far Eastern and Near Eastern artistic traditions.

LEWIS, BERNARD
Some English Travelers in the East.
Reprint from "Middle Eastern Studies", Vol.4, No.3; April 1968; pp. 296-315.

A well written article about the motives for travel to the East by Victorians. The travellers discussed are: Lady Mary Wortely Montagu, wife of the British Ambassador to Turkey 1717-1718; Adolphus Slade, a British Naval officer sent to Turkey in 1829, who was seconded to the Turkish Navy in 1849-1866; and Sir Charles Elliot, a British diplomat posted to Turkey.

LEWIS, BERNARD
Semites and Anti-Semites.
Reprint from "Survey", No.2, 79; London, Spring 1971; pp. 169-184.

The writer first debunks the myth of the Semitic and Aryan races. The terms primarily employed to distinguish languages, were first used in late 18th and early 19th centuries when European philologists made the discovery that various languages were related to one another and formed distinct categories. Racialists then distorted the terms to tailor their own prejudices. Lewis discusses the beginnings and causes of anti Jewish sentiment in the Arab World as originating in and having been imported from Europe in mid 19th and early 20th centuries. The writer also emphasizes the European roots of anti-semitism that go back to the beginnings of Christianity. In a recently published article, the writer contradicts his earlier premises and rashly argues that present day anti-semitism is an Arab inspired phenomenon.

LEWIS, BERNARD
The United States, Turkey and Iran.
Reprint of article from unknown source, c.1976; pp. 165-180.

Review of U.S. relations with Turkey and Iran since World War II and the Truman doctrine.

LEWIS, BERNARD
Translation from Arabic.
Reprint from the "Proceedings of the American Philosophical Society, Vol.124, No.1, February 1980"; Philadelphia, 1980; pp. 41-47.

In an excellent article the writer discusses the

difficulties involved in the task of the modern translator of
Arabic into English. Even though until the Renaissance and the
Reformation, Arabic was the most widely translated language in
the world, the modern translator is burdened with the legacy of
the horrid and inaccurate translations from the Middle Ages
through the 19th century in the "pseudo-biblical, mock-Elizabethan,
bogus oriental style" of English translators. The writer quotes
a letter written by the Jewish philosopher Maimonides to his
translator c.1199 who was translating a work of his from Arabic
into Hebrew (which reads like Hamlet's directive to actors), and
embodies the soundest advice.

LEWIS, BERNARD
        The Question of Orientalism.
        Article from "The New York Review of Books"; 24 June 1982;
pp. 49-56.

        Edward Said, Professor of literature at Columbia University,
in his book "Orientalism" (1979) argues that the terms "Orientalism" and "Orientalists" once used to denote Western scholarship
in Asian studies have acquired perjorative connotations as they
reflect the prejudiced colonial views of the 19th century European
scholars, and most of the present Orientalists are children of
that school and inheritors of the same prejudices and biases.
Said argues for a revamping of the present systems of Middle
Eastern studies at American and European universities along ideal-
ogical lines closer to his own thinking.
        Lewis' article, which is aimed at the refutation of Said's
thesis, suggests that Said's arguments are overstated and are
not relevant today. He argues that Said's thesis would lead to
the elimination of all academic centers of Eastern Studies in
Europe and the U.S. and would ban any Westerner from the serious
study of Eastern cultures. Thus only people of the East would be
entitled to pursue "Oriental" studies. Lewis further states that
Said is more concerned with ideology than scholarship. He points
to Said's less than perfect command of Arabic through references
to the latter's numerous errors of transcription from Arabic.
Lewis also unfortunately overstates his case. (Refer to Said,
Edward under Section A.)

LEWIS, BERNARD
        How Khomeini Made It.
        A review of the book "Reign of The Ayatollahs: Iran and the
Islamic Revolution" by Shaul Bakhash, from "The New York Review
of Books"; 17 January 1985; illustrated; pp. 10-13.

LEWIS, BERNARD
        The Shi'a.
        An article from "The New York Review of Books"; 15 August
1985; pp. 7-10.

840

LIFE MAGAZINE
   A Future to Outshine Ancient Glories - A Royal Reformer
Rebuilds His Nation.
   United States, c.1963; 9 pp. of colored illustrations; pp.
34-49.

   An article written especially for "Life" by Mohammad Reza
Shah describing his "Revolution from the Throne".

LIFE MAGAZINE
   Iran's Long Cry of Rage.
   Cover Story; United States, January 1980; illustrated; pp.
22-29.

   Includes an article entitled "For America: the Lessons of the
Crisis" by George Ball.

LIFE MAGAZINE
   Exile's End.
   United States, September 1980; illustrated; pp. 102-105.

   Article on and photographs of Mohammad Reza Shah's death and
funeral in Egypt.

LITVINSKY, B.A.; MARSAKOV, K.P.; and MUKHTAROV, A.M.
   Historiography of Tajikistan (1917-1969).
   Photocopy of reprint of papers delivered at the XIII International Congress of Historical Sciences, published by the Academy
of Sciences, Tajik SSR; Moscow, 1970; 80 pp.

   Three papers on the following: 1) Archaeology, Ancient History
and Numismatics, 2) History of Middle Ages and Modern Times (until
1917), 3) History of Soviet Society.

LIVSHITS, V.A.
   New Parthian Documents from South Turkmenistan.
   Photocopy from "Acta Antiqua Academiae Scientiarum Hungar-
icae", XXV, Fasc.1-4; Budapest, Hungary, 1977; pp. 157-186.

LOISIRS: REVUE MENSUELLE
   Interview with Dr. Ghassem Ghani.
   Cairo, October 1948; illustrated; 2 pp.

   In French. Brief biography and an interview with Ghassem
Ghani, Iranian Ambassador to Egypt at the time. From an Egyptian
magazine.

LONG, GEORGE W. and ROBERTS, J. BAYLOR
   Journey into Troubled Iran.
   Article in "National Geographic Magazine"; Washington, D.C.,

October 1951; 35 photographs; pp. 425-464.

Two Americans visit Iran in 1951 at the height of the Anglo-Iranian oil dispute. Nothing perceptive or interesting, but some good photographs.

LORENZ, JOSEPH P.
        Liberal Nationalism in Egypt and Iran.
        Typewritten Master's degree thesis, in folder; submitted to the Faculty of Law and Government, Columbia University; New York, c. 1965.

        "A Study of Western Impact on Traditional Islamic Society."

LORIMER, MAJOR D.L.R.
        Notes on the Gabri Dialect of Modern Persian.
        Reprint from the "Journal of the Royal Asiatic Society"; London, July 1916; pp. 423-489.

LORIMER, MAJOR D.L.R.
        The Popular Verse of the Bakhtiari of S.W. Persia - III: Further Specimens.
        Photocopy of reprint from "BSOAS", London University, Vol. XXVI, Part 1; 1963; pp. 55-68.

        Lorimer did pioneering studies on the Bakhtiari tribe and speech.

LORIMER, MAJOR D.L.R.
        A Bakhtiari Persian Text.
        Photocopy of reprint from "Indo-Iranica"; Wiesbaden, 1964; pp. 120-133.

LUKENS, MARIE G.
        Islamic Art.
        New York, 1965; large booklet; full page illustrations, some in color; numerous illustrations in text, some in color, and map; 48 pp.

        Published by the Metropolitan Museum of Art in New York to accompany its large collection of Islamic art.

LUKENS, MARIE G. and GRUBE, ERNEST J.
        The Language of the Birds.
        Reprint of articles in "Bulletin of the Metropolitan Museum of Art"; New York, May 1967; full page illustrations, some in color, and illustrations in text; pp. 317-352.

        A booklet consisting of two articles reprinted from the Metropolitan Museum's Bulletin: "Fifteenth Century Miniatures" by

Marie G. Lukens and "17th Century Miniatures" by Ernest J. Grube, which describe the eight miniature paintings illustrating a 15th century copy of "The Language of the Birds", a 12th century mystical poem by the Persian poet Farid e-din Attar, newly acquired for the Museum's collection.

LUKONIN, V.G.
An Experimental Dating of Some Sassanian Seals.
Papers presented by the U.S.S.R. Delegation at the XXV International Congress of Orientalists; Moscow, 1960; 16 pp.

LUTHER, KENNETH A.
Ravandi's Report on the Administrative Change of Muhammad Jahan Pahlavan.
Reprint from "Iran and Islam"; Edinburgh University Press, 1971; pp. 393-406.

An article on the dirth of material concerning the last of the Saljuq kings of Iraq, Tuqrol (1176-1194).

MACKENZIE, D.N.
     Gender in Kurdish.
     Photocopy of reprint from "BSOAS", London University, Vol.
XVI, Part 3; 1954; pp. 528-541.

MACKENZIE, D.N.
     The Origins of Kurdish.
     Reprint from the "Transactions of the Philological Society";
Great Britain, 1961; pp. 68-86.

MACKENZIE, D.N.
     Zoroastrian Astrology in the Bundahisn.
     Photocopy of reprint from "BSOAS", London University, Vol.
XXVII, Part 3; 1964; pp. 511-529.

MACKENZIE, D.N.
     Iranian Languages.
     Reprint from "Current Trends in Linguistics" No.5; Great
Britain, c.1968; pp. 450-477.

MACKENZIE, D.N.
     A Zoroastrian Master of Ceremonies.
     Photocopy of reprint from "W.B. Henning Memorial Volume, Asia
Major Library"; London, c.1968; pp. 264-271.

MACKENZIE, D.N.
     The Model Marriage Contract in Pahlavi With an Addendum.
     Reprint from "K.R. Cama Oriental Institute Golden Jubilee
Volume"; Bombay, 1969; pp. 103-112.

MACKENZIE, D.N.
     Mani's Sabuhragan (I).
     Photocopy of reprint from "BSOAS", London University, Vol.
XLII, Part 3; 1979; pp. 500-534.

MACKENZIE, D.N.
     Mani's Sabuhragan (II).
     Photocopy of reprint from "BSOAS", London University, Vol.
XLIII, Part 2; 1980; 12 full page plates; pp. 288-310.

MACLEOD, ALISON
     The Ordeal of a Central Banker: The Nobari Interview.
     Photocopy from "Euromoney"; London, February 1982; illus-
trated; pp. 22-44.

     Interview by Alison MacLeod with Ali-Reza Nobari, former
governor of the Central Bank of Iran, 1979-1981. Nobari, a
protégé of Bani-Sadr was an enthusiastic supporter of much of the
neo-Marxist economic legislation after the Revolution. Nobari
basically argues that if he had had a free hand Iran would be a
paradise now.

844

MAHDAVY, HOSSEIN
        Iran's Agrarian Problems and Recent Attempts at Reform.
        Copy of paper marked: "Preliminary draft: not for public-
ation"; prepared for Seminar at Harvard University on Problems of
Contemporary Iran, April 1965; 37 pp.

        The writer dismisses most of the attempts at reform and
points out that the relationship between peasants and landlords
has now been supplanted by peasants and corrupt government officials both civilian and military, and that the peasant's lot has
not really altered. He also argues that no thought was given to
future plans, i.e. whether there would be small holdings by
peasants or large agro-business projects and that the two are not
compatible. Writer: A gifted economist who was to remain abroad
from this point onwards and become a prominent member of the
secular opposition to the Shah. He returned to Iran after the
1979 Revolution but his enthusiasm for the Revolution was not
reciprocated.

MAHDAVY, HOSSEIN
        The Coming Crisis in Iran.
        Reprint from "Foreign Affairs"; New York, October 1965; pp.
134-146.

        A perceptive article that caused a minor sensation at the
time. Senator Fulbright asked the author to give his views to
the Senate Foreign Relations Committee. The Shah complained to
Hamilton Fish Armstrong, then the editor of Foreign Affairs, during the latter's visit to Tehran in 1967.

MAHDAVI, SHIREEN
        Women and the Shia Ulama in Iran.
        Reprint from "Middle Eastern Studies", Vol.19, No.1; London,
January 1983; pp. 17-27.

        "Prepared for presentation at the Fifteenth Annual Meeting
of the Middle East Studies Association, Seattle, Washington,
November, 1981."

MAHRAD, AHMAD
        Iranisches Jahrbuch 1983.
        Hildesheim, West Germany; 8vo, soft cover; 246 pp.

MALEK-ASLANI, M.
        Sulphur Prospects in Iran.
        Texas, 1967; 4to; map in text and folding maps; illustrations
on full pages; 53 pp. of text.

        Prepared for Tenneco Oil Company.

MALTI-DOUGLAS, FEDWA
	Discussion of New Books, Re-Orienting Orientalism.
	Reprint from the "Virginia Quarterly Review", Vol.55, No.4;
Autumn 1979; pp. 724-733.

	Review of Edward W. Said's book "Orientalism". The reviewer
takes the "middle line" between Said and Bernard Lewis. He does
accept the premise that "Oriental" studies reflect the misunderstanding and prejudices of their origins but believes it can be
rectified. He faults Said for overstating his case and for
including certain Colonial agents as typical "Orientalists" in
order to strengthen his argument against the academic community.

MANSOUR, JAVAD
	A Brief Review of Iran.
	Washington, D.C., c.1955; pamphlet; illustrated and front
cover map; 8 pp.

	Short sections on history, geography, economy by a then
Ministry of Foreign Affairs officer in Washington who became
Minister of Information in the late sixties.

MAP OF PERSIAN EMPIRE.
	c. mid 19th century; published in Moscow.

	Folding military and intelligence map of the "Persian Empire"
in mid 19th century with a key to post offices, railways, telegraph cables; spheres of Russian and British influence; army
posts; etc.. In Russian with hand-written English translations
of the items in the key.

MARGOLIOUTH, D.S.
	An Early Judeo-Persian Document from Kotan, in the Stein
Collection, with Other Persian Documents.
	Photocopy of reprint from the "Royal Asiatic Society";
October 1903; pp. 736-761.

MARSHALL, D.N.
	The Afghans in India under the Delhi Sultanate and the
Mughal Empire: A Survey of Relevant Manuscripts.
	New York, 1976; 4to, soft cover; 27 pp.

MASHIAH, YAAKOV
	Once Upon a Time.
	Reprint from "Acta Orientalia", XXXIII; Leiden, 1971; pp.
109-143.

	"A study of Yeki Bud, Yeki Nabud (Once upon a time), the
first collection of short stories by Sayyid Mohammad Ali Jamalzadeh."

The second chapter of a proposed biography of the renowned contemporary author. Writer: At Ohio State University.

MASHIAH, YAAKOV
In Search of an Insane Universe. A Study of Dar Al-Majanin, The Lunatic Asylum, by Sayyid Mohammad Ali Jamalzadeh.
Reprint from "Le Museon, Revue d'Etudes Orientales", Vol. LXXXVI, 1-2; Louvain, 1973; pp. 147-174.

A discussion of the first full length novel of Jamalzadeh, first published in 1942. Some 20 years earlier Jamalzadeh had published his first collection of short stories "Yeki Bud, Yeki Nabud". In the intervening period Jamalzadeh had published nothing. In succeeding years, he wrote and published over 50 works of fiction and commentaries.

MASSIGNON, LOUIS
L'Oeuvre Hallagienne d'Attar.
Bound article from the "Revue des Etudes Islamique"; Paris, c.1947; 4to; pp. 117-144.

Examination of the legend of Mansour Hallaj who claimed deity during the Abbassid Caliphate and was killed as a heretic.

MEDIEVAL NEAR EASTERN POTTERY
London, 1957; 2 pp. of text plus 28 black and white plates.

Booklet published by the Victoria and Albert Museum.

MEFTAH, ABDUL HOSSEIN
Iran: Crossroads of Invasions.
Text of lecture at the Imperial College, London on 29 March 1985; 8 pp.

The writer maintains Ann Lambton planned the Iranian Revolution of 1979 in 1965. Miss Lambton enlisted the help of Bernard Lewis who was sent on a mission to the U.S. (to teach at Princeton University) and plan the "destruction of the Iranian nation". Senators William Fullbright, Hubert Humphrey and Frank Church joined the plot. Then the B.B.C. entered the picture. The plan was to stop the industrialization of Iran, and Khomaini was the perfect candidate. Writer: "Former member of Royal Iranian Government."

MEHER BABA
Gems from the Discourses of Mehr Baba.
New York, 1945; small 16mo; soft cover; 64 pp.

Includes a biographical sketch of Mehr Baba, a 20th century pseudo Sufi teacher born in India of Persian parents, and extracts from his "Discourses".

MEISAMI, JULIE SCOTT
      Allegorical Techniques in the Ghazals of Hafez.
      Reprint from "Edebiyat 4"; 1979; 40 pp.

MELIKIAN CHIRVANI, A.S.
      Iranian Metal-Work and the Written Word.
      Article in "Apollo: The Magazine of the Arts"; London, April
1976; illustrated; pp. 286-291.

      Writer: Journalist for the International Herald Tribune
covering the art market and auctions.

MENGES, KARL H.
      Early Slavo-Iranian Contacts and Iranian Influences in Slavic
Mythology.
      Photocopy of reprint from "Zeki Velidi Togan'a Armagan Dan
Ayribasim"; Istanbul, 1955; 12 pp.

      In an interesting article the writer maintains that both
Persians and Slavs speak languages which belong to the Eastern
group of Indo-European languages. He argues that in all likeli-
hood, in pre-historical and early historical times, Persians and
Slavs were immediate neighbors in the "Ponto Caspian Steppes".

MENGES, KARL H.
      The European Word for Pearle of Dravidian Origin.
      Reprint from "Orientalia Suecana", Vol.XIX and XX (1970-1971);
Upsala, Sweden, 1972; pp. 205-215.

THE MESSAGE OF PEACE: A MONTHLY MAGAZINE FROM QUM.
      Vol.I, No.9-10; 14 May 1980; 43 pp. Vol.II, No.1; 13 June
1980; 43 pp.; Vol.II, No.2; 13 July 1980; 43 pp.

      Magazine appears to have been published by the Theological
Seminary in Qom.

MICHAELSON, JUDITH and KLEINMAN, LARRY
      Marion's Story: Javit's Wife Sees No Conflict, Says She'll
Keep Iranian Job.
      "The New York Post", 15 January 1976; pp. 1 and 3. Plus
articles entitled "The Woman's View of Javit's Dispute" by Jane
Perlez, and "Marion: Won't Quit, I Deserve the Job" by Judith
Michaelson, pp. 5 and 50.

      Disclosure of the wife of the senior New York Senator,
Jacob Javit, member of the Senate Foreign Relations Committee,
taking a job as a public relations advisor for Iran (ostensibly
for Iran Air). Additional article by Art Buchwald re same subject,
from the "International Herald Tribune"; January 22, 1976; p. 14.

MIDDLE EAST REVIEW - 1984
    London, 1984; 4to; illustrated in text; 311 pp.

    Yearly magazine; economic and political survey of the
countries of the Middle East, North Africa, Sudan, Mauritania,
Somalia, and Cyprus.

MIDDLETON, DREW
    Internal Unrest Adds to Warring Iran's Miseries.
    "International Herald Tribune", 4 February 1985; p. 6.

    The writer, the defense correspondent of the New York Times
since the retirement of Hanson Baldwin, covered the European
Theatre of World War II and is one of the noted authorities on
conventional warfare. He had visited Iran during the forties
through the sixties. His writings on the Iran-Iraq War have
been superior.

MILANI, FARZANEH
    Woman and Family in Iran.
    Typewritten article on Forough Farrokhzad; c.1980; 24 pp.

MILES, GEORGE C.
    Abarqubadh, a New Umayyad Mint.
    Photocopy of reprint from "The American Numismatic Society",
Museum Notes IV; 1950; illustrated; pp. 115-120.

MILES, GEORGE C.
    Some New Light on the History of Kerman in the First Century
of Hijrah.
    Reprint from "The World of Islam", Studies in honor of
Philip K. Hitti; London, 1959; pp. 85-98.

MILES, GEORGE C.
    Book Review - The Iconography of Umayyad Coinage.
    Reprint from "Ars Orientalis III"; 1959; pp. 207-213.

    Review of book by John Walker: "A catalogue of the Mohammadan
coins in the British Museum." Vol.I, 1941, Vol.II, 1956.

MILES, GEORGE C.
    Inscriptions on the Minarets of Saveh, Iran.
    Photocopy of reprint from "Studies in Islamic Art and
Architecture", in honor of Professor K.A.C. Creswell; Center for
Arabic Studies, The American University of Cairo Press, 1965;
illustrated; pp. 163-178.

MILES, GEORGE C.
    A Hoard of Kakwayhid Dirhems.
    Photocopy of reprint from "The American Numismatic Society",

Museum Notes 12; 1966; pp. 165-193 and four plates.

MILES, GEORGE C.
     The Earliest Arab Gold Coinage.
     Photocopy of reprint from "The American Numismatic Society",
Museum Notes 13; 1967; illustrated; pp. 205-229.

MILES, GEORGE C.
     Two Unpublished Arab-Sassanian Dirhems of Abdullah B. Umayyah.
     Photocopy of reprint from "The American Numismatic Society",
Museum Notes 14; 1968; pp. 155-157 and one full page plate.

MILES, GEORGE C.
     Coinage of the Ziyarid Dynasty of Tabaristan and Gurgan.
     Photocopy of reprint from "The American Numismatic Society",
Museum Notes 18; 1972; illustrated; pp. 119-137.

MILES, GEORGE C.
     Coins of the Assassins of Alamut.
     Photocopy of reprint from "Orientalia Lovaniensia Periodica",
Vol.3; Belgium, 1972; illustrated; pp. 155-163.

MILES, GEORGE C.
     Another Kakwayhid Note.
     Reprint from "The American Numismatic Society", Museum Notes
18; 1972; illustrated; pp. 139-148.

MILLER, WILLIAM GREEN
     Geographical Review: Hosseinabad, a Persian Village.
     Reprint from "The Middle East Journal"; Washington, D.C.,
Autumn 1964; pp. 483-498.

     An early study of the effect of land reform on a Persian
village. The same village has been the subject of further
studies at intervals of ten years by others, providing a unique
record of the social and economic evolution of a village from the
eve of land reform to 1983.

MILLER, WILLIAM GREEN
     Political Organization in Iran: From Dowreh to Political
Party. Part I.
     Reprint from Middle East Journal, Washington D.C., Spring
1969; pp. 159-167.

     The article is an important, original and thoughtful
contribution, later expanded upon by other writers. William
Miller was a member of the State Department, served in Iran as a
consular officer in Esfahan in 1960 and later as a member of the
political section of the U.S. Embassy in Tehran 1961-1964. He
resigned from the Foreign Service over differences with U.S.
policy in Iran. The writer was offered post of U.S. Ambassador

850

to Iran after the Revolution but declined for personal reasons.

MILLER, WILLIAM GREEN
      Political Party Organization in Iran: From Dowreh to
Political Party. Part II.
      Reprint from "The Middle East Journal"; Washington, D.C.,
Summer 1969; pp. 343-350.

MILLER, WILLIAM GREEN
      The United States and the Continuing Iranian Revolution.
      Paper dated February 1980 for private circulation; 29 pp.

      An excellent review of U.S.-Iran relationship from 1906 to
the present. The writer points out that the basic cause of failure of U.S. policy makers has been the lack of effort to "understand Iran from the point of view of Iranians".

MILLER, WILLIAM GREEN
      The Impact of the Iranian Revolution, the Iran-Iraq War, and
the Arab-Israeli issue on the Gulf States and Western interests.
      Discussion paper for the 11 February 1982 meeting of the
Discussion Group on the Middle East, Council on Foreign Relations;
25 pp.

      "The greatest threat to U.S. political interests in the area
is not from the Soviets but from the continuing bitterness and
the corrosive effect of the Arab-Israel conflict, the continuing
Iran-Iraq war and most important, the enmity, misunderstanding and
fear by Islamic fundamentalists like Ayatollah Khomaini of the
influence of Western culture."

MILLER, WILLIAM GREEN
      The Possibilities for a New United States-Iranian Relation-
ship.
      Typewritten manuscript. Discussion paper presented to the
"Conference on the Iranian Revolution and the Islamic Republic;
New Assessments", organized by the Woodrow Wilson International
Center for scholars, Washington, D.C., May 1982; 18 pp.

      The writer argues that after Khomaini's death there will be
a struggle for power between Communists supported by the Russians
and the extreme clerical right. The U.S. can play a constructive
role by supporting elements that adhere to the 1906 Constitution.

MILLER, WILLIAM G.
      Maintaining the Status Quo or Broadening the Political Base
- The Case of Iran.
      Paper delivered at a conference held by the Aspen Institute
at Wingspread, Wisconsin in October 1983; 24 pp.

The writer discusses the failure of U.S. policy towards
Iran. He believes that if the U.S. had followed a different
course in 1953, in 1962 or even in 1978, "we would see today a
moderate constitutional government in power. (The U.S.) had
the power to pursue a different course." The writer also believes
that the continuation of a religious fundamentalist regime after
Khomaini's death is by no means a foregone conclusion. "The
question of succession depends on whether Khomaini outlives his
aged rival Ayatollahs who still have substantial religious
influence."

MILLER, WILLIAM GREEN
        The Lessons of Iran.
        Review of Gary Sick's "All Fall Down", "Boston Globe";
30 June 1985; pp. A12 and 14.

MILLS, MARGARET ANN
        Cupid and Psyche in Afghanistan: An International Tale in
Cultural Context.
        New York, Spring 1978; 4to, soft cover; 28 pp.

        Occasional paper Number 14 published by the Afghanistan
Council of the Asia Society. Writer: Harvard University.

THE MINIATURE IN PERSIAN ART.
        Chicago, 1963; booklet/catalogue; illustrated; 24 pp.

        Designed to accompany a loan exhibition held by the Arts Club
of Chicago, 9 April-9 May 1963. A comprehensive exhibition.

MINORSKY, V.
        Caucasica in the History of Mayyafariqin.
        London, c.1947; 8vo; pp. 27-96 and one plate.

        Reprint from an unidentified journal subsequently bound in
hard cover. A compilation of the passages in the 12th century
history of the town of Mayyafariqin, situated on a western
tributary of the Tigris River.

MINORSKY, VLADIMIR
        Jihan-Shah Qara-Qoyunlu and His Poetry.
        Photocopy of reprint from "BSOAS", London University, Vol.
XVI, Part 2; 1954; pp. 271-267.

MINORSKY, VLADIMIR
        A Mongol Decree of 720/1320 to the family of Shaykh Zahid.
        Reprint from "BSOAS", London University, Vol.XVI, Part 3;
1954; pp. 517-527.

MINORSKY, VLADIMIR
        Thomas of Metsope on the Timurid Turkman Wars.

852

        Photocopy of reprint from unknown publication, Vol.XII;
Lahore, Pakistan, 1955; 26 pp.

MINORSKY, VLADIMIR
        The Qara-Qoyunlu and the Qutb-Shhas.
        Reprint from "BSOAS", London University. Vol.XVII, Part 1;
1955; pp. 50-73.

MINORSKY, VLADIMIR
        The Aq-Qoyunlu and Land Reforms (Turkmenica, 11).
        Reprint from "BSOAS", London University; Vol.XVII, Part 3;
1955; pp. 449-462.

MINORSKY, VLADIMIR
        The Older Preface to the "Shah-Nama".
        Reprint from "Studi Orientalistici in Onore di Giorgio Levi
della Vida", Vol.11; Rome, 1956; 21 pp.

MINORSKY, VLADIMIR
        Pur-I Baha "Mongol" Ode (Mongolica 2).
        Photocopy of reprint from "BSOAS", London University, Vol.
XVIII, Part 2; 1956; pp. 261-279.

MINORSKY, VLADIMIR
        Mongol Palace-Names in Mukri Kurdistan (Mongolica 4).
        Photocopy of reprint from "BSOAS", London University, Vol.
XIX, Part 1; 1957; pp. 58-82.

MINORSKY, VLADIMIR
        Shaykh Bali-Efendi on the Safavids.
        Photocopy of reprint from "BSOAS", London University, Vol.
XX; 1957; pp. 437-450.

MINORSKY, VLADIMIR
        Bibliography of the publications of Professor V. Minorsky.
        Reprint from "BSOAS", London University, Vol.XIV, Part 3;
1960; pp. 665-681.

        "Studies presented to Vladimir Minorsky by his colleagues
and friends."

MINORSKY, VLADIMIR
        A Greek Crossing on the Oxus.
        Photocopy of reprint from "BSOAS", London University, Vol.
XXX, Part 1; 1967; pp. 45-53.

OBITUARY: VLADIMIR FEDOROVICH MINORSKI (written by D.M. Lang).
        Photocopy of reprint from "BSOAS", London University, Vol.
XXIV, Part 3; 1966; pp. 694-699.

Minorsky (1877-1966), studied law at Moscow University.
Then, with a view to entering the diplomatic service, he entered
the Lazarev Institute of Oriental Languages (1900-1903) where he
learned Persian and Arabic. In 1902 he visited Iran for the first
time. Influenced by the writings of E.G. Browne, his interest in
Persian studies gained momentum. In 1903, he entered the Russian
Foreign Service and he served several times in Persia as a diplomat.
Upon returning to Moscow he studied under V.V. Barthold. After
the Russian Revolution he went to Paris, where he taught at
various centers, and was influenced by the great Persian
scholar Mohammad Qazvini. In 1932 at the invitation of Denison
Ross he went to England and from 1932, he taught at London
University, retiring in 1944 but continuing his writings and
studies.

OBITUARY OF PROFESSOR VLADIMIR MINORSKI (written by Ilya Gershevitch).
    Reprint from the "Journal of the Royal Asiatic Society";
London, April 1967; pp. 53-57.

MINUTES OF THE MEETING OF THE CHICAGO INSTITUTE ON MIDDLE EAST.
    Held during a three day period in May 1974; 15 pp.

MIRAN, M. ALAM
    The Function of National Languages in Afghanistan.
    New York, February 1977; 4to, soft cover; 10 pp.

    Occasional Paper Number 11 of the Afghanistan Council of the
Asia Society.

MOAYYAD, HESHMAT
    Zum Problemkreis und Stand der Persischen Lexikographie.
    Reprint from "Annali dell Instituto Universitario Orientale
di Napoli", Nuova Serie, Vol.XII; Rome, 1962; pp. 1-31.

MOAYYAD, HESHMAT
    Nachtrag zum Deutsch - Persischen Worterbuch von Eilers.
    Reprint from preceding publication, same issue; pp. 32-81.

MOAYYAD, HESHMAT
    Review of "Index Iranicus", Vol.I, 1910-1958 by Iraj Afshar.
    Reprint from "Annali dell Instituto Universitario Orientale
di Napoli", Nuova Serie, Vol.XIII; Rome, 1963.

    In German.

MOAYYAD, HESHMAT
    Eine Wiedergefundene Schrift Ueber Ahmad-E Gam und Seine
Nachkommen.
    Reprint from "Annali dell Instituto Universitario Orientale
di Napoli", Nuova Serie, Vol.XIV; Rome, 1964; pp. 255-284, and

854

two full page plate reproductions of the manuscript discussed.

A discussion of the manuscript "Rowzat ol Riyahain" which
the author found near Harat in 1964. The manuscript was published
in its entirety in 1966.

MOAYYAD, HESHMAT
Review of "Deutsch-Persisches Woterbuch" by Wilhelm Eilers.
Reprint from "Oriens" Vols.18-19; Leiden, 1965-1966; pp.
407-410.

In German.

MOAYYAD, HESHMAT
Review of "Deutsch - Persischer Sprachfuhrer" by Issa Chehabi.
Reprint from "Oriens" Vols.23-34; Leiden, 1970-1971; pp. 544-
546.

In German.

MOAYYAD, HESHMAT
Review of "Vis and Ramin" translated from the Persian of
Fakhr Ud-Din Gurgani by George Morrison.
Reprint from "Journal of Near Eastern Studies"; United
States, c.1972; pp. 213-215.

The writer in his review also touches on the similarity
between the story of Vis and Ramin, written in mid 11th century
A.D. and the Celtic legend of "Tristan and Isolde". While
acknowledging the "amazing similarity ... both in the general
structure of the story and a number of decisively important
details" the writer takes the view that there is no tangible
evidence of connection between the two tales.

MOAYYAD, HESHMAT
Review of "Persisch - Deutsches Worterbuch" by H. Junker and
B. Alavi.
Reprint from "Oriens", Vols.25-26; Leiden, c.1972; pp. 396-
399.

In German.

MOAYYAD, HESHMAT
Review of "Lehrubuch der Persischen Sprache" by Bozorg Alavi
and Manfred Lorenz.
Reprint from the "International Journal of Middle Eastern
Studies 3"; Great Britain, 1972; pp. 372-380.

The same issue contains reviews of Iraj Afshar's "Index
Iranicus" by Iraj Dehghan, and Albert Kudsi-Zadeh's "Sayyid Jamal
Al-Din Al-Afghani: An annotated bibliography" by Nikki R. Keddie.

MOAYYAD, HESHMAT
       Some Remarks on the Nasirean Ethics by Nasir Ad-Din Tusi.
       Reprint from "Journal of Near Eastern Studies", Vol.31, No.3;
United States, July 1972; pp. 179-186.

       In 1964 G.M. Wickens published his translation of Khaje Nasir
e-Din's (1201-1274) greatest work "Akhlaq Nasiri". The writer has
referred to the Persian text which formed the basis for Wickens'
translation and rectifies certain shortcomings in Wickens' work.
The review, however, is a general survey of other recent works
(up to 1972) on Tusi.

MOAYYAD, HESHMAT
       Parvin's Poems – A Cry in the Wilderness.
       Reprint from "Islamwissenschaftliche Abhandlungen"; Wiesbaden,
1974; pp. 164-190, with 6 plates.

       An excellent recounting of the life of Parvin Etesami (1907-
1941), probably the best poetess of 20th century Iran, interspersed with an analysis of her poetry. A girl brought up by the
rigid standards of 19th century Persia, Parvin remained shy, timid
and withdrawn. Her marriage was a failure. The writer makes the
point that had she lived beyond 1941, the whole "liberating"
influence of the era which ushered in a second literary renaissance in 20th century Iran (albeit for a brief period) would have
had an equally liberating influence on her life and poetry, and
her work would have taken on new dimensions. Moayed has
recently translated and published some of Parvin's poems (refer
to Etesami in Section A).

MOAYYAD, HESHMAT
       Review of Fritz Meier's book "Abu Said-I-Abul Khayr".
       Reprint from "Journal of the American Oriental Society"; Vol.
102, No.2; 1982; pp. 381-382.

       The writer is highly laudatory of Meier's work and considers
it as the definitive work on Abu Said Abul Khayr (967-1049 A.D.),
one of the early mystic sages.

MOGADAM, M.
       Mithra, the Incarnate Saviour.
       Paper presented to the Second International Congress of
Mithraic Studies; Tehran, c.1970; 15 pp.

       In an absurd article, the writer argues that Jesus of
Nazareth and Mithra were one and the same and Jesus was born in
southeastern Persia. It is the Romans that confused the event
and thought Jesus was born in Bethlehem. The learned writer also
argues that the concept of immaculate birth is Persian in origin
as well.

856

MOHAMMAD REZA SHAH
     How the Americans Overthrew Me: The Shah's Own Story.
     In 2 Parts. 2 articles from "Now" magazine; Great Britain;
illustrated; 7 December 1979, pp. 20-26 and 32-34; 14 December
1979, pp. 20-34.

     "Adapted by H.J. Weaver from 'Reponse à L'Histoire' by
Muhammad Reza Pahlavi, to be published (in December) in Paris."
With photographs added by "Now" magazine. Written during his
fatal illness (refer to entries under the writer in Section A).

MOHANDESSI, MANOUTCHEHR
     Hedayat and Rilke.
     Photocopy of reprint from "Contemporary Literature"; United
States, Summer 1971; pp. 209-216.

     The writer sets forth the thesis that Hedayat had read some of
Rilke's works and had been greatly influenced by them, and may
have unconsciously incorporated certain material from Rilke's
works in his "Blind Owl".

MONNERET DE VILLARD, UGO
     The Fire Temples.
     Reprint from the "Bulletin of the American Institute for
Persian Art and Archaeology", Vol.V, No.4; New York, December 1936;
illustrated in text and full page illustrations; pp. 175-234.

     Re: Sassanian Architecture.

MOOREY, P.R.S.
     Ancient Bronzework from Luristan.
     Photocopy of reprint from unknown journal; Great Britain, c.
1968; 8 pp.

MOOSA, MATTI
     The Translation of Western Fiction into Arabic.
     Reprint from "The Islamic Quarterly", Vol.XIV, No.4; Great
Britain, 1972; pp. 202-236.

     The translation of Western fiction into Arabic during the
19th and 20th centuries was the most important element in the
development of modern Arabic fiction. The article, although it
does not deal with the Persian scene, is equally applicable to
Iran. Serious translation of Western fiction into Persian began
a little later (in the twenties) and had a profound effect on
modern Persian fiction and poetry.

MOREWEDGE, PARVIZ
     Ibn Sina (Avicenna) and Malcolm and the Ontological Argument.
     Photocopy from "The Monist", Vol.54, No.2; Illinois, 1970;
pp. 234-249.

Writer: State University of New York.

MOREWEDGE, PARVIZ
     Contemporary Scholarship on Near Eastern Philosophy.
     Reprint from "The Philosophical Forum", Vol.II, No.1 (New
Series); Boston University, Fall 1970; pp. 122-140.

     Further discussions of Ibn Sina's philosophical contributions.
The writer maintains the general approach of Western students of
philosophy is that it is basically Greek philosophy, modified by
Islamic culture. He argues that this precept ignores the fact
that thinkers such as Ibn Sina did not merely comment on Greek
philosophy but in many instances were authors of original
thought.

MOREWEDGE, PARVIZ
     The Logic of Emanationism and Sufism in the Philosophy of
Ibn Sina (Avicenna), Part I.
     Reprint from the "Journal of the American Oriental Society",
Vol.91, No.4; United States, October-December 1971; pp. 467-475.

MOREWEDGE, PARVIZ
     The Logic of Emanationism and Sufism in the Philosophy of
Ibn Sina (Avicenna), Part II.
     Reprint from the "Journal of the American Oriental Society",
Vol.92, No.1; United States, January-March 1972; pp. 1-18.

MOREWEDGE, PARVIZ
     A Major Contribution to the History of Islamic Philosophy:
A Review Article.
     Reprint from "The Muslim World", Hartford Seminary Foundation,
Vol.LXII, No.2; United States, 1972; pp. 148-157.

     Review of "A History of Islamic Philosophy", by Majid Fakhry.

MOREWEDGE, PARVIZ
     Philosophical Analysis and Ibn Sina's "Essence - Existence"
Distinction.
     Reprint from the "Journal of the American Oriental Society",
Vol.92, No.3; United States, July-September 1972; pp. 425-435.

MOREWEDGE, PARVIZ
     Ibn Sina's Concept of the Self.
     Photocopy of reprint from the "Philosophical Forum";
published by Boston University, Fall 1973; pp. 49-73.

     The writer in an excellent article maintains that Ibn Sina's
subjects of enquiry were not limited to Islamic theological
concepts of the day but embraced subjects that have contemporary

858

philosophical relevance.

MORGAN, MARY and ULLMAN, OCSI
        Central-Asian Ikats.
        London, 1974; large 8vo, soft cover; illustrated, one in
color; 4 pp.

        Includes a 4 pp. booklet insert of the aims and forthcoming
exhibition of the Textile Gallery London; in the autumn of 1974.

MORGENSTIERNE, GEORG
        Balochi Miscellanea.
        Reprint from "Acta Orientalia"; Leiden, 1948; pp. 253-292.

MORGENSTIERNE, GEORG
        The Development of Iranian R + Consonent in the Shughni
Group.
        Reprint from "Asia Major" the W.B. Henning Memorial Volume;
London, c.1968; pp. 334-342.

MORONY, MICHAEL G.
        Continuity and Change in the Administratitive Geography of
Late Sassanian and Early Islamic Al-Iraq.
        Photocopy of reprint from "Iran", Vol.XX; published by the
British Institute of Persian Studies, 1982; 49 pp.

MORRISON, GEORGE
        Flowers and Witchcraft in the Vis o Ramin of Fakhr Ud-Din
Gurgani.
        Reprint from "Acta Iranica", "Commemoration Cyrus" celebrat-
ing the 2500 Anniversary of the Foundation of the Persian Empire,
1971; Leiden, 1974; pp. 249-259.

        Gurgani began writing his poem in springtime (Now Rouz: the
New Year) and completed it in the autumn and presented it to his
patron as a present for the feast of Mehregan (the autumnal
equinox). Hence, there is a profusion of references to flowers,
nightingales, trees and gardens; and even though most of the
characters are ruled by fate there are individuals in the story
who control people and events through witchcraft.

MORTIMER, EDWARD
        Iran's Brand of Islam - a religion of opposition.
        Article from the "Times"; London, 24 November 1978; p. 10.

MORTIMER, EDWARD, et al.
        The "Shiite Challenge".
        "The Times"; London, 19 November 1984.

        Part I of two articles by Edward Mortimer and various "Times"

correspondents tracing the spread of Islamic militancy in Iran
and the Arab Middle East six years after Khomaini's Revolution.
A country by country survey.

MORTIMER, EDWARD, et al.
        The Spreading Faith.
        "The Times"; London, 20 November 1984.

        Part II and the conclusion of an investigation by Edward
Mortimer and a team of "Times" foreign correspondents into the
spread of Islamic militancy.

MORTIMER, EDWARD
        Article from "The Times"; London, 27 May 1985; illustrated
with photographs of Dr. Mosaddeq and the three Rashidian brothers.

        Written on the day of the broadcasting of the "Iran" segment
of Granada Television Series "End of Empire". The article basically deals with the same material as the "Observer" article (refer
to Hawkes, Nigel in Section B) and shows how Britain through misin-
formation and playing upon the U.S. paranoia in the days of Senator
Joseph McCarthy convinced the Americans to take an active hand in
the plot to overthrow Mosaddeq and thwart a "Communist takeover".

MORTIMER, EDWARD
        To the Tehran Station.
        "The New York Review of Books"; 30 January 1986; pp. 13 and
14.

        Review of Roy Mottahedeh's "The Mantle of the Prophet".

MOSSADEGH, MOHAMMAD
        A Short Biography of the Prime Minister of Iran.
        Tehran, c.1951; frontispiece and 5 pp. plus a list of public-
ations of Dr. Mosaddeq in Persian and French.

MOTTAHEDEH, ROY P.
        Bureaucracy and the Patrimonial State in Early Islamic Iran
and Iraq.
        Reprint of a paper read at a conference in Hamadan, Iran in
1977; unknown publication; pp. 25-36.

        The writer discusses the body of bureaucrats created in late
9th century and their contribution to the continuity of the administrative system and the preservation of learning.

MOTTAHEDEH, ROY P.
        The Buyids.
        Photocopy of reprint of entry in the "Dictionary of the
Middle Ages" (Joseph R. Strayer, editor in chief), Vol.2; New York,
c.1979.

MOTTAHEDEH, ROY P.
        The Shu'ubiyah Controversy and the Social History of Early
Islamic Iran.
        Reprint from the "International Journal of Middle Eastern
Studies", Vol.7, 1976; Princeton, New Jersey, 1980; pp. 161-182.

MOTTAHEDEH, ROY PARVIZ
        Iran's Foreign Devils.
        Reprint from "Foreign Policy", No.38; United States, Spring
1980; pp. 19-34.

        An article written after the seizure of the hostages
discussing possible motives of the organizers.

MOTTAHEDEH, ROY PARVIZ
        A Note on the Tasbib.
        Photocopy of reprint from "Studia Arabica and Islamica",
American University of Beirut; 1981; pp. 347-351.

        A brief explanation of the financial and legal institution
of "Tasbib" in Islamic administration. The institution was used
as a means to remunerate a public servant by assigning to him
the unpaid tax liability of a defaulting third party. In this
way the public servant had the right to collect the tax directly
from the liable source. The practice helped to reduce the admin-
istratiive work load and expenditures, but was also abused by
administrators.

MUHAMMAD, SEYED
        Forest Development Policy in Iran (Background, Problems and
Proposals).
        53 page manuscript dated October 1960.

NAIPAUL, V.S.
Tehran Winter.
Article from "The New York Review of Books", 8 October 1981;
pp. 23-29.

"Abstract Journalism." Later incorporated in writer's book,
"Among the Believers" (refer to Section A).

NASER E-DIN SHAH'S STATE VISIT TO GREAT BRITAIN IN 1889.
Photocopy of five pages from the visitors' book of Baron
Ferdinand Rothschild's English country house, on the occasion of
the visit of Naser e-Din Shah, 10 July 1889.

Signatures include those of: The British - The Prince of
Wales, Lord Rothschild, George Curzon, Lord Northbrook, Lord
Abercorn, et al.. The Persians - The Shah, Ali Asghar Khan Amin
ol-Soltan (Atabak), Mirza Reza Khan Arfa (Danesh), Amin Homayoun,
et al..

NASR, SEYYED HOSSEIN
Sacred Art in Persian Culture.
Iran, 1970; soft cover; 26 pp.

A publication of the Festival of Arts, Shiraz - Persepolis,
1970.

NASR, SEYYED HOSSEIN
Elements of Continuity in the Life of Mysticism and
Philosophy in Iran.
Reprint of paper delivered before the International Congress
of Iranology, Shiraz, October 1971; 13 pp.

A well written article which argues that Islam, with its
great tendency for assimilation, incorporated many pre-Islamic
Persian religious principles.

NASR, SEYYED HOSSEIN
Islamic Philosophy in Contemporary Persia: A Survey of
Activity During the Past Two Decades.
Research monograph No.3 published by the Middle East Center,
University of Utah, Salt Lake City, 1972; 20 pp.

A survey of philosophical inquiry and teaching trends in
Iran during 1950-1970. The writer identifies three groups
concerned with philosophy during the period. First, the tradit-
ionally educated who are versed in Islamic philosophy; second,
those who have both a traditional and a modern education combining
the traditional with a modern approach; and finally those who are
concerned with secular modern Western philosophy. The writer
then deals primarily with the first two groups.

862

NASR, SEYYED HOSSEIN
     Abu Rayhan Al-Biruni.
     Reprint from "Hamdard Islamicus" Quarterly Journal, Vol.II,
No.2; Pakistan, 1979; pp. 91-97.

     A short biography of the great Persian scholar, scientist
and historian (973-1051 A.D.).

NASR, SEYYED HOSSEIN
     Post-Avicennan Islamic Philosophy and the Study of Being.
     Reprint from "Reason, Action and Experience"; Hamburg, 1979;
pp. 87-93.

NASR, SEYYED HOSSEIN
     A Muslim Reflection on Religion and Theology.
     Reprint from "Journal of Ecumenical Studies", Vol.17, No.1;
United States, Winter 1980; pp. 112-120.

     A commentary on an article written by a prominent Catholic
theologian.

NASR, SEYYED HOSSEIN
     Reflections on Methodology in the Islamic Sciences.
     Reprint from "Hamdard Islamicus", Quarterly Journal, Vol.III,
No.3; Pakistan, 1980; pp. 3-13.

NASR, SEYYED HOSSEIN
     The Concept of Reality and Freedom in Islam and Islamic
Civilization.
     Reprint from "The Philosophy of Human Rights", edited by
A.S. Rosenbaum; Westport, Connecticut, 1980; pp. 95-101.

     The writer states that the "foundation of human rights is
essentially theological and is rooted in the obligations owed by
human beings to God".

NASR, SEYYED HOSSEIN
     On the Teaching of Philosophy in the Muslim World.
     Reprint from "Hamdard Islamicus", Quarterly Journal, Vol.IV,
No.2; Pakistan, 1981; pp. 53-72.

     A paper prepared in connection with the First International
Conference on Muslim Education, held in Mecca in 1977. The
writer basically argues that in order to be able to refute "alien"
thoughts, Moslems must be well versed in Islamic philosophy, and
once that has been secured, it is well to be acquainted with
Western philosophy to determine what is contrary to basic Moslem
teachings.

NASR, SEYYED HOSSEIN
     Eternity and Temporal Order - A View of Evolution from the

Islamic Perspective.
     Reprint from "Rivista di Biologia", Vol.77, No.2; Perugia,
Italy, 1984; pp. 211-232.

NASR, SEYYED HOSSEIN
     Islamic Work Ethics.
     Reprint from "Hamdard Islamicus", Quarterly Journal, Vol.VII,
No.4; Pakistan, Winter 1984; pp. 25-35.

     In a well reasoned article, the writer argues that the
concept of work ethic in Islam is similar if not even more exact-
ing than the Judeo-Christian concept.

NAVEH, JOSEPH and SHAKED, PAUL
     Ritual Texts or Treasury Documents?
     Photocopy of reprint from "Orientalia", Vol.42, Fasc.3;
United States, 1973; pp. 445-457.

NEGAHBAN, EZAT O.
     A Glance at Iranian Archaeology.
     Article published by the "High Council of Culture and Art";
Tehran, November 1973; illustrated on full page plates; 45 pp.

     A survey by an eminent Iranian archaeologist who conducted
excavations in Iran (including the Marlik find) in the early
sixties. (Refer to Section C under writer's name.)

NEGARESTAN: MUSEUM OF EIGHTEENTH AND NINETEENTH CENTURY IRANIAN
ART.
     Tehran, 1976; folding leaflet; illustrated in color; 6 pp.

     Gives facilities, times of opening and history of the museum
and its collection.

NETZER, AMNON
     Daniyal-Name: An Exposition of Judeo-Persian.
     Reprint from "Islam and Its Cultural Divergence", University
of Illinois Press, Urbana, Illinois, c.1975; pp. 145-164.

     Discussion of a manuscript at the British Museum. Writer:
At University of Jerusalem.

NETZER, AMNON
     Islam in Iran: Search for Identity.
     Reprint from "The Crescent in the East, Islam in Asia Major";
London, 1982; pp. 5-22.

     The writer argues that Arabs accepted Islam without any
difficulty because they had no pre-Islamic tradition. The
Persians, while accepting Islam, unconsciously tried and still

try to relate it to their pre-Islamic culture e.g. the molding of
Imam Ali in the shape of Rostam and creating a striking resemb-
lance between the two. The writer believes the conflict exists
even in today's Islamic Republic of Iran.

NETZER, AMNON
        An Isfahani Jewish Folk-Song.
        Photocopy from "Irano-Judaica", Ben-Zvi Institute; Jerusalem,
1982; pp. 180-203.

        An interesting article that deals with the evolution of
language in the Jewish community of Esfahan.

NEUSNER, JACOB
        Babylonian Jewry and Shapur II's Persecution of Christianity
from 339 to 379 A.D.
        Photocopy of reprint from "Hebrew Union College Annual", Vol.
XLIII; United States, 1972; 26 pp.

        Writer: Professor at Brown University discusses the policy
adopted by Shahpur II, arising from the suspicion that the Persian
Christian sympathized with his Christian enemies, the Roman
Empire.

NEW BOOKS QUARTERLY: On Islam and the Muslim World; Vol.I, No.I.
        London, Autumn 1980; small journal; 103 pp.

        Published by the Islamic Council of Europe and intended to
appear quarterly. This first issue "is devoted exclusively to
the First International Exhibition of Books on Islam and the
Muslim World" held 23-25 September 1980 at S.O.A.S., University
of London.

NEW YORK TIMES
        The Shah Departs, Finally.
        Editorial; 17 January 1979; p. A22.

NEW YORK TIMES
        Iran Faces Major Economic Difficulties.
        12 February 1979; p. A12.

        Includes "A Chronology of Major Events in Iranian Turmoil".

NEW YORK TIMES
        Eyeless in Iran.
        29 July 1979; pp. 16-17.

        Unattributed article. "A study of the Carter Administration's
response to the Iranian crisis, ... based upon scores of interviews with senior civilian and military policy makers, intelligence officers and members of Congress. It documents the errors

in intelligence gathering, analysis and policy making ... that led Jimmy Carter to impose a massive reorganization on the intelligence community."

NEW YORK TIMES
    Texts of U.S. Replies to Iran on Conditions for Releasing Hostages.
    29 December 1980; p. A10.

    Also includes a continuation from page 1 of an article headed "U.S. Discloses Proposals It Made to Tehran".

NEW YORK TIMES
    The Hostages, Day 444: Families Wait as the Nation Watches: Near-Euphoria of Hostages' Families Gives Way to Last-Minute Uncertainty.
    20 January 1981; p. A3.

    Includes on reverse side (p.A4) "Text of Agreement Between Iran and the U.S. to Resolve the Hostage Situation".

NEW YORK TIMES
    America in Captivity: Points of Decision in the Hostage Crisis.
    "New York Times Magazine" Special Issue; c. May, 1981; illustrated; 148 pp.

    The entire issue is devoted to "An Inquiry by the New York Times Staff", A.M. Rosenthal, Terence Smith, John Kifner and others, into the events leading up to and the handling of the crisis.

NEWSWEEK
    Iran's Birthday Party.
    25 October 1971; pp. 16-17.

    Article by Loren Jenkins re celebrations at Persepolis marking 2,500 years of Persian monarchy. "The ultimate in kitsch ... Blend of immitation Louis XV and plastic with no Persian art objects or carpets."

NEWSWEEK
    The Master Builder of Iran.
    14 October 1974; pp. 27-33.

    Includes an interview with Mohammad Reza Shah and a biography section entitled "Who's Really Who in Iran". Newsweek selects the following people as those who exercise power in Iran: General N. Nassiri, General Hossein Fardoust, M. Yeganeh, Habib Sabet, Nader Ardalan and K. Ferdowsi. An article worthwhile for its absurdity.

866

NEWSWEEK
Pushing for Cheaper Oil.
3 March 1975; pp. 28-33.

Includes also an article entitled "Pan Iran Airways" report-
ing on the Iranian government's proposed loan of $245 million to
Pan American Airways, plus a cartoon of the Shah holding up two
Pan Am pilots with a dollar bill and entitled "Hijacked". The
article is apprehensive about the increasing influence of Iran
in the world of international finance and laudatory towards Henry
Kissinger for his "handling of Middle Eastern Rulers".

NEWSWEEK
Iran: Bloom off the Boom.
1 March 1976; pp. 24-26.

"The end of the economic boom." Also includes an interview
with Mohammad Reza Shah.

NEWSWEEK
Crusader in Exile.
6 November 1978; pp. 31-32.

Article on Khomaini in exile in France, including one of the
first interviews. The Western media thought it had another Gandhi.

NEWSWEEK
Iran: At the Brink?
13 November 1978; pp. 30-32.

NEWSWEEK
Showdown for the Shah.
Cover story; 20 November 1978; pp. 14-16.

There is in addition a report of a conversation with the Shah
entitled "Tea with the Shah" by Arnaud de Borchgrave, pp. 21-22,
and a report on tensions inside the American community in
Tehran entitled "'Yonky' Go Home", p. 23. Borchgrave sees the
"Red" hand behind the turbulance and is unable to understand the
Khomaini phenomenon.

NEWSWEEK
Iran at the Brink.
Cover story; 8 January 1979; pp. 14-19.

"Iran in Chaos"; article states that "Bakhtiar has a chance".

NEWSWEEK
Khomeini Power.
Cover story; 12 February 1979; pp. 42-48.

"Iran's Mystery Man", Khomaini, makes the cover of Newsweek. Most of the information on its subject is hazy and he remains a "mystery" to the writers.

NEWSWEEK
U.S. vs. Iran: Calm but Tough.
26 November 1979; pp. 10-16; plus cover story: "Has the U.S. Lost its Clout"; pp. 21-24, and pp. 26.

The first weeks after the seizure of the hostages.

NEWSWEEK
A Grim Thanksgiving.
Cover story; 3 December 1979; pp. 10-26.

NEWSWEEK
Iran: Is There a Way Out?
Cover story; 10 December 1979; pp. 8-14.

Khomaini on the cover again with the Shah underneath his shadow. Treatment of the Shah as the "Flying Dutchman". And an interview with Henry Kissinger who claims nothing would have happened in Iran had he been running things in the U.S..

NEWSWEEK
Tightening the Screws.
Cover story; 17 December 1979; pp. 8-14.

Re economic sanctions.

NICHOLSON, R.A.
Persian Lyrics.
Reprint of a section from "The Augustan Books of Poetry"; London, c.1930; pp. 5-30.

Selection of verses ranging from Mowlana Jalal e-Din to Iraj Mirza.

NIKITINE, B.
Seyyed Mohammad Ali Djemalzadeh - Pionnier De La Prose Moderne Persane.
Reprint from "La Revue des Etudes Islamiques"; Paris, 1959; pp. 23-33.

Short biography.

NODERER, E.R.
When the foot was on the other shah.
Article from "The Chicago Tribune Magazine"; 10 October 1971; illustrated; pp. 48-51 and p. 58.

Written from the journals kept by the writer during the Russian-British occupation of Iran in 1941 during World War II.

NORTON, AUGUSTUS RICHARD
Making Enemies in South Lebanon: Harakat Amal, the IDF, and South Lebanon.
Reprint from the "Middle East Insight", Vol.3; no place of publication indicated; 1984; illustrated; pp. 13-20.

The writer, an American Army officer who teaches at West Point Military Academy, argues that it was sheer folly for the Israelis to attack Lebanon in June of 1982. The southern Shi'ites interest could no longer be reconciled with the Fedayeen pressure in Lebanon and they could have come to blows sooner or later. The Israelis misreading the long term implications of Amal's militancy, nevertheless attacked. The writer discusses the origins and organization of Amal.

NOORZOY, M.S.; BRUNNER, C.J. and KERR, G.B.
An Analysis of Several Recent Afghan Laws.
New York, October 1977; 4to, soft cover; 67 pp.

A collection of "Papers presented at the Afghanistan Studies Association panel of the Middle East Studies Association annual meeting, 1976".

OAKES, JOHN B.
        The Persian Mind.
        "New York Times"; 30 September 1975; p. unknown.

        One of the first Western journalists to detect that something
was amiss during the economic boom.

OBERDOFER, DON
        Envoys See Captives: The Making of a Crisis: U.S. Agonizes
Over an Exile's Entry.
        Photocopy from "The Washington Post"; 11 November 1979; pp.
A1 and A13.

        An even-handed analysis of the Shah's plight.

OBERLING, PIERRE
        A Note on Tattooing and Branding Among the Aghach Eris of
South-Western Iran.
        Photocopy of reprint from "Ethnos", Nos.1-4; Ethnographical
Museum of Sweden, Stockholm, 1962; pp. 126-128.

OBERLING, PIERRE
        Georgians and Circassians in Iran.
        Photocopy of reprint from "Studia Caucasica", No.1; The Hague,
1963; map; pp. 127-143.

        The writer discusses the policy of Shah Abbas I to bring
Georgians and Circassians to Persia, principally to Esfahan. Shah
Esmail II had already brought large numbers of Georgians and
Circassians (over 30,000) to Persia as prisoners. During Shah
Abbas's rule larger numbers were brought in. The best known of
the Georgian settlements was in Ferydan, west of Esfahan. There
were, however, settlements in Khorasan at Abbas Abad (half way
between Shahroud and Sabzevar), Mazandaran at Ashraf (Behshahr of
today), Gilan and other parts of the country. Most Georgians
became Moslems and by the end of the 16th century they probably
numbered 250,000. Some of the women found their way to the Royal
Harem and became influential. It has been suggested that the
influx of the Georgians and Circassians into the houses of the
nobility and the Royal Harem had a disasterous influence on the
administration of the country as the women tried to advance their
offsprings, which led to conspiracies and dynastic disputes.

OBERLING, PIERRE
        The Turkie Tribes of Southwestern Persia.
        Reprint from "Ural-Altaische Jahrbücher", Vol.35, Fas.B,
1963; West Germany, 1964; pp. 164-180.

        Discussion of the Afshari tribes of Khuzestan.

870

OBEYD-I-ZAKANI
        Gorby and the Rats.
        Photocopy of translation of "Mush-O-Gurbeh" by Omar S. Pound;
London, 1972; 20 pp.

        The most popular children's poem in Persian, translated
superbly.

THE OBSERVER
        Woman Leads Fight Against the Ayatollah.
        31 March 1985.

        An account of a 30 year old woman's promotion to co-leader-
ship of the Mojahedeen Khalq; her marriage to Massoud Rajavi,
the leader of the Mojahedeen; the comments of the number-four
person in the Mojahedeen hierarchy who was her former husband and
his decision "willingly to divorce his wife for a greater cause".

O'DONOVAN, PATRICK
        Dust Settles on the Shah's Picnic.
        "The Observer"; London, 17 October 1971; p. 5.

        Re the Persepolis "party".

THE OIL CRISIS: IN PERSPECTIVE
        "Daedalus" Magazine; United States, fall 1975; 302 pp.

        Series of articles on the central theme of the then "oil
crisis", by various contributors.

OKAZAKI, SHOKO
        Shirang-Sofla: The Economics of a Northeast Iranian Village.
        Photocopy of reprint from "The Developing Economies" VII-3;
Institute of Asian Economic Affairs, Tokyo, Japan, September 1969;
pp. 261-283.

OKRENT, CHRISTINE
        Hoveyda.
        Cover and article from "Paris Match"; 20 April 1979; illus-
trated; pp. 30-38.

        Article on the former Prime Minister's imprisonment, mock
trial and execution.

OLSON, WILLIAM J.
        The Succession Crisis in Iran.
        Article in "The Washington Quarterly", published by the
Center for Strategic and International Studies, Georgetown University; Washington, D.C., Summer 1983; pp. 156-161.

ONO, MORIO
      On Socio-Economic Structure of Iranian Villages - With
Special Reference to Deh.
      Reprint from "The Developing Economies" V-3; Institute of
Asian Economic Affairs, Tokyo, Japan, September 1967; pp. 446-462.

OTTO-DINIZ, SARA; McCAFFREY, JACQUELINE PINSKER; and SCHMANDT-
BESSERAT, DENISE
      At the Court of the Great King: The Art of the Persian
Empire.
      Austin, Texas, 1978; large 8vo, soft cover; illustrations;
30 pp. of text.

      Children's booklet designed to accompany the Exhibit
"Ancient Persia: The Art of an Empire" held at the University of
Texas at Austin, 12 February - 16 April 1978.

P

PAHLAVI, ASHRAF; HOVEYDA, FEREYDOUN and GROSS, GEORGE E.
Series of Articles from "The New York Times"; January 1980;
p. A23.

1) "I Will Fight These Slanders" by Ashraf Pahlavi.
2) "'Corruption Ran Wild' in Iranian Royalty" by Fereydoun
Hoveyda.
3) "Befriending the Shah - Moral Considerations" by George
E. Gross

PAINTINGS FROM THE MUSLIM COURTS OF INDIA.
London, 1976; small 4to, soft cover; illustrations, some in
color, map; 99 pp.

Catalogue of an exhibition held at the British Museum, 13
April to 11 July 1976. Prepared by R.H. Pinder-Wilson.

PAPER, HERBERT H. and JAZAYERY, MOHAMMED ALI
The Writing System of Modern Persian.
Reprint from the "American Council of Learned Scoieties",
Publication Series B. No.4; United States, 1955; 30 pp.

PAPER, HERBERT H.
Judeo-Persian Bible Translations: Some Sample Texts.
Photocopy of reprint from "Studies in Bibliography and Book-
lore", Vol.VIII, Nos.2-4; published by the Library of Hebrew
Union College - Jewish Institute of Religion; Cincinnati, Ohio,
Spring 1968; pp. 99-113.

PAPER, HERBERT H.
Ecclesiastes in Judeo-Persian.
Reprint from "Orientalia", Vol.42, Fasc.1-2, 1; United States,
1973; pp. 328-337.

From a manuscript acquired by an American bibliophile.

PARIS-MATCH
La Mort du Shah.
Cover Story; 8 August 1980; illustrated; 22 pp.

PARVIS TANAVOLI: FIFTEEN YEARS OF BRONZE SCULPTURE.
New York, 1976; large booklet/catalogue; illustrated; 95 pp.

Designed to accompany a loan exhibition of the works of a
modern Iranian sculptor held at New York University, 8 December
1976 to 12 January 1977, and sponsored by National Iranian Radio
and Television on the occasion of the American Bicentennial. The
catalogue includes an interview with the artist.

PATTULLO, SUSAN JAYE
Additions to the Selected Bibliography for the Art of Ancient

Iran.
Reprint from unknown publication; New York, c.1980.

Writer: Columbia University.

PAUL, BILL
Caveat Lender: Chase Bank and Others Face Court Challenges on Huge Loans to Iran.
Photocopy of article from "The Wall Street Journal"; New York, 29 March 1980; pp. 1 and 31.

An inaccurate and unreliable account.

PEARSON, J.D. and RICE, D.S. (compiled by)
Islamic Art and Archaeology: A register of work published in the year 1955.
Cambridge, 1960; booklet; 65 pp.

"With contributions from Yu. E. Borshchevskiy, L.A. Mayer, R. Ettinghausen." The second volume. The first, a register of work published in the year 1954, appeared in 1956 under the same title.

LES PEINTRES POPULAIRES DE LA LEGENDE PERSANE.
Paris, c.1975; small 8vo, soft cover; illustrated, some in color; 92 pp.

Introduction and captions to illustrations in French and English. Designed to accompany an exhibition at the Maison d'Iran in Paris. Collection of "Naive" paintings from the previous 150 years. An exhibition of very inferior Persian painting called "Naive Art" for want of any other description.

PERELMAN, S.J.
Sizzling in the Streets of Tehran.
Extract from a book by Perelman entitled "Eastward Ha!" published in "The New York Post"; 14 October 1977; p. 29.

An inconsequential piece by the American humorist, written during his "80 days around the world".

PERSIA: SWANS ART TREASURE TOURS.
Great Britain, 1977; large 8vo, soft cover; illustrated in color plus map; 7 pp.

Brochure advertising the Swan-Hellenic conducted tours in Persia in the 1978/79 season.

PERSIAN AND INDIAN MINIATURES FROM THE COLLECTION OF EDWIN BINNEY, 3rd.

874

Portland, Oregon, 1962; booklet; illustrated, some in color; 48 pp.

Catalogue of an exhibition at the Portland Art Museum, 28 September to 29 November 1962. Text and catalogue by Edwin Binney.

PERSIAN ART: AN ILLUSTRATED SOUVENIR OF THE EXHIBITION OF PERSIAN ART AT BURLINGTON HOUSE.
London, 1931; 19 pp. of text and 101 black and white plates.

Introduction includes a section entitled "Some Aspects of Persian Art" by Roger Fry.

PERSIAN FRESCO PAINTINGS.
Publication of the American Institute for Persian Art and Archaeology; New York City, October 1932; entire number 4; 18 pp. of illustrated text plus 44 black and white plates.

Introduction by Arthur Upham Pope. Designed to accompany an exhibition, held under the auspices of the Institute and the Trustees of the Museum of Modern Art, of Persian fresco paintings "reconstructed by Mr. Sarkis Katchadourian from the seventeenth century originals in Isfahan". Poor "reconstructions", and nothing to merit an exhibition.

PERSIAN LITERATURE WORKSHOP.
The University of Texas at Austin; 13-15 April 1977; 2 pp.

A list of books and articles on particular approaches to translation of literature from another language (particularly Persian) into English.

PERSIAN MINIATURES: AN EXHIBITION OF SEVENTEEN PAGES FROM THE HOUGHTON SHAHNAMEH.
London, 1979; illustrated, some in color; 45 pp.

Designed to accompany an exhibition of seventeen miniatures at Thos. Agnew and Sons, London, 3 July to 24 August 1979. Another sale of the pages from the ill fated Shahnama.

PERSIAN PAINTINGS: FROM MINIATURES OF THE XIII-XVI CENTURIES.
London, 1947; large booklet; 9 pp. of text plus 12 color plates.

Introduction by Basil Gray. Miniatures from various collections in France, England and Egypt.

PERSPECTIVE: A REVIEW OF IRAN'S OIL INDUSTRY.
Iran, c.1961; large 8vo, soft cover; illustrated and map; 16 pp.

An outline history of the development of the oil industry
in Iran from early explorations in the late 19th century;
published by NIOC to commemorate the decennial of the nationalization of Iran's oil industry.

PHILIP, A.B.
A Persian Visitor.
Article from unidentified (British) magazine; 1948; illus-
trated; p. 5.

Compares Mohammad Reza Shah's first visit to London in 1948
with the visit of Naser e-Din Shah in 1873.

A PICTORIAL RECORD OF THE DELEGATES TO THE UNITED NATIONS CONFER-
ENCE ON INTERNATIONAL ORGANIZATIONS.
United States, June 1945; spiral-bound booklet; 62 pp.

Photographs of delegates to the founding conference of the
United Nations in San Francisco in April 1945, including members
of the Iranian delegation.

PIEMONTESE, ANGELO M.
An Italian Source for the History of Qagar (sic) Persia: The
Reports of General Enrico Andreini (1871-1886).
Reprint from "East and West", New Series, Vol.19, Nos.1-2;
Rome, March-June 1969; pp. 147-175.

Andreini, an Italian officer from Lucca in Tuscany, was
expelled from the Tuscan army "for disgraceful and incorrigible
conduct" in 1853. He was then forced to seek a career elsewhere.
He went to Persia in 1857 and became an infantry inspector with
the rank of captain. His career progressed and in 1872 he
became a general in the Persian army. In order to promote Italian
interests in Persia, he established contacts with the various
Italian courts, and soon thereafter he became the official
representative of the Italian Government in Persia   Until the
arrival of the first Italian Minister in Tehran (1866) he sent
regular reports on the economic conditions of Persia to the
Italian Government. The writer has found 437 of these reports
which show that Andreini was a perceptive reporter who easily
adjusted to and understood his surroundings. A very useful
addition to Persian 19th century scholarship.

PINDER-WILSON, R.H.
Persian Painting of the Fifteenth Century.
London, 1958; 4to, soft cover; illustrated in color; 24 pp.

Published by the Faber Gallery of Oriental Art. Introduction
and notes by R.H. Pinder-Wilson.

PINDER-WILSON, RALPH
______
     Elegance and Ornament in Islamic Glass.
     Article in "Apollo: The Magazine of the Arts"; London, April
1976; pp. 282-286.

PLENDERLEITH, H.J.
______
     Scientific Examination of an 11th Century Persian Silver
Salver.
     Reprint from "The Museums Journal", Vol.XXXIII; London,
November 1933; 8vo, soft cover; pp. 280-284 plus 2 black and
white plates.

     With an introduction by Arthur Upham Pope the then Director
of the American Institute for Persian Art and Archaeology.
Writer: At British Museum.

POPE, ARTHUR UPHAM
______
     The Historic Significance of Stucco Decoration in Persian
Architecture.
     Reprint from "The Art Bulletin", Vol.XVI; New York, 1934;
illustrated; pp. 321-332.

POPE, ARTHUR UPHAM
______
     Iranian and Armenian Contributions to the Beginnings of
Gothic Architecture.
     Photocopy of reprint from the "American Quarterly", Vol.I,
No.2; 1946; pp. 125-148 text and pp. 149-172 illustrations.

     In an interesting article, the writer discusses the signific-
ant contributions of Near Eastern architecture to Gothic architecture.

POPE, ARTHUR UPHAM
______
     The Garden Idea in Persia.
     Reprint of article from unknown journal, c.1950; 12 pp.

POPE, ARTHUR UPHAM
______
     The New Persian Renaissance.
     Reprint of a speech delivered before the Fifth Congress of
Iranian Art and Archaeology; 11 April 1968; 8 pp.

     In a self serving paper, the writer in effect argues that
Persian art has become known to the West only from the late
twenties and mostly through his efforts.

PORADA, EDITH
______
     Of Deer, Bells and Pomegranates.
     Photocopy of extract of article from "L'Iranica Antiqua",
Vol.VII; Leiden, 1967; pp. 99-120.

PORADA, EDITH
    True or False? Genuine and False Cylinder at Andrews Univer-
sity.
    Photocopy of reprint from "Andrews University Seminary
Studies", Vol.VI, No.2; Michigan, July 1968; pp. 134-149.

PORADA, EDITH
    Battlements in the Military Architecture and in the Symbolism
of the Ancient Near East.
    Photocopy of reprint from unknown journal; c.1970; 12 pp. and
four full page illustrated plates.

PORADA, EDITH
    Some Thoughts on the Audience Reliefs of Persepolis.
    Reprint from "Studies in Classical Art and Archaeology"; New
York, c.1970; pp. 37-43 and 4 pp. of plates.

PORADA, EDITH
    Bibliography for the Art of Ancient Iran.
    Reprint from "The Journal of the Ancient Near Eastern Society
of Columbia University", Vol.9; c.1971; illustrated; pp. 67-83.

PORADA, EDITH
    Ancient Persian Bronzes.
    Article in "Apollo: The Magazine of the Arts"; London,
February 1979; illustrated; pp. 140-144.

POSTER ART IN IRAN.
    Tehran, c.1978; booklet/catalogue; illustrated, some in
color; 76 pp.

    Published by the Tehran Museum of Contemporary Art. Intro-
duction in English and Persian. The catalogue attempts "to relate
a brief history of the development of the poster as an influential
art form in Iran" and is illustrated with primarily contemporary
examples.

POURHADI, IBRAHIM V.
    Soviet Tajik Literature.
    Photocopy of reprint from "The Middle East Journal"; United
States, Winter 1966; pp. 104-114.

    The Soviet policy of severing the links of the Soviet Moslem
with his Islamic past and the introduction of the Cyrillic alpha-
bet have caused young Tajik writers to forget poetry and "fatal-
istic" writings and instead produce uniformly dreary short stories
and novels. The writer argues that one should not blame "the
artist but rather the gloomy studio in which he has to work".

POURHADI, IBRAHIM
    A Selected and Annotated Bibliography of Persian Textbooks

Including Bilingual Dictionaries, Poetry and Proverbs.
    Publication series No.1, Iranian Embassy, Washington, D.C.;
c.1975; 17 pp.

POURJAVADI, NASROLLAH and WILSON, PETER LAMBTON
    From Kings of Love: The History and Poetry of the Nimatullahi
Sufi Order.
    Photocopy of reprint from unknown publication; London, 1978;
pp. 81-87.

POWERS, THOMAS
    A Book Held Hostage.
    Photocopy of a review of "Countercoup; The Struggle for the
Control of Iran" by Kermit Roosevelt from "The Nation"; United
States, 12 April 1980; pp. 437-440.

    Roosevelt's book was "withdrawn from publication" at the
author's request until the American hostages in Tehran had been
released. What is not mentioned is that the book was taken out
of circulation at the insistence of British Petroleum until
certain "offending" pages had been expurgated. Reviewer: Author of
the book "The Man Who Kept the Secrets: A biography of Richard
Helms". (Refer to Section A.)

PRESENT PERSIA; THE NATION OF IRAN
    Iran, 1971; 8vo, soft cover; booklet; illustrated; 10 pp.

    Published by the Documentation Center of Iran.

PRIVATE EYE
    Iranian Affairs: Caught Reporter.
    Cover and pages from "Private Eye", 19 March 1976. Includes
article on p. 17.

    A short biography of a key man in Anglo-Iranian relations
during the preceding 30 years. Subject: Shapoor Reporter
rendered to the British and Iranian Governments a variety of
services including those in his capacity as "economic consultant
to major British interests in Iran". Reporter was knighted by the
British Government for his "extraordinary" commercial services.

PROGRAMME DES CEREMONIES DU MARIAGE DE S.A.I. LE PRINCE HERITIER
AVEC S.A.R. LA PRINCESSE FOWZIEH.
    Iran, 1939; 8vo, soft cover; illustrated; 66 pp.

    Text in French and Persian. Schedule of events on the
journey to Egypt by the Iranian heir to the throne and Iranian
representatives, and their stay in Egypt to celebrate his marriage
to Princess Fowzie, sister of King Farouk; 24 February to 1 April,
1939. This was the future Mohammad Reza Shah's first marriage.

PRZEWORSKI, STEFAN
<u>   Luristan Bronzes in the Collection of Mr. Frank Savery,</u>
British Consul-General at Warsaw.
    As "Communicated to the Society of Antiquaries"; from
"Archaeologia", Vol.LXXXVIII; Oxford, 1940; 4to, soft cover;
illustrated; pp. 229-269.

THE QASHQA'I OF IRAN.
        Manchester, England, 1976; small 4to, soft cover; illustrated,
some in color and map; 95 pp. text plus 48 plates.

        Catalogue designed to accompany an exhibition at the Whit-
worth Art Gallery, University of Manchester, 24 April to 29 April
1976, as part of the World of Islam Festival in the U.K. in 1976.
Exhibit of life and artifacts of the Qashqa'i tribe.

QUINN, SALLY
        A Sumptuous Party of Parties by the King of Kings.
        "Washington Post", 11 October 1971; pp. B1-B3.

        Persepolis celebrations for the 2,500th Anniversary of
Iranian Monarchy.

QUINN, SALLY
        Iranian Nights and Washington Daze.
        "The Washington Post", Style Section; 19 May 1975; illus-
trated; pp. B1 and B3.

        Re Shah's visit. President and Mrs. Betty Ford were the
hosts.

RAMAZANI, R.K.
       Security in the Persian Gulf.
       "Foreign Affairs", Vol.57, No.4; United States, Spring 1979;
pp. 821-835.

RAMAZANI, R.K.
       Iran: Burying the Hatchet.
       "Foreign Policy", No.60; United States, Fall 1985; pp. 52-75.

       In a well reasoned article, the writer argues that Iran is
much too important to the West, especially the U.S., to be ignored
or regarded with unabated hostility and suspicion. When Khomaini
disappears from the scene, there could come about a change of
atmosphere in Tehran that may be conducive to some sort of
rapprochement. The writer pleads that the groundwork should be
laid now by the U.S. by at least muting its strident pronouncements on Iran. Iran has apparently made some gestures and its
high officials have uttered some vague comments about the desir-
ability of some relations with the U.S. These should be explored
by the administration, and the ritualistic condemnation of the
U.S. by the fringe elements in Iran should be ignored.
       The writer further argues that U.S. foreign policy towards
Iran revolves around a much too facile domino theory that unless
Iran is isolated, the countries of the Persian Gulf region would be
consumed by the fires of revolution. It has become apparent, the
writer points out, that revolutionary Shi'ism molded after that
of Khomaini is neither welcome nor exportable in the region.

RAPOPORT, Y.A.
       Some Aspects of the Evolution of Zoroastrian Funeral Rites
(according to Archaeological Finds).
       Photocopy of reprint of papers presented by the U.S.S.R.
delegation to the XXV International Congress of Orientalists;
Moscow, 1960; 10 pp.

REDJALI, SIMIN
       The Role of Women in Education in Iran.
       Photocopy of typewritten speech delivered at the Inter-
national Women's Congress in Madrid, 7 to 14 June 1970, by the
Secretary General of the Women's Organization of Iran; 12 pp.

REID, JAMES J.
       The Qajar Uymaq in the Safavid Period, 1500-1722.
       Reprint from "Iranian Studies", Vol.XI; United States, 1978;
pp. 117-143.

REID, J.
       The Qaramanlu: The Growth and Development of a Lesser Tribal
Elite in 16th and 17th Century Persia.
       Photocopy of reprint from "Studia Iranica", Tome 9, Fas.2;

882

Leiden, 1980; pp. 195-209.

REID, JAMES J.
        Rebellion and Social Change in Astarabad, 1537-1744.
        Reprint from the "International Journal of Middle East
Studies", No.13; United States, 1981; 35-53.

        In an excellent article, the writer discusses the intermittent
revolts of the Central Asian tribes from early 16th century to the
revolts of the Afshars in early 18th century and the Qajars at the
end of the 18th century.

RENEW, WINTER 1970
        8vo, soft cover; illustrated; 36 pp.

        A journal published in Iran by the Association of Returnee
Professional Groups which "aims at providing a means of communication among Iranians educated abroad".

REPORTS OF THE STUDY GROUPS: FIRST IRANIANS STUDENTS' CONVENTION,
DENVER, COLORADO, SEPTEMBER 1953.
        The reports of five study groups on: education, agriculture,
social advance, development of mutual understanding between U.S.
and Iran, and industrial development. Published by the Iranian
Students Association; one illustration; 22 pp.

        A very stormy convention. It was held a week after the coup
of August 1953 which overthrew Mosaddeq. The overwhelming majority
of students were pro Mosaddeq but with different shadings and
motives. The small group of Iranian Communists were the best
organized and were forwarding plans for a coalition with National
Front supporters which was rejected. At a subsequent Convention,
(Berkeley 1954) the lines drawn were much more clearly defined.
The Communists attempted to take over the Iranian Students Association but were voted down. Ironically, the Communist elements
fared better in Iran where, with a change of heart and allegiance,
one of them rose to ministerial rank. From among their student
counterparts in Europe there similarly arose in the sixties and
seventies a dozen high ranking officials in the Shah's regime.

REY, LUCIEN
        Persia in Perspective.
        Article from "New Left Review", No.19; Great Britain, March-
April 1963; maps; pp. 32-55.

        Writer: Taught briefly at Tehran University.

THE REZA ABBASI CULTURAL AND ARTS CENTER: LIST OF OBJECTS.
        Iran, 1976; large 8vo, soft cover; 132 pp.

A catalogue of the collection of metalwork, pottery, manuscripts, paintings, jewelry, lacquer-work, etc. Parallel
descriptions of objects in English and Persian.

RICHTER-BERNBURG, LUTZ
     Amir-Malik-Shahanshah-adud Ad-Daulais Titulature Re-Examined.
     Photocopy of reprint from "Iran" XVIII, 1980; The British
Institute of Persian Studies; pp. 83-102.

RIESTAHL, RUDOLF M.
     An Exhibition of Persian and Indian Miniature Paintings from
the Collection of Demotte, Inc.
     New York, 1934; 8vo, soft cover; 41 pp. of text and 12 full
page plates in monochrome.

     An extremely useful catalogue in that it shows what was
available for purchase even in the mid thirties: Three miniatures
from the famous Demotte Shahnama, five Teimurid, and many early
Safavid miniatures. It would have been useful if there had been
a price list as the sale was at the height of the Depression.

ROBINSON, B.W.
     Some Modern Persian Miniatures.
     Article in "The Studio", Vol.CXXXV, No.660; London, March
1948; illustrated, some in color; pp. 69-100 and advertisements.

     An art journal which includes in this number the above
article by B.W. Robinson subtitled, "Contemporary examples,
exhibited by the British Council in London last July, are
described against the background of their historical tradition".
Probably one of the first articles on late Qajar and early
Pahlavi painters.

ROBINSON, B.W.
     Persian Paintings.
     London, 1965; 18 pp. of text plus 36 monochrome plates.

     Published by the Victoria and Albert Museum; illustrations
include works in other collections. Well chosen pieces by a
noted expert in the field who has done more than anyone to bring
18th and 19th century Persian painting as well as calligraphy to
the attention of the West.

ROBINSON, B.W.
     Persian Painting in Bond Street.
     Article in "Apollo: The Magazine of the Arts"; London, April
1976; illustrated, some in color; pp. 318-321.

     The entire issue is devoted to "Islamic Art".

884

ROBINSON, B.W.
        The Kingdom of Qajar.
        Milan, 1985; pp. 61-84 and 15 full page color plates.

        The text is basically from Robert Ker Porter's book "Travels
in Georgia, Persia, Armenia and Ancient Babylon ...".

RODINSON, MAXIME
        Islam Resurgent.
        Article from "Gazelle Review of Literature on the Middle
East", No.6; London, 1979; 8vo, soft cover; 119 pp.

        Also contains a series of book reviews including two by
Fred Halliday and Nikki Keddie on recent publications on Iran.

RODMAN, PETER W.
        "The Hostage Crisis: How not to Negotiate".
        Article from "The Washington Quarterly", Vol.4, No.3;
Washington, D.C., Summer 1981; pp. 9-25.

        An unconvincing article as the writer is vague in his
alternatives and remedies even with the benefit of hindsight.

ROEMER, HANS ROBERT
        Probleme der Hafizforschung und der Stand Ihrer Lösung.
        Photocopy of an article published by the Akademie der
Wissenschaften und der Literatur in Mainz in "Abhandlungen der
Klasse der Literatur, Jahrgang 1951, Nr.3"; Wiesbaden; pp. 3-98.

ROMANOWSKI DE BONCZA, V. (designed by)
        Costumes Militaires de l'Empire Perse Depuis sa Fondation.
        Greece, c.1966; First Part; 3 pp. of text in French and 16
colored plates in a folder.

        Depicts the military costumes of the Achaemenids.

ROSENTHAL, FRANZ
        Al-Biruni Between Greece and India.
        Reprint from "Biruni Symposium, Persian Studies", No.7;
Columbia University, New York, 1976; 12 pp.

ROTHSTEIN, NATALIE
        The Ardabil Carpet.
        London, 1976; Victoria and Albert Museum published 9 broad-
sheets of its masterpieces. This is "Sheet Five".

        A detailed and illustrated description of the Ardabil Carpet
considered the finest existing carpet in the world. It is dated
946 A.H./1540 A.D. and was woven either in Tabriz or Kashan.
A similar carpet is owned by the Getty Museum at Malibu, California (see separate entry under Stead, Rex).

ROUDAKI HALL ON THE OCCASION OF THE TENTH ANNIVERSARY OF IRAN'S
WHITE REVOLUTION
        Iran, c.1972; 4to, soft cover; illustrated; 94 pp.

        In English and Persian. Events at Roudaki Hall in Tehran
during the Anniversary celebrations. Mostly photographs of
artists who had performed in that interim.

ROULEAU, ERIC
        Khomeini's Iran.
        "Foreign Affairs"; United States, Fall 1980; pp. 1-20.

        Writer: Chief Middle East correspondent and editorial writer
at the French daily, "Le Monde", and an acute observer of
contemporary Iran.

RUBIN, BARRY
        Iran, the Ayatollah, and U.S. Options.
        Article in "The Washington Quarterly"; published by The
Center for Strategic and International Studies, Georgetown University; Washington, D.C., Summer 1983; pp. 142-155.

RUSSELL, JAMES R.
        Zoroastrian Problems in Armenia: Mihr and Vahagn.
        Photocopy of reprint from "Zoroastrian Problems"; c.1970;
7 pp.

SABRI-TABRIZI, G.R.
    Human Values in the Works of Two Persian Writers.
    Reprint of article from unknown journal, c.1970; 8 pp.

    Jalal Al-Ahmad and Samad Behrangi are the two writers
discussed in this article.

SAID, EDWARD
    Crazy America.
    Article from "The London Review of Books"; 19 March – 1 April
1981; pp. 11 and 12.

    An article on the U.S. press coverage and perception of the
Iranian hostage crisis and their final release, which the writer
considers as hysterical, shallow and given to superficial general-
ization.

SAFINIA, MRS. M.
    Laws Passed in Favour of Iranian Women in Recent Years.
    Photocopy of a speech delivered to a seminar to study the
family situation and the effects of the Family Protection Law;
Tehran, c.1968; 4 pp.

    The speaker was a lawyer and a member of the Women's Organiz-
ation of Iran.

SALE, RICHARD
    Carter and Iran: From Idealism to Disaster.
    Photocopy from "The Washington Quarterly"; Washington, D.C.,
Autumn 1980; pp. 75-87.

    Writer: A journalist engaged in writing a book on U.S.
foreign policy in Iran. The article contains many errors of fact.

SAMADI, H.
    Les Découvertes Fortuités Klardasht, Garmabak, Emam et
Tomadjan (Mazanderan et Guilan).
    Tehran, November 1959; illustrated; 46 pp.

    Author: Curator of the National Museum of Tehran.

SANAI, MAHMOUD
    Mysticism in Persian Poetry.
    Photocopy of reprint from the "Journal of the Iran Society";
London, July 1951; 19 pp.

    Writer: A Persian psychologist and a man of letters who died
in London in 1985.

SANAI, MAHMOUD
    Avicenna.

Photocopy of reprint from "The Lancet"; London, 14 August 1954; 7 pp.

A short biography of Avicenna written on the occasion of his millenary.

SANGHVI, RAMESH
Shahanshah.
Published by "Transorient Books"; London, 1969; 31 pp.

A short biography by an Indian public relations man.

SAQQAKHANEH
Iran, 1977; small 4to, soft cover; illustrated; some in color; 44 pp.

Catalogue designed to accompany an exhibition held at the Tehran Museum of Contemporary Art, 22 October 1977. An exhibition of the "vernacular aspects of contemporary art in Iran". Religious ritual motifs and symbols in contemporary Persian art. A mediocre exhibition.

SASSANIAN SILVERWARE
Leningrad, 1973; folder containing 16 large-postcard-size color reproductions.
From the Hermitage Collection, No.11, published by Aurora Art Publications, Leningrad; one of a series "from the art collection of Soviet Museums". Captions are in Russian and English.

SAVORY, ROGER M.
The Significance of the Political Murder of Mirza Salman.
Photocopy of an abridged version of a paper read at the XXVIth International Congress of Orientalists, held at New Delhi in January 1964, reprinted from "Islamic Studies, Journal of the Central Institute of Islamic Research", Vol.III, No.2; Karachi, June 1964; pp. 181-191.

The writer points out that every individual who held the title of Vakeel (Vice Regent of the Shah) from the beginning of the Safavid dynasty until the accession of Shah Abbas was murdered or rendered totally inactive by the Qezelbash. Mirza Salman never held the title but had aspired to that office.

SAVORY, ROGER M.
Some Notes on the Provincial Administration of the Early Safavid Empire.
Photocopy of reprint from "BSOAS", London University, Vol. XXVII, Part 1; 1964; pp. 114-129.

The writer discusses the complex administrative system of

888

the provinces under the early Safavid rule. As there was no
concept of state, as such, and instead there was the concept of
the "God protected Kingdom", the distinction between temporal and
spiritual realms were not sharply defined. Thus, the same lack
of boundaries and the presence of rivalries in the administration
of the central state stretched into and affected the administration of the provinces.

SAVORY, ROGER M.
     The Struggle for Supremacy in Persia after the Death of
Teimour.
     Photocopy of reprint from "Der Islam", Band 40, Haft 1;
Berlin, 1964; pp. 35-65.

     Discussion of events from the death of Teimour to Shah
Ismail I.

SAVORY, ROGER M.
     A Curious Episode of Safavid History.
     Offprint of article from "Iran and Islam"; Edinburgh Univer-
sity Press, 1971; pp. 461-472.

     The writer discusses the chaos that ensued after Shah
Tahmasp's death and the growing power of the Qezelbash in
determining his successor, leading to the murder of Shah Ismail II
and the enthronement of Sultan Mohammad Khodabandeh and the rise
of pseudo pretenders to the throne. The writer discusses the
fight for supremacy amongst the various elements, the Tajiks, the
Circassians, the Georgians and the Qezelbash; and the intrigues
in the royal harem amongst the Circassian wives and their off-
spring.

SAVORY, ROGER M.
     British and French Diplomacy in Persia, 1800-1810.
     Photocopy of reprint from "Iran, Journal of the British
Institute of Persian Studies", Vol.10; London, 1972; pp. 31-44.

     The writer concludes that despite feverish diplomatic
activity by the British and the French, the winners were the
Russians who annexed vast territories of Persia.

SAVORY, ROGER M.
     Iran's Cultural Heritage and Its Relevance Today.
     Paper read 24 February 1977 at the University of Texas at
Austin; 26 pp.

     An excellent paper which basically argues that worthwhile
Persian traditions must be maintained in order for it to become
a stable society. The writer also pleads for moderation in Iran's
pursuit of Western technological skills.

SCHACHT, JOSEPH
> Islamic Law in Contemporary States.
> Reprint from "The American Journal of Comparative Law", Vol.
8, No.2; United States, Spring 1959; pp. 133-147.

The inability of Islamic Law to answer questions resulting from the rapid political, social and economic development of certain countries of the Islamic world in the late fifties. Writer: Professor of Arabic and Islamic Studies at Columbia University.

SCHACHT, JOSEPH
> Sociological Aspects of Islamic Law.
> Paper read at the Center for the Study of Law and Society at University of California, Berkeley, 25 April 1963; 27 pp.

SCHAFER, EDWARD H.
> Iranian Merchants in T'ang Dynasty Tales.
> Reprint from "Semetic and Oriental Studies", Vol.XI; University of California, 1951; pp. 403-422.

An interesting and original article dealing with Persian merchants in China from the Sassanian period to 10th century A.D. The Persian merchant was perceived as shrewd, wealthy, generous and "strange". The merchants travelled to China both by overland routes and by sea to the port of Canton; the sea route taking about five months.

SCHIMMEL, ANNEMARIE
> A Sincere Muhammadan's Way to Salvation.
> Photocopy of reprint of article from unknown journal, 1973; pp. 221-242.

The experiences of one Khaje Mir Dard of Delhi (1721-85) "describing the mystical way which led him from his former state of intoxication and poetical exuberance to the quiet and sober attitude of a sincere Muhammadan".

SCHMIDT, J. HEINRICH
> L'Expédition de Ctésiphone en 1931-1932.
> Reprint from "De la Revue Syria, 1934"; Paris, 1934; 23 pp.

SCHNEIDER, LAURA T.
> Landscape in Islamic Art.
> Photocopy of reprint from "Mid East"; Washington, D.C., 1967; illustrated; pp. 8-16.

An interesting article wherein writer states that the landscape for the Persian painter remained basically unchanged from mid 13th to the 18th century; the same stream, the same cloud, etc. The writer argues that the artist did not need to change

890

the landscape even when striving for various effects. Equally
applicable to Arab paintings of 12th through 14th centuries,
although the landscape differed somewhat. Both schools, however,
had a tendency to show only pieces of the background unlike the
complete and detailed aspects in much of Western painting.

SCHROEDER, ERIC
     Iranian Painting - An introduction.
     New York, 1940; 8vo, soft cover; 12 pp. of text and 8 full
page illustrations.

     Written for the Persian Art Exhibition in New York in 1940.

SCHWARTZ, MARTIN
     Iranian Draw - "To Lead Astray".
     Photocopy of reprint from the "Journal of the Royal Asiatic
Society"; London, October 1966; pp. 119-122.

SCHWARTZ, MARTIN
     Miscellanea Iranica.
     Reprint of article from "W.B. Henning Memorial Volume",
Published by Asia Major; London, c.1967; pp. 385-394.

SCIOLINO, ELAINE
     Iran's Durable Revolution.
     Article in "Foreign Affairs", Vol.61, No.4; New York, Spring
1983; pp. 893-920.

     Writer: A knowledgeable journalist covering Iran since the
Revolution. Formerly a reporter for Newsweek, she has visited
Iran several times since 1978. She is presently with the New
York Times.

SCIOLINO, ELAINE
     Documents Detailing Israeli Missile Deal with the Shah.
     "New York Times", April 1986; p. A17.

     The same material covered by Martin Baily of "The Observer"
on 7 March 1986, interspersed with interviews with some of the
participants at the meeting in Israel.

SELECTED GRAPHICS FROM THE PRIVATE COLLECTION OF FARAH PAHLAVI,
HER IMPERIAL MAJESTY, THE SHAHBANOU OF IRAN.
     Tehran, 1976; booklet; illustrated in color; 30 pp.

     Introductions and descriptions of exhibits in both English
and Persian. Catalogue of an exhibition at the Negarestan
Museum, Tehran, held in July 1976 on the occasion of the 50th
anniversary of the Pahlavi Dynasty. Why it should have been
celebrated by Picassos, Legers, and Chagalls is baffling.

A SELECTION FROM THE FOROUGHI COLLECTION
     Iran, 1977; booklet; illustrated in color; 50 pp.

     Introduction and captions to illustrations in parallel
English and Persian. Catalogue of the Reza Abassi Arts Center's
exhibition from the collection of Mohsen Foroughi: "Iranian
artifacts from the 2nd Millenium B.C. to the late 18th Century
A.D.." The best private collection in Iran in its field.

A SELECTION FROM THE COLLECTION OF MOHAMMAD-ALI MASS'OUDI:
SPECIMENS OF IRANIAN CALLIGRAPHY SINCE THE 9th CENTURY A.D.
     Tehran, c.1978; 4to, soft cover; illustrated in color; 94 pp.

     Introduction and catalogue descriptions in both English and
Persian. Catalogue of an exhibition at the Reza Abassi Cultural
and Arts Center in Tehran. One of the superior private collections of Persian calligraphy.

SEPEHRI, SOHRAB
     The Sound of Water's Footsteps.
     Translated by Massud Farzan, published in "Mundus Artium",
Vol.5, Nos.1 and 2; no place of publication indicated; 1972; pp.
14-17.

     Sepehri, better known as a painter, is also one of the
better contemporary poets. A good poem with a very good translation.

SEVEN MILLENIA OF PERSIAN POTTERY; THE GLUCK COLLECTION.
     Japan, 1978; small 4to, soft cover; illustrated, some in
color, and map; 62 pp.

     Catalogue of an exhibition of objects from the book "A
Survey of Persian Handicraft" by Jay and Sumi Gluck held at the
Tekisui Museum, Japan, 2-22 April 1978. Text in Japanese;
captions to illustrations in Japanese and English.

SEVENTH ASIAN GAMES: BULLETIN 2. OFFICIAL REPORT OF APRIL 1973.
     Tehran, 1974; booklet; illustrated; 15 pp.

     In Persian and English. Issued by the Organizing Committee,
Tehran, where the "Asian Olympics" was held.

SHABAN, M.A.
     Khurasan at the Time of the Arab Conquest.
     Photocopy from "Iran and Islam"; no date or place of
publication indicated; pp. 479-490.

     The writer discusses the easternmost region of the
Sassanian Empire, which was the last area conquered by the Arabs

in Central Asia, Marv being designated as its capital.

SHAFA, SHOJAEDDIN
    Facts About the Celebrations of the 2500th Anniversary of
the Founding of the Persian Empire by Cyrus the Great (1971).
    Tehran, 1971; small 8vo, soft cover; illustrations and maps;
31 pp.

    Background history to and plans for the 2500th Anniversary
celebrations in Iran in 1971. A justification for the extrava-
ganza of 1971 by one of the promoters of the event. The writer was
the cultural affairs spokesman for the Court.

THE SHAHANSHAH'S PROPOSAL FOR A NEW OIL PRICING SYSTEM.
    Full page advertisement in the "New York Times", 11 November
1974; p. 18.

    Contains the full text of the Shah's press conference in
Tehran on 2 November 1974, that was designed "to tear down
misinterpretations" in the American press of the Shah's remarks.

SHAHBAZI, A. SH.
    An Achaemenid Symbol, 1. A Farewell to "Fravahr" and
"Ahuramazda".
    Photocopy of reprint from "Archaeologische Mitteilungen aus
Iran", Band 7; Berlin, 1974; pp. 135-144.

SHAHBAZI, A. SH.
    From Parsa to Taxt-E Jamsid.
    Photocopy of reprint from "Archaeologische Mitteilungen aus
Iran", Band 10; Berlin, 1977; pp. 197-207.

SHAHBAZI, A. SH.
    The Traditional Date of Zoroaster, Explained.
    Photocopy of reprint from "BSOAS", London University, Vol.
XL, Part 1; 1977; pp. 25-36.

    The writer argues that Zoroaster lived before 1000 B.C. (as
opposed to the more accepted date of about 500 B.C.).

SHAHBAZI, A. SH.
    Darius Haft Kisvar.
    Photocopy of reprint from "Archaeologische Mitteilungen aus
Iran"; Berlin, 1983; illustrated; pp. 239-246.

SHAHBAZI, A. SH.
    The Birthdate of Firdawsi (3rd Dey 308 Yazdigardi = 3 Jan-
uary 940).
    Photocopy from "Zeitschrift der Deutschen Morbenlandischen
Gesellschaft", Band 134, Haft 1; Wiesbaden, 1984; pp. 98-105.

In an excellent article the writer discusses the two datings
of Ferdowsi's birth from internal evidence within the Shahnama
itself as set forth by J. Mohl and Theodore Noldeke. The writer,
by further analysis, arrives at the date given above, which is
very close to Mohl's date with a minor adjustment for the number
of days in the Yazdigardi year. Noldeke's reasoning supported by
S.H. Taqizadeh influenced the Iranian Government to accept 324
(Y), 934 A.D. as the birth date and the centenary celebrations of
1934 was based on that date. Mohl and Noldeke were the greatest
Western authorities on the Shahnama. Mohl translated the Shahnama
in seven volumes from 1838 to 1878 and Noldeke's work is between
1896 and 1907. Since 1905 all studies on the life of Ferdowsi
are based upon the findings and conclusions of these two scholars.
No other authority on the subject has yet commented on the present
writer's thesis as set out above.

SHAHID, IRFAN
     The Iranian Factor in Byzantium During the Reign of Heraclius.
     An offprint from Dumbarton Oaks papers, No.26; United States,
1972; pp. 295-320.

     The Sassanid influence on Byzantine institutions.

SHAHID, IRFAN
     Theodore Noldeke's "Geschichte der Perser und Araber zur Zeit
der Sasaniden"; An Evaluation.
     Reprint from the "International Journal of Middle East
Studies", No.8; United States, 1977; pp. 117-122.

SHAHID, IRFAN
     Muhammad and Alexander.
     "Third Andrew W. Mellon Distinguished Lecture", delivered at
Georgetown University, 2 May 1978; 11 pp.

     Discussion of two men of military genius who changed the
course of history and shaped the world today.

SHAKED, SHAUL
     Esoteric Trends in Zoroastrianism.
     Photocopy of reprint from "The Israel Academy of Sciences
and Humanities Proceedings", Vol.III, No.7; Jersualem, 1969; 49 pp.

SHAKED, SHAUL
     Eschatology and the Goal of the Religious Life in Sassanian
Zoroastrianism.
     Reprint from "Types of Redemption", conference held at
Jerusalem, 14 to 19 July 1968; Leiden, 1970; pp. 223-230.

SHAKED, SHAUL
     Qumran and Iran: Further Consideration.
     Photocopy of reprint from "Israel Oriental Studies" II; Tel-

Aviv, 1972; pp. 433-444.

SHAKED, SHAUL
Some Legal and Administrative Terms of the Sassanian Period.
Photocopy of reprint from "Acta Iranica"; Leiden, 1975; pp. 213-225.

SHAKED, SHAUL
Jewish and Christian Seals of the Sassanian Period.
"Studies in memory of Gaston Wiet." Photocopy of reprint from "Institute of Asian and African Studies", The Hebrew University of Jerusalem; Jerusalem, 1977; pp. 17-31, and one plate.

SHAKED, SHAUL
Mihr the Judge - I. Middle Persian Miyancig.
Paper sent to be read at the Second International Congress of Mithraic Studies held in Tehran in 1975. Printed in unknown publication c.1980; 31 pp.

SHAKI, MANSOUR
The Social Doctrine of Mazdak in the Light of Middle Persian Evidence.
Reprint from "Archiv Orientalni", Vol.46, No.4; Prague, 1978; pp. 281-306.

SHARIATI, ALI
Selection and/or Election (Vesayat va Showra).
Tehran, 1979; 8vo, soft cover; 16 pp.

Lecture delivered in Mecca c. 1969. The writer maintains that if instead of an oligarchy the people had chosen a successor to the Prophet, 250 years of the religious leadership by Imams would have ensued, and Islamic rule would have been based on political awareness and institutions which would have prevented the schism between Shi'ites and Sunnis.

SHARIATI, ALI
Red Shi'ism.
Tehran, 1979; 8vo, soft cover; 24 pp.

Lecture delivered at Hosseiniye Ershad in September 1972. The term Red Shi'ism refers to the Shi'ite concept of martyrdom.

SHARIATI, ALI
One Followed by an Eternity of Zeros.
Tehran, 1979; 8vo, soft cover; 25 pp.

A lecture at Hosseiniye Ershad c.1972.

SHARIATI, ALI
Yea, Brother! That's the Way It Was.

Tehran, 1979; 8vo, soft cover; 20 pp.

Lecture at Hosseiniye Ershad c.1972.

SHAWCROSS, WILLIAM
Through History with Henry A. Kissinger.
Review of the book "White House Years" by Henry Kissinger
in "Harper's Magazine"; New York, November 1980; pp. 35-44 and
89-97.

The reviewer examines in some detail Kissinger's all too
brief account of that administration's policy towards Iran and
its consequences. In Shawcross's view "the policies themselves,
and Kissinger's account of them, demonstrate well his inadequacies
as both statesman and historian". Shawcross believes that the
Nixon and Kissinger policy of appointing the Shah as the guardian
of the region, promising him every weapon short of nuclear arms
on their visit to Tehran in May 1972, played a part in the
late Shah's loss of touch with his people and eventual fall.
Reviewer: Author of the book "Sideshow: Kissinger, Nixon and the
Destruction of Cambodia".

SHEEAN, VINCENT
Rival Imperialism in Persia: Phases of the New-Old Central
Asian Conflict between Great Britain and Russia.
Article in "Asia"; United States, February 1927; illustrated;
pp. 135-149.

The third of a series of articles on Persia by an American
journalist who argues that even though "British influence in
Persia has very frequently appeared to strike at the independence
of that unfortunate nation", and even though Britain has an
economic grip on Persia by its control of the Anglo-Iranian Oil
Company; nevertheless, British interests in Persia are strategic
and are aimed to "stave off the evil day" that the Russians make
a bid to take over the country. (Refer to writer under Section
A.)

SHEIKHOLESLAMI, A. REZA
The Sale of Offices in Qajar Iran, 1858-1896.
Photocopy from "Iranian Studies"; United States, Spring-
Summer, 1971; pp. 104-118.

The writer treats the subject within the context of a
"Patrimonial State" and as a natural extension of the concept of
an office as a "piece of property". The office holder accepted
his office as merely a personal service to the Shah and hence
had no duty to the state. The three elder sons of Naser e-Din Shah,
Zell ol Soltan, Kamran Mirza and the Crown Prince, later Mozafar
e-Din Shah, at one time administered about four-fifths of the coun-

896

try. The Shah's household got a share of the other offices.·
Intermediate office holders paid the Princes or the chief minister
for the award of an office and in order to recoup the money, the
burden fell on the people in the form of levies and fixed taxes.
An excellent article on a subject that deserves lengthier treatment as the idea of the royal family owning the entire country
and offices being held at the whim of one person continued past
the period under discussion. The "Patrimonial State" lingers on
even today.

SHEPHERD, DOROTHY G.
       Banquet and Hunt in the Medieval Islamic Iconography.
       Article published by the Walters Art Gallery; Baltimore,
1974; pp. 79-92.

SHERER, BILL
       A Psychological Exegesis of the Zoroastrian Creation Myth.
       "Term Paper for Religions and Philosophies of Ancient Iran",
submitted to Professor Shaul Shaked, Hebrew University of
Jerusalem, 19 December 1980; 28 pp.

SHINJI, FUKAI
       A Persian Treasure in the Shoso-in Repository.
       Photocopy from "Japan Quarterly", April-June, Vol.VII, No.2;
Tokyo, 1960; 7 pp. of text and 2 pp. of plates.

       Sassanian art in the collection of the Chinese Emperor in
mid 8th century (refer to article by Edward Schafer on Persian
merchants).

THE SHIRAZ WATER WORKS: SHIRAZ, IRAN.
       New York, June 1951; 8vo, soft cover; illustrated and charts;
33 pp.

       A philanthropic contribution by the late Mohammad Namazi,
who also built a modern hospital in the city of his birth.

SHOJAI, D.A.
       The Structure of Fitzgerald's Rubaiyat of Omar Khayyam.
       Reprint from the "Papers of the Michigan Academy of Science,
Arts and Letters", Vol.LII, 1966; Michigan, 1967; pp. 369-382.

       The writer argues that Fitzgerald was basically interested
in the structure, and meaning was secondary. Furthermore,
Fitzgerald wanted the poem to be understood by the English reader.

SHOJAI, D.A.
       Court Poetry in the Period of Ferdowsi.
       Article from unknown journal, c.1970; pp. 134-139.

SHOJAI, D.A.
The Conflict of Authority as a Unifying Theme in the Shah-
nameh.
Photocopy of reprint from "Literature East and West", Vol.XV,
No.1; Austin, Texas, 1971; pp. 96-107.

An excellent article.

SHOJAI, D.A.
Review of: In Search of Khayyam by Ali Dashti, translated by
L.P. Elwell-Sutton.
Reprint from "Iranian Studies", Vol.V, Nos.2-3; United States,
Spring and Summer 1972; pp. 112-119.

The writer at first doubts the usefulness of the translation
of a mediocre work and ends by finding redeeming features in the
work and the translator's effort.

SHOJAI, D.A.
The Fatal Rage: Heroic Anger in Modern Iranian Fiction.
Paper presented at the joint meeting of the Middle East
Studies Association and the Society for Iranian Studies; Boston,
7 November 1974; 18 pp.

An inquiry into the anger shown in the work of contemporary
writers as a symptom of their alienation from society and their
despair. Works of F. Esfandiary, S. Chubak, B. Alavi and S.
Hedayat are cited.

SHOJAI, D.A.
Western Influence on the Development of Modern Iranian
Literature.
Photocopy of a paper delivered at the Princeton University
Conference on Near Eastern Society in Literature; Princeton, 21 May
1976; 12 pp.

SHOKOOHY, MEHRDAD
Monuments of the Early Caliphates at Darzin in the Kirman
Region.
Article in the "Journal of the Royal Asiatic Society"; London,
1980; illustrations in full page and in text; pp. 1-20.

SHOR, JEAN AND FRANK
We Dwelt in Kashgai Tents.
Article from "The National Geographic Magazine"; United
States, June 1952; illustrations; pp. 805-832.

SHRIMSLEY, ANTHONY
The Young Shah Speaks: "I have decided to sacrifice my life
until my last breath."

"The Mail on Sunday"; London, 2 May 1982; p. 7.

SIMSAR, MUHAMMAD AHMED
Oriental Manuscripts of the John Frederick Lewis Collection in The Free Library of Philadelphia.
Philadelphia, 1937; 8vo; illustrated; unpaginated.

SKJAERVO, O.
Case in Inscriptional Middle Persian. Inscriptional Parthian and the Pahlavi Psalter.
Photocopy from "Studia Iranica", Tome 12, Fasc.2; Leiden, 1983; in two parts: Part 1, pp. 47-62; Part II, pp. 151-181.

SKRINE, C.P.
From Baluchistan to the Mediterranean by Car.
Article in the "Journal of the Royal Central Asian Society", Vol.XIX, Part I; London, January 1932; 8vo, soft cover; pp. 68-88 and maps.

As an appendix, the article contains a "Note on the Preservation of Persian Fauna", by Colonel R.L. Kennion, pp. 86-88.

SMITH, JOHN MASSON Jr.
Mongol and Nomadic Taxation.
Photocopy from "Harvard Journal of Asiatic Studies", Vol.30; United States, 1970; pp. 46-85.

SMITH, MYRON BEMENT
The Wood Mimbar in the Masdjid-i-Ddjami, Naiin.
Reprint from "Ars Islamica", Vol.V, Part 1; no place of publication indicated; 1938; illustrated; pp. 21-35.

Includes an "Epigraphical Notice" by Paul Wittek. The writer in an excellent article describes the mambar in one of the oldest Persian mosques.

SMITH, STEVE
Policy Preferences and Bureaucratic Position: The Case of the American Hostage Rescue Mission.
Article in "Interantional Affairs", Vol.61, No.1; no place of publication indicated; Winter 1984/1985; pp. 9-27.

An article on the background to the decision, the mechanism of decision-making and the participants. Writer: Teacher at University of East Anglia.
In the same issue appears an article by Sir Anthony Parsons on "Aspects of Foreign Policy". Not directly related to Iran, but dealing with British attitudes to "Cultural Diplomacy".

SMITH, TERENCE
Iran: Five Years of Fanaticism.

"The New York Times Magazine"; 12 February 1984; pp. 21-36.

Includes also articles entitled "Paris: The Iranian Exiles" by Richard Z. Chesnoff p. 23, and "Lebanon: The Iranian Presence" by Thomas L. Friedman, p. 34.

SORROUDI, SOROUR
     Akhavan's "The Ending of the Shahnameh": A Critique.
     Photocopy from "Iranian Studies", Vol.II, No.2-3; United States, 1969; pp. 80-99.

Includes the Persian text of the poem with a translation by Soroudi. An analysis of an important poem by one of the leading poets of Contemporary Iran: Mehdi Akhavan Sales known by his pen name of M. Omid. The end of the Shahnama was in reality even worse than imagined by the poet.

SOUTHGATE, MINOO S.
     Portrait of Alexander in Persian Alexander-Romances of the Islamic Era.
     Photocopy of reprint from "Journal of the American Oriental Society", Vol.97, No.3; United States, July-September 1977; pp. 278-284.

While Zoroastrian Persians hated Alexander and his invasion of Persia, Moslem Persians have romanticized him as a brave conqueror and a wise king. The writer presents a composite portrait of Alexander from the study of Persian romance tales. She traces the origin of the legends and argues that when the Persian poets took over, the tales became even more fanciful. Nezami celebrates him not only as a conqueror but also as a prophet; some made him into a Moslem and are joyous at his defeat of Darius; and in Jami, he performs supernatural deeds. An excellent summary and well written. Writer: Baruch College, City University of New York.

SOUTHGATE, MINOO
     The Negative Images of Blacks in Some Medieval Iranian Writings.
     Reprint from "Iranian Studies", Vol.XVII, No.1; United States, Winter 1984; pp. 3-36.

An interesting article but over-stated and goes out of its way to make a point. Negative images of alien nations can be found in any body of literature, beginning with Homer and the classical tragedians. The writer, however, makes a most original point that this "negative attitude" came about despite the fact that Persia was never invaded or attacked from Africa. The Mongols and Turks who invaded and destroyed Persia are never treated with the same degree of resentment.

SPICEHANDLER, EZRA
     The Persecution of the Jews of Esfahan under Shah Abbas II
(1642-1666).
     Reprint from "Hebrew Union College Annual", Vol.XLVI;
Jerusalem, 1975; 26 pp.

     As the title suggests. Later Safavid kings became more
oppressive and persecuted the majority as well as minorities.
The article singles out the sinister influence of Mohammad Baqer
Majlesi. Writer: At Hebrew Union College, Jerusalem.

SPIECKER, KARLHEINZ
     Demag News; 1967.
     The Bulletin of Demag A.G., Duisburg (A German steel and
machine tool company); Duisburg, 1967; large 8vo, soft cover;
illustrated, some in color, and diagrams; 22 pp.

     A report "on the two first Iranian steel rolling mills"
which Demag helped to build.

SPOONER, BRIAN
     Notes on the Toponymy of the Persian Makran.
     Photocopy of reprint from "Iran and Islam"; no place of
publication indicated; c.1970; pp. 517-533 and map.

SPOONER, BRIAN
     Irrigation and Society: The Iranian Plateau.
     Photocopy of revised version of paper delivered at Symposium
on Impact of Irrigation on Society; Long Beach, California,
1 April 1972; 38 pp.

SPRACHMAN, PAUL
     Private Parts and Persian Insult Poetry.
     Offprint of article from "Maledicta"; no place of public-
ation indicated; 1982; pp. 238-248.

     A well written and interesting article.

STEAD, REXFORD
     The Ardabil Carpets.
     Malibu, California, 1974; small 4to, soft cover; illustrated,
some in color; 50 pp.

     Monograph produced by the J. Paul Getty Museum in Malibu,
California. A detailed examination and description of the matched
pair of Ardabil carpets, masterpieces of early Safavid carpet
artistry; one at the Victoria and Albert Museum in London since
the turn of the century, and the other given to the Los Angeles
County Museum by J. Paul Getty in 1953. Writer: Deputy Director
of the Los Angeles County Museum of Art.

STEEL, RONALD
The Makings of Classical Tragedy.
Book review of 3 books: "The Rise and Fall of the Shah" by
Amin Saikal; "Faces in a Mirror: Memoirs from Exile" by Ashraf
Pahlavi; and "The Fall of the Shah" by Fereydoun Hoveyda; from
"The New York Times Book Review"; 1 June 1980; pp. 1 and 38.

Writer: A noted historian, who had previously written, inter
alia, "Pax Americana" and the definitive biography of Walter
Lippmann.

STEIN, SIR AUREL
Alexander's Campaign on the Indian North-West Frontier.
Article in the "Journal of the Central Asia Society", Vol.
XVII, Part 2; London, April 1930; map; pp. 147-170.

STEIN, DONNA, et al.
A Brief Chronology of Pop Art.
Iran, c.1976/7; 6 pp.

Small folding leaflets giving a chronology of important pop-
art exhibitions from 1951-1974 in both Persian and English. Also
an article entitled "Printing Pop Art" in Persian and English.
Distributed by the Tehran Museum of Contemporary Art. An attempt
to justify purchases of Pop Art by Iranian museums.

STEIN, DONNA
Early Photography in Iran.
Reprint from "History of Photography: an International
Quarterly", Vol.7, No.4; United States, October-December 1983;
illustrated; pp. 257-291.

An interesting and original contribution.

STERN, FRITZ
The Giant from Afar: Visions of Europe from Algiers to Tokyo.
Photocopy from "Foreign Affairs"; New York, October 1977;
pp. 111-135.

The writer visited various capital cities, including Tehran,
for a perspective of the West from the East. Writer: A distinguished historian, presently professor of history at Columbia
University. This article was intended to form the nucleus of a
never completed book.

STERN, S.M.
Yaqub the Coppersmith and Persian National Sentiment.
Photocopy of reprint from "Iran and Islam"; no place of
publication indicated; c.1965; pp. 535-555.

The writer argues that of the nations conquered by the Arabs,

the Persians had the strongest sense of national identity. The
writer recounts the first revolt against the conquering Arabs
by Yaqub Lays of Sistan during the second half of 9th century A.D.
Persian writers and historians immediately turned Yaqub into a
descendent of the pre-Islamic kings of Iran. The writer also
discusses the popular poetry of the era glorifying Yaqub.

STEVENS, MARY ANNE (edited by)
      The Orientalists: Delacroix to Matisse; European Painters
in North Africa and the Near East.
      Catalogue of an exhibition of the Royal Academy of Arts in
London, 24 March to 27 May 1984; illustrated, some in color;
256 pp.

      The best exhibition to date of such works.

STEVENS, SIR ROGER
      European Visitors to the Safavid Court.
      Photocopy of a paper delivered at a public lecture on 22
January 1974; Great Britain; 30 pp.

      An excellent paper. The writer is specially conversant with
early travel books. (Refer to Section A under writer's name.)

STONE, I.F.
      War for Oil?
      Article from "The New York Review of Books"; 6 February 1975;
pp. 7-10.

      In the aftermath of the OPEC oil price rise in November 1973,
Robert Tucker wrote an article in "Commentary" advocating the
break-up of OPEC by seizing the Arabian oil fields along the
Persian Gulf, i.e. outright war against the Arabs. Even Iran,
considered by Tucker as a friend of Israel, was not secure or
exempt from his wrath. A frightening scenario proposed by the
neo-conservatives. I.F. Stone, one of the most clearheaded
journalists of his age, points out the absurdity of it all.

STRAUS, RICHARD, and WOLLACK, KEN
      Treading Softly in the Volatile Gulf.
      Article in the "Los Angeles Times"; 27 May 1984; p. 1.

STRONACH, DAVID and YOUNG, T. CUYLER Jr.
      Three Seljuq Tomb Towers.
      Photocopy of reprint from "Iran, Journal of the British
Institute of Persian Studies", Vol.IV; London, 1966; 20 pp. of
text, illustrated in text and 24 pp. of plates.

THE STUDY OF MODERN PERSIA IN THE UNIVERSITY OF CAMBRIDGE: II
      Typewritten manuscript of a lecture, principally a descript-

ion of the career of Professor Reynold Alleyne Nicholson, Professor of Arabic at Cambridge. The name of the lecturer, venue and date is unidentified; c. late 1930's; 5 pp.

SULLIVAN, WILLIAM H.
Dateline Iran: The Road Not taken.
Photocopy of article from "Carnegie Endowment - Foreign Policy No. 40" (title of article is pencilled in); United States, c. end of 1979; pp. 57-63.

An account of political events within Iran, and the conflict between the U.S. State Department and National Security Council Advisor Zbigniew Brzezinski in the winter months of 1978/79, as seen from the U.S. Ambassador's point of view. The road advocated was set forth too late, the writer having gone on home leave June-August 1978. The proposal was set forth in late November when the country was coming apart. (Refer to Section A under writer's name.

T

TAFAZZOLI, AHMAD
     A List of Trades and Crafts in the Sassanian Period.
     Reprint of article from "Archaeologische Mitteilungen aus
Iran, Neue Folge", Band 7; Berlin, 1974; pp. 191-196.

     An excellent article which describes the four classes of
society in the Sassanian period: 1- The Priests, 2- The Warriors,
3- Scribes and Bureaucrats and 4- Artisans and Peasants. As in
modern times, the priests (in this case, Zoroastrian) considered
themselves the most important and indispensible part of society.

TAFAZZOLI, AHMED
     Some Middle-Persian Quotations in Classical Arabic and
Persian Texts.
     Photocopy of reprint from "Fondation Culturelle Iranienne";
Louvain, 1974; pp. 337-349.

TAGLIABUE, JOHN
     Iran-U.S. Arbitration Opening: Tribunal to Sift Claims of
Companies.
     "New York Times"; c.1982; Business Section; pp. D1 and D8.

TAL'-WI-WI AND TAL'-WI-WI IN THE PINES.
     Arizona, c.1949; unpaginated.

     Illustrated spiral-bound brochure of an Arizona ranch and
farm owned by Dale Bumstead; the brochure is dedicated to
Mohammad Reza Shah on the occasion of his stay as a guest in 1949.

TALES AND LEGENDS IN PERSIAN MUGHAL AND TURKISH MINIATURES.
     Catalogue of an Exhibition from 3 September 1979 to 2 March
1980; London, 1979; 5 pp.

TAQIZADEH, SEYED HASSAN
     The Word Suno in the Vendidad.
     Photocopy of reprint from "BSOS", London University, Vol.
IX, Part 2; c.1936; pp. 321-325.

TAQIZADEH, SEYED HASSAN
     An Ancient Persian Practice Preserved by a Non-Iranian
People - The Mandaean Calendar.
     Photocopy of reprint from "BSOS", London University, Vol.
IX, Part 3; c.1936; pp. 603-619.

TAQIZADEH, SEYED HASSAN
     Various Eras and Calendars Used in the Countries of Islam.
     Photocopy of reprint from "BSOS", London University, Vol.
IX, Part 1; c.1937; First Part; pp. 107-132.

TAQIZADEH, SEYED HASSAN

Various Eras and Calendars Used in the Countries of Islam.
Photocopy of reprint from "BSOS", London University, Vol.X,
Part I; c.1937; Second Part; pp. 903-922.

TAQIZADEH, SEYED HASSAN
Old Iranian Calendars.
London, 1938; 8vo; 57 pp.

A short "study of the history of the Iranian system of time-
reckoning". Published in book form but included amongst the
articles as it relates to and is, in essence, a continuation of
articles on the same subject by the writer included herein.

TAQIZADEH, SEYED HASSAN
The Iranian Festivals Adopted by the Christians and Condemned
by the Jews.
Reprint from "BSOAS", London University, Vol.X, Part 3; 1941;
pp. 632-653.

TAQIZADEH, SEYED HASSAN
The Early Sassanians - Some Chronological Points Which
Possibly Call for Revision.
Reprint from "BSOAS", London University, Vol.XI, Part I; 1943;
pp. 6-51.

The writer, basing his study on contemporary sources, including
the calendar, suggests new dates for the reigns of Ardeshir I and
Shapur I.

TAQIZADEH, SEYED HASSAN
The "Era of Zoroaster".
Photocopy of reprint from the "Journal of the Royal Asiatic
Society"; London, April 1947; pp. 33-40.

The writer establishes the date of Alexander's conquest, the
Selucid rule in Persia, the ascension of the Parthians and the
defeat of Ardavan, the last of the Parthian kings, by Ardashir,
the founder of the Sassanid dynasty. The article is solely
concerned with the date of the "coming of the religion" in
Sassanian times and not with the date of Zoroaster's birth, etc.

TAQIZADEH, SEYED HASSAN
The Old Persian Calendars Again.
Photocopy of reprint from "BSOAS", London University, Vol.
XIV, Part 3; 1952; pp. 600-611.

TAQIZADEH, SEYED HASSAN
The Background of the Constitutional Movement in Azarbaijan.
Reprint from the "Middle East Journal"; United States, Autumn
1960; translated by Nikki R. Keddie, annotated by N. Keddie and

Abdol Hossein Zarinkoub; pp. 456-465.

Text of a speech delivered at the Tabriz National Library in April 1959 on the 50th anniversary of Howard Baskerville's death, a young American who was killed fighting for the Constitutionalists in the revolution of 1906-1909; a shortened version of a speech Taqizadeh had delivered in Tehran some two years earlier at the Mehregan CLub. The earlier version, although covering less than 70 pages is one of the most comprehensive and perceptive accounts of the events leading up to the 1906 Revolution.

S.H. Taqizadeh (1878-1970) was, for brief periods in his life, one of the leading political figures of 20th century Iran. An intelligent and erudite man, he is considered a scholar of distinction, although he wrote very little, mostly articles in a Persian paper in Berlin (Kaveh) during World War I and the years immediately following the war. He was one of the most important political figures in the Constitutional Movement and was elected to the first Iranian Parliament from Tabriz. When Mohammad Ali Shah ordered the shelling of the Parliament and arrested and murdered the prominent Constitutionalists, Taqizadeh sought refuge at the British Legation in Tehran and later fled to Turkey. After a brief return, he went into self-imposed exile in Europe, where he spent almost three decades, some in official capacities. He served briefly as Minister of Finance during the ill-fated extension of the Oil Concession in 1933. He served as Minister to London during the World War II years and the years immediately thereafter. Upon his return he served as a Senator and President of the Iranian Senate. His importance on the political scene rested to some degree on his seniority in the Freemasonry hierarchy. A major contribution of Taqizadeh was his sponsorship and encouragement of young Persian scholars. Altogether a controversial man with an uneven political record not helped by some debatable political decisions at crucial moments of his life.

TAQIZADEH, SEYED HASSAN
       The Dates of Mani's Life.
       Reprint from "Asia Major, New Series", Vol.VI, Part I; London, c.1960; po. 106-121.

       "Translated from the Persian, introduced and concluded by W.B. Henning.

TARAPOR, MAHRUKH
       Islamic Calligraphy.
       United States, 1979; booklet; illustrated; 8 pp.

       Published by the Asia Society Inc. and prepared to accompany the exhibition, at the Asia House, New York, 11 January-11 March 1979. An inferior exhibition.

TARN, W.W.
Selucid - Parthian Studies.
Reprint from "Proceedings of the British Academy", Vol.XVI;
London, 1930; 33 pp.

Re the Chinese nomads who attacked northeast Persia in the
second century B.C.

TAVAKKOLI, A.
The First Constitution of the Ministry of Foreign Affairs
Drafted by Mirza Saiid Khan Mutamin ol Mulk in 1881-1882.
Reprint from the "Bulletin of the Ministry of Foreign
Affairs",1, 2; Tehran, 1951; 7 pp.

A very brief history.

TEHRAN TIMES
37-year oppression in Iran; 18 months of Shah's exile end.
Photocopy from the "Tehran Times"; 28 July 1980.

TEHRANIAN, MAJID
The Curse of Modernity: The Dialectics of Modernization and
Communication.
Reprint from the "International Social Science Journal", Vol.
XXXII, No.2; United States, 1980; pp. 247-263.

Well written and often witty but inconclusive and covers
familiar grounds.

TEIXIDOR, JAVIER
The Kingdom of Adiabene and Hatra.
Reprint from "Berytus", Vol.XVII; Copenhagen 1967; 11 pp.

TEXTILE MUSEUM JOURNAL, VOL.III, NO.3.
Washington, D.C., December 1972; illustrations in text; 82
pp.

Contains series of articles and book reviews on, inter alia,
"Symbolic Meanings in Oriental Rug Patterns" and a review of
"The Turkaman of Iran" by Anthony N. Landreau.

TEXTILE MUSEUM JOURNAL, VOL.III, NO.4.
Washington, D.C., December 1973; illustrated and map; 48 pp.

Contains, articles on "Anatolian Rugs" and on
"Kurdish Kilim Weaving in the Van-Hakkari District of Eastern
Turkey".

THACKSTON, W.M. Jr.
Introductory Notes to Persian Prosody.
Photocopy of article from unknown publication; no date; 37 pp.

THORDARSON, FRIDRIK
       Ossetic and Caucasian - Stray Notes.
       Photocopy of reprint from the "Norwegian Journal of Linguistics", University of Oslo, Vol.27, No.1; 1973; pp. 85-92.

       Writer: Professor of Persian Studies at University of Oslo.

THORDARSON, FRIDRIK
       Georg Morgenstierne, 1892-1978.
       Reprint from "Hommages et Opera Minora", Vol.XXII; Leiden, 1981; 7 pp.

THURGOOD, LIZ
       The "King of Kings" who ruled by tyranny.
       "The Guardian"; London, 27 July 1980; illustrated; p. 11.

       A review of the Shah's life and rule, on the day after his death. The writer, an English girl who worked for the "Tehran Journal", an English language newspaper published in Tehran. She later became a "stringer" for the Guardian. An early devotee of the Revolution, her coverage of events in 1978-1979 showed her bias.

TIKKU, GIRHARI L.
       Mysticism in Kashmir in the 14th and 15th Centuries.
       Reprint from "The Muslim World", Hartford Seminary Foundation, Vol.LIII, No.3; Hartford, Connecticut, July 1963; pp. 226-233.

       Writer: Taught at U.C.L.A.

TIKKU, GIRHARI L.
       Some Socio-Religious Themes in Modern Persian Fiction.
       Photocopy from unknown publication; c.1970; pp. 165-179.

       In an excellent article, the writer demonstrates how, from the turn of the century, the molla in Persian fiction is depicted as a hypocrite or a rogue in the mold of a Tartuff.

TIME MAGAZINE
       Man of the Year: Mohammad Mossadegh.
       7 January 1952; pp. 18-21.

       A misleading and highly biased description of the subject. The article even questions Iran's ownership of and right to nationalize its oil.

TIME MAGAZINE
       25 August 1967; p. 45.

       An article on an exhibition of Persian art at the Victoria

and Albert Museum.

<u>TIME MAGAZINE</u>
      Oil, Grandeur and a Challenge to the West.
      Iran/Cover Story; 4 November 1974; pp. 28-38.

     Time considered the Shah as one of the "three or four" most important people in the world (after the oil price rise).

<u>TIME MAGAZINE</u>
      Iran: Cramping the Shah's Style.
      16 February 1976; p. 27.

     Concentrates on arms purchases by Iran and on the growing opposition inside the country.

<u>TIME MAGAZINE</u>
      Torture as Policy: The Network of Evil.
      Human Rights/Cover Story, 16 August 1976; pp. 11-14.

     An investigation of the official use of torture around the world, including Iran. A terrifying report.

<u>TIME MAGAZINE</u>
      The Shah's Divided Land.
      18 September 1978; pp. 32-40.

     Written in the aftermath of "Black Friday". Also includes an interview with the Shah by Strobe Talbott.

<u>TIME MAGAZINE</u>
     Another Crisis for the Shah: A grim week of strikes, slow-downs and lingering discontent.
      13 November 1978; pp. 34-35.

     The editors of Time were just becoming aware that something serious was happening in Iran.

<u>TIME MAGAZINE</u>
      The Shah's fight for survival.
      Show-down in Iran/Cover Story, 20 November 1978; pp. 12-16.

     The issue includes an article by Time's State Department correspondent entitled "Carter's Urgent Priority: Heading Off Chaos". It is about this point that the West began to think the "impossible" may happen.

<u>TIME MAGAZINE</u>
      Iran: The Military is in Charge.
      27 November 1978; pp. 23-24.

The issue includes an article entitled "The Shah Is Not Giving Up" on the same page. An all too brief a period of renewed optimism.

TIME MAGAZINE
Iran: Relative calm, but the test is yet to come.
4 December 1978; p. 39.

The issue includes an article entitled "Who Lost Iran?".

TIME MAGAZINE
Iran: Entering a Dangerous Hour.
11 December 1978; pp. 28 and 31.

Time saw the Ashura marches as fateful.

TIME MAGAZINE
The Weekend of Crisis.
Iran/Cover Story, 18 December 1978; pp. 8-12.

A summary written by Strobe Talbott.

TIME MAGAZINE
Hard Choices in Tehran.
25 December 1978; pp. 32-33, 37-38.

"Like his base of support, the Shah's options are narrowing fast." Time now "seriously" doubts whether the Shah can survive and suggests that his departure may restore calm.

TIME MAGAZINE
The Khomaini Era Begins.
Cover Story, 12 February 1979; pp. 32-40.

Khomaini on the cover. The word "Ayatullah" makes it into an English Dictionary. Time is ambivalent and hazy about its subject.

TIME MAGAZINE
Guns, Death and Chaos.
Cover Story, 26 February 1979; pp. 26-33.

"Iran: Anarchy and Exodus." A sense of surprise runs throughout the article. Time editors had apparently expected otherwise.

TIME MAGAZINE
Blackmailing the U.S.
Cover Story, 19 November 1979; pp. 18-22.

The taking of the hostages and Khomaini's declaration,
"America is the Great Satan". An examination of U.S. policy
towards the Shah from the fifties through the seventies.

TIME MAGAZINE
Iran: The Test of Wills.
Cover Story, 26 November 1979; pp. 14-28.

An analysis of the few options open to the U.S.

TIME MAGAZINE
Angry Attacks on America.
Cover Story, 3 December 1979; pp. 10-21.

"Grapes of Wrath." Article questions U.S. policy toward
Iran from the World War II period.

TIME MAGAZINE
The Storm Over the Shah.
Cover Story, 10 December 1979; pp. 16-27.

The last appearance of the Shah on a Time cover. The magazine,
a supporter of the former regime, also seems to be abandoning
the Shah.

TIME MAGAZINE
The Hostages in Danger.
17 December 1979; pp. 12-19.

Reports on the Shah's new book, Iranian students, the
theology of Khomaini, and a Time Essay entitled "Islam against
the West?" pp. 20 and 23.

TIME MAGAZINE
Man of the Year: Ayatullah Khomeini.
7 January 1980; pp. 8-32.

Cover picture and cover story entitled "The Mystic Who Lit
The Fires of Hatred: Iran's Ayatullah Khomeini seized his nation
and shook all Islam". Includes an interview with Khomaini.

TIME MAGAZINE
War in The Persian Gulf.
Cover Story, 6 October 1980; pp. 10-17.

Iraq's invasion and the need by Iran for its "frozen funds"
in the U.S. and Europe.

TIME MAGAZINE
Will The Gulf Explode?

Cover Story, 7 October 1980; pp. 12-21.

An article describing Iraq's surprise at how Iran had not caved in. Time is equally surprised.

TIME MAGAZINE
Hostage Breakthrough.
Cover Story, 26 January 1981; pp. 12-24.

TIME MAGAZINE
Blurred View from the Embassy: Captured papers reveal a confused U.S. Policy about the Shah.
15 February 1982; p. 29.

So far 51 volumes of documents seized at the time of the take-over of the U.S. Embassy have been published. (Refer to "Documents from the Nest of Spies" under Section A.)

TIME MAGAZINE
444 Days of Agony: The Fall of the Shah: Keeping Faith, Part II.
18 October 1982; Special Section; pp. 24-41.

An excerpt from former President Jimmy Carter's book, "Keeping Faith". The selected extracts deal with the Iranian hostage crisis.

THE TIMES
Special Art Number; London, 5 January 1931; 24 pp.

Issued to coincide with the International Exhibition of Persian Art held at Burlington House in London.

THE TIMES
The Shah in Rome - No Definite Plans for Future.
London, 19 August 1953.

Written on the eve of "operation Ajax", the article depicts Mosaddeq as a tool of the Communists. A second article titled "Republic Demanded - Communist Statement" is on the same page.

THE TIMES
Popular Will in Persia.
London, 24 August 1953; p. 5.

"The rising of August 19 can be considered unprecedented in Persian history. It stands in sharp contrast with the artificial risings staged by the pro Moussadek groups and backed by the Tudeh Party ..."

THE TIMES
      Persian Attitude to Britain. General Zahedi to "Go Slow".
London, 26 August 1953; p. 6.

      General Zahedi is depicted as the "man of the people".

THE TIMES
      Investment in Iran: A Special Report.
Special Section; London, 25 October 1974; illustrated; pp.
I-XII.

THE TIMES
      Tehran: A Special Report on one of the leading business
centres of the Middle East.
Special Section; London, 6 May 1977; illustrated; pp. I-XII.

      A series of articles by "The Times" correspondents on the best
sources for British firms to earn their share of "petrodollars".

THE TIMES
      Iran Leader Pledges Revolution 'export'.
London, 5 February 1980; p. 7.

TOGAN, ZEKI VELIDI
      The Earliest Translation of the Quran into Turkish.
Photocopy of reprint from the "Review of the Institute of
Islamic Studies", Vol.IV, Parts 1-2; Istanbul, 1964; 19 pp.

TOLSTOV, S.P.
      Scythians of the Aral Sea Area and Khorezm.
Photocopy of paper delivered at the XXV International Congress of Orientalists, Moscow, 1960; 67 pp.

TOUMA, HABIB HASSAN
      The 'Maqam' Phenomenon: An Improvisation Technique in the
Music of the Middle East.
Reprint from the "Journal of Ethnomusicology", Vol.XV, No.1;
1971; pp. 38-48.

      The Arab "maqam" is the Persian "dastgah".

TOURIST BROCHURES.
      1.   Khuzistan, Iran: Cultural Holiday in the Sun; Tehran,
          1974.
      2.   Iran: Ancient Persia; Tehran, 1974.
      3.   Discover Persia's Desert Cities; c.1974.
      4.   Caviar Coast: Northern Iran; Tehran, 1974.
      5.   Iran: Persepolis: Persia (in French); c.1974.
      6.   Isfahan, Iran is real Persia; Tehran, 1974.
      7.   Shiraz, Iran: Gateway to the city of roses and poetry;
          Tehran, 1974.

914

All illustrated, folding tourist brochures.

TREASURES OF THE ASHMOLEAN MUSEUM.
Oxford, 1970; illustrated, some in color, and index; 96 pp.

"An illustrated souvenir of Art, Archaeology and Numismatics from photographs by Olive Godwin, Michael Dudley and Caroline Carpenter." The Persian collection, although limited, is very good.

TSUGE, GEN'ICHI
Rhythmic Aspects of the "Avaz" in Persian Music.
Reprint from the "Journal of Ethnomusicology", Vol.14; No.2; May 1970; pp. 205-227.

A study of the rhythmic core of Persian music.

TURNER, LOUIS and BEDORE, JAMES
The Trade Politics of Middle Eastern Industrialization.
"Foreign Affairs", Vol.57; No.2; New York, Winter 1978/9; pp. 306-322.

The article decribes some preliminary findings and concentrates specifically on "Saudi and Iranian ambitions in petrochemicals and refining" as they are the leading OPEC oil producers. It states that "within these two chosen industries the Saudis and Iranians are most likely to emerge as significant exporters of industrial products". Authors: Members of the research staff at the Royal Institute of International Affairs (Chatham House), London.

TYLER, ANNE
Your Place is Empty.
Short story from "The New Yorker" magazine, 22 November 1976; pp. 45-54.

The story of an Iranian mother-in-law's first visit to her son and American daughter-in-law in the U.S.. Extremely well written and the writer catches all the nuances and moods.

UTAS, BO
	Notes on Some Public and Semi-Public Libraries in the Near
and Middle East Containing Persian and Other Moslem Manuscripts.
	Photocopy from "Acta Orientalia", XXXIII; Leiden, 1971;
pp. 169-192.

	Turkey, Iran, Afghanistan and Pakistan. A useful article,
probably the first on the subject in English. There are, however,
several important omissions of libraries in Iran and Turkey.

V

VANDEN BERGHE, L.
Le Tombeau Achémenide de Buzpar.
Reprint from "Vorderasiatische Archaologie"; Berlin, c.1962;
illustrated in text and separate plates; pp. 243-258.

VEYSEY, ARTHUR
The Party's on the Shah.
Article from "The Chicago Tribune Magazine", 10 October 1971;
illustrated; pp. 45-47.

Subtitle: "1971: The Ruler of Iran is all set to foot the
bill for his country's 2,500th birthday."

VIEILLE, PAUL
Iran and Islam.
"Gazelle Review of Literature on the Middle East", No.9;
London, 1981; 8vo, soft cover; 72 pp.

Series of book reviews including two by Paul Vieille and
M. Nishabouri on recent publications on Iran and two by Karen
Dawisha and Elizabeth Monroe on recent publications on the
Persian Gulf.

WALLACE, MIKE

The Shah of Iran on Israel, Corruption, Torture.
Photocopy of article from unidentified American newspaper;
22 October 1976.

Excerpts from the transcript of a Mike Wallace interview
with the Shah to be screened on CBS's "Sixty Minutes" program.
A damaging interview by the Shah.

WASHINGTON POST

President Greets Shah as 300 Picket in Park.
Friday, 16 May 1975; p. A2.

The issue includes the above article by staff writer Martha
Hamilton, and another entitled "Top-Level Talks Set for Shah",
without a byline.

WEISKOPF, MICHAEL

The Kuh Dasht Hoard and the Parthian "Dark Ages".
Reprint from "ANSMN"; United States, 1981; pp. 125-152 and
3 plates.

An article describing Parthian coins found in Lorestan.

WEISS, GERHARD H.

In Search of Silk: Adam Olearius' Mission to Russia and
Persia.
Minneapolis, Minnesota, 1983; 8vo, soft cover; 42 pp. and
map.

A lecture delivered in May 1982 in Minneapolis. The work
follows Olearius' account of his journey as secretary to the
Holstein Mission to Russia and Persia under the patronage of the
Court of Frederick III, the Duke of Holstein, in the 1630's.
(See Section A under Olearius.) Writer: Member of the Department
of German, University of Minnesota.

WELCH, ANTHONY

Painting and Patronage Under Shah Abbas I.
Photocopy of paper prepared for the Isfahan Colloquium at
Harvard University, 21-24 January 1974; 41 pp. and bibliography.

In an excellent article, the writer discusses the overwhelming influence of Shah Abbas on art during his rule. Shah
Abbas was more interested in the "arts of official connection",
i.e. architecture, city planning; and "arts of economic utility",
i.e. ceramics, textiles and carpets; than in the more personal
"arts of the book". The writer maintains, however, that during
the period many painters came forth and created what is now known
as the "Esfahan style, even though they are not of a homogenous

nature". The writer adds that the diversity of style and the heterogeneous nature of the paintings can be attributed to two factors: "The wide ranging personal taste of the king and the emergence of other patrons."

WELCH, STUART C.
78 Pictures from a World of Kings, Heroes and Demons: The Houghton Shahnameh.
The Metropolitan Museum of Art Bulletin, Vol.XXIX, No.8; April 1971; illustrated plus colored illustrations on front and back cover; pp. 341-357.

WELCOME TO IRAN
Tehran, c.1975; 8vo, soft cover; illustrated in color plus maps (one folding); 38 pp.

A tourist handbook and guide to the "Asian Highway", the Iranian section of which runs along the northern border of the country from Bazargan on the Turkish frontier to the Afghan border post of Kalkaleh, and includes the principle towns along the route. Published by the Iranian Ministry of Information and Tourism as part of the "South Asia Tourism Year" of 1975.

WERTIME, JOHN T.
Flat-Woven Structures Found in Nomadic and Village Weavings from the Near East and Central Asia.
Reprint from the "Textile Museum Journal", Vol.18; United States, 1979; illustrated; pp. 33-54.

WERYHO, JAN W.
Sistani-i-Persian Folklore.
Reprint from "Indo-Iranian Journal", Vol.5, No.4; Leiden, c.1965; pp. 266-307.

Writer: Professor at McGill University, Montreal.

WERYHO, JAN W.
"Persian" versus "Iranian" (The Word Fars as an Ethnic Term).
Reprint of article published by the Institute of Islamic Studies, McGill University, Montreal, 1973; 19 pp.

In a very cautious and inconclusive article the writer states that "Persia" and "Iran" are synonymous. He maintains, however, that there is a difference in the terms "Persian" and "Iranian", since the term Persian cannot apply to all the subjects of Iran. The distinctions are not entirely made clear.

WEYMOUTH, LALLY
1-	"Iraqi Leader Charges U.S. Prolongs War."
Article in the "Los Angeles Times", 13 May 1984; pp. 1 and 3.

2-   "How Iraq is Trying to Drag Others into the War."
      Article in the "Los Angeles Times", 20 May 1984; pp. 1 and 3.
3-   "How Soviets Figure in Iraqi Plans."
      Article in the "Los Angeles Times", 27 May 1984; pp. 1 and 3.

      The writer's concern is the effect of the war on Israel.

WHITLEY, ANDREW; GRAHAM, ROBERT and HOUSEGO, DAVID
      Three articles by the foreign staff of "The Financial Times"
under the general heading "Former Financial Times correspondents
in Tehran look back on the life of the Shah and provide personal
views of his style of government".
      "The Financial Times", London, 28 July 1980; p. 2.

WINDENGREN, GEO.
      The Mithraic Mysteries in the Greco-Roman World with Special
Regard to Their Iranian Background.
      Reprint from "Accademia Nazionale dei Lincei", Vol.76; Rome,
1966; pp. 433-455.

      Writer: Professor at Upsala University, Sweden.

WINDENGREN, GEO.
      The Principle of Evil in Eastern Religions.
      Photocopy of reprint of article published by Northwestern
University Press; Evanston, Illinois, 1967; pp. 21-55.

WINDENGREN, GEO.
      Primordial Man And Prostitute: A Zervanite Motif in the
Sassanid Avesta.
      Reprint from "Studies in Mysticism and Religion"; Jerusalem,
1967; pp. 337-352.

WINDENGREN, GEO.
      Reflections on the Origin of the Mithraic Mysteries.
      Photocopy of reprint from "Perennitas"; Athens, c.1970;
pp. 647-668.

WINDENGREN, GEO.
      Speculations in the Rasa'il Ikhwan Al-Safa and Some Hurufi
Texts.
      Reprint from "Macrocosmos-Microcosmos", Instituto Di Studi
Filosofici; Rome, 1980; pp. 297-312.

WILBER, DONALD N.
      Language and Society: The Case of Iran.
      Reprint from "Behavior Science Notes", Vol.2; No.1; 1967;
pp. 22-30.

      The writer makes an interesting point that the language used

in Persia reflects those patterns of behavior which have been
time tested to withstand the stresses and hardships resulting
from centuries of warfare and foreign domination. The writer,
however, undercuts his arguments by citing wrong examples, and
by assigning non-existant meanings to words, etc.

WILKE, ULFERT
        Calligraphic Ceramics from Eastern Iran.
        United States, 1974; 4to, soft cover; 32 pp. and 38 full
page ceramics illustrations, all in black and white.

        Catalogue of an exhibition at the University of Iowa Museum
of Art, Iowa City, 7 November-15 December 1974. All 10th century
pottery from Naishabur and an excellent collection.

WILKINSON, CHARLES K.
        The Achaemenian Remains at Qasr-I-Abu Nasr.
        Reprint from the "Journal of Near Eastern Studies", Vol.XXIV,
No.4; Chicago, October 1965; pp. 341-345 text and 12 pp. of
plates.

        The site discussed is some 30 kilometers from Persepolis.

WILKINSON, CHARLES K.
        Christian Remains from Naishapur.
        Reprint from "Forschungen Zur Kunst Asiens"; Istanbul, 1970;
illustrated; pp. 79-87.

        In an interesting article it is convincingly argued that
there were Christians in Naishabur in the 9th, 10th and 11th
centuries, and that there was relative freedom of religion
as evidenced by the symbols of different religious faiths appear-
ing on Naishabur pottery.

WILLIAMS, MAYNARD OWEN
        Afghanistan Makes Haste Slowly.
        From the "National Geographic Magazine"; Washington, D.C.,
December 1933; illustrations and photographs; pp. 731-769.

        The writer had written extensively on Central Asia and
Afghanistan.

WILLIAMS, RICHARD
        Russia's Muslim Neighbor.
        Article from "The Listener"; London, 21 September 1950; pp.
365-366.

        Writer: The BBC's Middle East Correspondent.

WILSON, SIR ARNOLD T.

History of the Mission of the Fathers of the Society of
Jesus, Established in Persia by The Reverend Father Alexander of
Rhodes.
Reprint from "BSOS", University of London, Vol.III, Part 4;
1925; 8vo, soft cover; pp. 675-706.

A translation of a work compiled by Father Jacqeus de
Machault and published in Paris, 1659.

WINDFUHR, GERNOT L.
A Linguist's Criticism of Persian Literature.
Reprint from "Neue Methodologie in der Iranistik"; Wiesbaden,
1974; pp. 331-352.

Writer: University of Michigan at Ann Arbor.

WINDFUHR, G.L.
Isoglosses: A Sketch on Persians and Parthians, Kurds and
Medes.
Reprint from "Acta Iranica"; Leiden, 1975; pp. 457-472.

WINDFUHR, GERNOT L.
Vohu Manah: A Key to the Zoroastrian World - Formula.
Reprint of article published by the Department of Near
Eastern Studies, University of Michigan "In Honor of George G.
Cameron", 1976; pp. 269-310.

THE WOMEN'S ORGANIZATION OF IRAN: 1966-1969.
Tehran, c.1969; small 8vo, soft cover; 19 pp.

A brief history of the status of women in Iran and of the
objectives and activities of the Women's Organization of Iran
since its founding in 1966 under the presidency of Princess Ashraf
Pahlavi.

THE WOMEN'S ORGANIZATION OF IRAN: (THE) CONSTITUTION.
Tehran, c.1969; small 8vo, soft cover; 12 pp.

WONDERS OF THE AGE
Catalogue of an exhibition of Persian Safavid Paintings; 10
August-28 October 1979; London 1979; 3 pp.

Published by the British Library.

WORLD OF ISLAM.
Great Britain, 1976; booklet; illustrated and map; 32 pp.

The story of Islam told in form of numerous small illustrations, prepared for children.

WORLD OF ISLAM FESTIVAL 1976: CALENDAR OF EVENTS
        Great Britain, 1976; small booklet; 36 pp.

        Calendar of principle events: Exhibitions, concerts, read-
ings, lectures, seminars, conferences, publications, films, and
fringe events during the Festival held in London, April-July 1976.

WORLD NEWS AND COMMENTARY
        Iran: Trying So Much So Fast.
        Cover Story; United States, 12 January 1976; illustrated; pp.
6-9

        Includes an interview with Iranian Prime Minister Amir Abbas
Hoveyda, entitled "Iran Wants the West's Technology, Not Its
Ideology".

WREN, CHRISTOPHER and SCHANCHE, DON
        Shah, 60, Dies in Exile in Cairo.
        "The International Herald Tribune", 28 July 1980; pp. 1, 2,
4 and 7.

        Articles on the Shah's death, his reign, reactions in the
U.S. and Tehran, funeral arrangements, plus editorial.

WRIGHT, SIR DENIS
        The Failed Despot.
        Cover and article from "The Spectator"; London, 2 August
1980; pp. 6-7.

        Written soon after Mohammad Reza Shah's death in Cairo as an
obituary. The writer states that "the Shah lived too long. Had
he died in 1972 or 1973, he would have gone down in history as
one of the greater post World War II leaders ... but he will
be remembered as the king who failed, the despot who brushed
aside all the unpalatable advice, surrounded himself with
sycophants and undesirables, tolerated massive corruption amongst
those closest to him, and flouted human rights to such an extent
that he was eventually rejected by his own people and forced to
abandon a country all but ruined by policies of his own making".
Besides his professional judgment, the writer, who was British
Ambassador to Tehran from 1963-1971, also makes certain personal
assessments, e.g. the Shah "feared the British" and had "a life
long distrust of the British and those Iranians whom he considered
as Anglophiles".

WROBEL, BRIAN
        Human Rights in Iran: Testimony on Behalf of Amnesty Inter-
national by Brian Wrobel ... Before the Subcommittee on International Organizations of the Committee on International Relations, House of Representatives, United States Congress, 28 Feb-

ruary 1978.
	London, 1978; large 8vo, soft cover; 63 pp.

	Published by Amnesty International.

YARMOHAMMADI, LOTFOLLAH
     A Preliminary Bibliogrpahy of Contrastive Linguistics:
Persian and English (Primarily).
     Reprint from "Kherad O Kushesh", Vol.IV, No.11-111; Tehran,
May 1973; 18 pp.

YARSHATER, E.
     The Dialect of Shahrud (Khalkhal).
     Reprint from "BSOAS", London University, Vol.XXII, Part I;
1959; pp. 52-68.

     A paper on Shahrudi, an Iranian dialect spoken in Khalkhal,
in Azarbaijan Province.

YARSHATER, E.
     The Tati Dialect of Kajal.
     Reprint from "BSOAS", London University, Vol.XXIII, Part 2;
1960; pp. 275-286.

     A paper on Kajali, a Tati dialect spoken in a small number
of villages in Khalkhal.

YARSHATER, E.
     Some Common Characteristics of Persian Poetry and Art.
     Reprint of a paper read to the IV International Congress of
Iranian Art and Archaeology, May 1959, published in "Studia
Islamica"; Paris, 1962; pp. 61-71.

YARSHATER, EHSAN
     A Book Review of Gilbert Lazard's "Les Premiers Poètes
Persans (IXe-Xe Siècles)".
     Reprint from the "Journal of the American Oriental Society",
Vol.88, No.3; July-September 1968; pp. 605-607.

YARSHATER, EHSAN
     The Tati Dialects of Tarom.
     Reprint from the "W.B. Henning Memorial Volume, Asia Major
Library"; London, c.1969; pp. 451-467, and map.

     Tarom is a district of Khamsa, south of Khalkhal and north
of Soltanie.

YARSHATER, EHSAN
     Distinction of the Feminine Gender in Southern Tati.
     Reprint from Vol.III of "Studia Classica e Orientalia, of
the Instituto di Glottologia della Universita di Roma"; Rome,
1969; pp. 281-301.

YARSHATER, EHSAN
     Cultural Development in Iran.

Reproduction of chapter 6 of "Iran: Past, Present and Future"; c.1971; pp. 407-419.

YARSHATER, EHSAN
Iran and Afghanistan.
Offprint from "Current Trends in Linguistics, 6; Linguistics in South West Asia and North Africa"; The Hague, c.1971; pp. 669-689.

A paper on trends in linguistics in Iran and Afghanistan.

YARSHATER, EHSAN
Were the Sassanians Heirs to the Achaemenids?
Reprint of paper presented at an international conference on La Persia nel Medioevo, held in Rome, 31 March-5 April 1970; Rome, 1971; pp. 517-531.

Published by the Accademia Nazionale dei Lincei.

YARSHATER, EHSAN
Safavid Literature: Progress or Decline.
Reprint from "Iranian Studies", Vol.VII, Nos.1-2; United States, Winter-Spring 1974; pp. 217-270.

The writer is not as harsh as other commentators. He sees some merit in the literature of that era.

YARSHATER, EHSAN
The Jewish Communities of Persia and Their Dialects.
Reprint from "Memorial Jean de Menasce"; Louvain, 1974; pp. 453-466.

YARSHATER, EHSAN
Affinities Between Persian Poetry and Music.
Reprint from "Studies in Art and Literature of the Near East", published by the Middle East Center, University of Utah, 1974; pp. 59-78.

YARSHATER, EHSAN
Lists of the Achaemenid Kings in Biruni and Bar Hebraeus.
Reprint from "Biruni Symposium" Persian Studies Series No.7; Iran Center, Columbia University, 1976; pp. 49-65.

YARSHATER, EHSAN
The Hybrid Language of the Jewish Communities of Persia.
Reprint from the "Journal of the American Oriental Society", Vol.97, No.1; New Haven, Conn., January-March 1977; pp. 1-7.

YARSHATER, EHSAN
A Book Review of Mary Boyce's "Zoroastrians: Their Religious

Beliefs and Practices".
Reprint from "Journal of Asian History", Vol.14, No.2;
London and Boston, 1979; pp. 152-155.

YOHANNAN, A. and JACKSON, A.V. WILLIAMS
Some Persian References to Zoroaster and His Religion.
Photocopy of reprint from the "Journal of the American
Oriental Society", Vol.XXVIII; United States, 1907; pp. 183-188.

YOHANNAN, J.D.
Emerson's Translations of Persian Poetry from German Sources.
Reprint from "American Literature", Vol.14, No.4; January
1943; pp. 408-420.

Emerson's translations into English of some ghazals of Hafez
from Joseph Von Hammer's German translation and some fragments
from other German sources.

YOHANNAN, J.D.
The Influence of Persian Poetry upon Emerson's Work.
Reprint from "American Literature", Vol.15, No.1; March 1943;
41 pp.

The influence of Hafez, Sa'di and Mowlana Jallal e-Din upon
Emerson's transcendentalist thoughts.

YOHANNAN, J.D.
Did Sir Richard Burton Translate Sa'adi's Gulistan?
Photocopy of reprint from the "Journal of the Royal Asiatic
Society"; London, October 1950; pp. 185-188.

In 1883, Burton, Edward Rehatsek, an Austro-Hungarian
Orientalist who had spent most of his life in India, F.F.
Arbuthnot and others formed the Kama Shastra Society for the
publication of Oriental Erotica. The writer believes that Burton,
although he knew some Persian, could not not have translated
Sa'di. The writer convincingly argues that it must have been
Rehatsek, and after their deaths the manuscript was incorrectly
attributed to Burton.

YOHANNAN, JOHN D.
The Persian Poetry Fad in England 1770-1825.
An abridgement of a Ph.D. dissertation, Department of English,
New York University, 1947; reprinted from "Comparative Literature",
Vol.IV, No.2; Spring 1952; pp. 137-160.

The writer traces the influence of Sir William Jones'
"Oriental" scholarship and the fascination of the English romantic
poets with Persian poetry: Byron, Thomas Moore, Walter Scott,
Coleridge and others.

YOHANNAN, J.D.
One Hundred Years of Fitzgerald's Ruyaiyat of Omar Khayyam
Reprint of article from Greek Magazine; Athens, 1960; pp.
199-274.

The writer gives a brief account of the Fitzgerald translation, later translations, the public attitude towards Omar
Khayyam, interspersed with some interesting observations and
facts.

YOUNG ARTISTS OF THE NEAR EAST.
United States, 1956; 22 pp. plus 12 monochrome plates.
A lengthy introduction plus catalogue to a travelling
exhibition sponsored by the Near East College Association and
introduced at the Carnegie Endowment International Center, New
York City, 22 October to 7 November 1956.

Nothing interesting or worthwhile.

YOUNG, GAVIN
The Shah.
"The Observer", Review Section; London, 16 November 1975; pp.
25 and 29.

YOUNG, T. CUYLER
Iran in Continuing Crisis.
Reprint from "Foreign Affairs"; United States, January 1962;
pp. 275-292.

A very interesting article. The writer was remarkably
prescient.

YOUNG, T. CUYLER
U.S. Policy in Iran Since World War II.
Copy of typewritten paper marked "Confidential: For Seminar
on Problems of Contemporary Iran, Harvard University, 17 April
1965"; 37 pp.

The writer traces U.S. popularity in Iran during World War II
and how she was not regarded as an "invader", but as a benevolent
ally. After the war, this goodwill suffered somewhat as a result
of the polarization of the world and the inevitable consequences of
the U.S. emerging as the leading world power. Young believes that
America's first real test in Iran occurred during the oil
nationalization crisis of 1951-1953. With the resolution of the
oil dispute, the U.S. gained political ascendency in Iran for the
first time, but with a "clear handicap and strike against it from
which U.S.-Iranian relations have never recovered and from which
they suffer to this day". The U.S. compounded its negative image
by pushing Iran into the CENTO Pact. The writer in conclusion

argues that it is more important for the U.S. "to have basically
a friendly Iranian people than the present relatively amenable
regime whose endurance, especially in crisis, is questionable".
The writer also believes that the years of the Shah's rule are
numbered and the U.S. should seek alternatives. He is quick to
add, however, that a dramatic withdrawal of support would produce
chaos in Iran. The immediate remedies recommended are gentle
persuasion to open up the system and the "arrest of the ever
increasing emphasis on purchase of arms and building of armed
forces". Young's thinking had undergone a change during the
fifties and he was one of the first academics to question the
direction of U.S. policy in Iran. As he became more critical, he
became more isolated and was ignored by Washington.

YOUNG, T. CUYLER
        Princeton University Department of Oriental Studies: Report
to the President for the Year 1 July 1965-30 June 1966.
        Nine typewritten pp. plus a list of graduate students and
faculty publications during the year.

YOUNG, T. CUYLER
        Princeton University Department of Oriental Studies: Report
to the President for the Year 1 July 1966-30 June 1967.
        11 typewritten pp. plus a list of graduate students and
faculty publications during the year.

YOUSOFI, GHOLAM HOSEYN
        Dehkhoda's Place in the Iranian Constitutional Movement.
        Reprint from "Zeitschrift der Deutschen Morgenlandischen
Gesellschaft", Band 125; Heft 1; Wiesbaden, 1975; pp. 117-132.

        Ali Akbar Dehkhoda (1879-1955), one of the foremost Persian
scholars of the 20th century, also played a prominent role in
the Constitutional Movement of 1905-1909. Dehkhoda wrote satir-
ical articles and light verse in the immensely popular paper Sur
Esrafil under the nom de guerre "Dakhou". Dehkhoda attacked the
prominent courtiers for their corruption and avarice. His paper
would be suppressed from time to time but it continued publication until the summer of 1908 reaching its 32nd issue when its
editor and founder Jahangir Khan Sur Esrafil was murdered by
Mohammad Ali Shah. Dehkhoda's lasting contribution is his
compilation of the Persian Encyclopedia, completed after his death
by the noted scholar Mohammad Mo'in.

ZAEHNER, R.C.
Zoroastrian Survivals in Iranian Folklore.
Article in two parts; probably unpublished; c.1960; 60 pp.

An amusing article. The writer, in a semi serious vein at
the outset, shows the influence of Persian legends taken from
Mithraism on the sculptures and monuments near the entrance to
the Sistine chapel. There is then a rambling discussion of a
fictitious character who Zaehner later used as the author of his
book "No Heaven for Gunga Din".

ZAVARZADEH, MAS'UD
The Persian Short Story Since the Second World War: An
Overview.
Reprint from "The Muslim World", Vol.LVIII,
Seminary Foundation, 1968; pp. 308-316.

A good article in an over-written field. Writer: At Indiana
University.

ZONIS, MARVIN
Human Rights and American Foreign Policy: The Case of Iran.
Photocopy of a typewritten manuscript marked "The University
of Chicago, March, 1977"; probably unpublished; 45 pp.

In the opening paragraph the writer quotes from the Qabus
Nama in which a prince advises "his son on the principles of
ruling, 1082 A.D." as follows:
"The welfare of the people must be carefully guarded by the
king. It is through the people that the country is made prosper-
ous ... Therefore, let there be no place in your heart for
extortion; the dynasty of kings who recognize rights endures
long and becomes old, but the dynasty of extortioners swiftly
perishes, because fair treatment means prosperity, and extortion
means a depopulated land ... The sages say that the well-
spring of thriving conditions and of gladness in the world is a
just king, while the source of desolation and misery is a king
who is an oppressor."
This sets the tone of the writer's thesis and he argues that
the income from oil revenues has put the regime to sleep and has
made it insensitive towards its people. The merchants, industrial-
ists and businessmen have done so well from the oil revenues that
they have become silent; large numbers of the moderate opposition
have been lulled into impotence. There is thus no demand for
civil liberties, political reform or any concession by the government. Instead there have risen groups whose opposition is so
intense that they resort to terrorism, and the regime in response
has become even more arbitrary in administering justice. The
writer argues that the U.S. should exercise its leverage for
human rights and that only a fair and impartial administration of
justice could save the regime.

www.ingramcontent.com/pod-product-compliance
Lightning Source LLC
Chambersburg PA
CBHW070754240726
48654CB00007B/73